HANIF KUREISHI: COLLECTED SCREENPLAYS I

Hanif Kureishi was born and brought up in Kent. He read philosophy at King's College, London. In 1981 he won the George Devine Award for his plays *Outskirts* and *Borderline*, and in 1982 he was appointed Writer-in-Residence at the Royal Court Theatre. In 1984 he wrote *My Beautiful Laundrette*, which received an Oscar nomination for Best Screenplay. His second screenplay *Sammy and Rosie Get Laid* (1987) was followed by *London Kills Me* (1991) which he also directed. *The Buddha of Suburbia* won the Whitbread Prize for Best First Novel in 1990 and was made into a four-part drama series by the BBC in 1993. His version of Brecht's *Mother Courage* has been produced by the Royal Shakespeare Company and the Royal National Theatre. His second novel, *The Black Album*, was published in 1995. With Jon Savage he edited *The Faber Book of Pop* (1995). His first collection of short stories, *Love in a Blue Time*, was published in 1997. His story *My Son the Fanatic*, from that collection, was adapted for film and released in 1998. *Intimacy*, his third novel, was published in 1998, and a film of the same title, based on the novel and other stories by the author, was released in 2001 and won the Golden Bear award at the Berlin Film Festival. His play *Sleep with Me* premièred at the Royal National Theatre in 1999. His second collection of stories, *Midnight All Day*, was published in 2000. His most recent novel is *Gabriel's Gift* (2001).

HANIF KUREISHI

Collected Screenplays

VOLUME I

My Beautiful Laundrette
Sammy and Rosie Get Laid
London Kills Me
My Son the Fanatic

faber and faber

This collection first published in 2002
by Faber and Faber Limited
3 Queen Square, London WC1N 3AU

Typeset by RefineCatch Ltd, Bungay, Suffolk
Printed in England by Bookmarque Ltd

My Beautiful Laundrette first published in 1986
© Hanif Kureishi, 1986

Sammy and Rosie Get Laid first published in 1988
© Hanif Kureishi, 1988

London Kills Me first published in 1991
© Hanif Kureishi, 1991
Still © Jaques Prayer

My Son the Fanatic first published in 1997
© Hanif Kureishi, 1997
Photographs by Joth Shakerley © Zephyr Films, 1997

This collection and Introduction © Hanif Kureishi, 2002

A CIP record for this book
is available from the British Library

ISBN 0–571–21433–9

2 4 6 8 10 9 7 5 3 1

CONTENTS

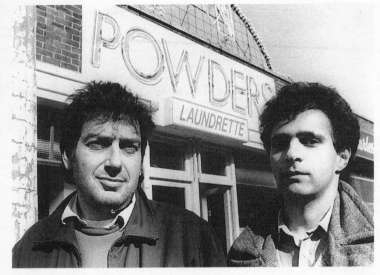
Hanif Kureishi with director Stephen Frears (left) on location for *My Beautiful Laundrette* in 1985.

INTRODUCTION: SEX AND SECULARITY

To me writing for film is no different to writing for any other form. It is the telling of stories, only on celluloid. However, you are writing for a director and then for actors. Economy is usually the point; one objective of film writing is to make it as quick and light as possible. You can't put in whatever you fancy in the hope that a leisured reader might follow you for a while, as you might in a novel. In that sense films are more like short stories. The restrictions of the form are almost poetic, though most poems are not read aloud in Cineplexes. Film is a broad art, which is its virtue.

Nevertheless, it didn't occur to any of us involved in *My Son The Fanatic*, for instance, that it would be either lucrative or of much interest to the general public. The film was almost a legacy of the 1960s and '70s, when one of the purposes of the BBC was to make cussed and usually provincial dramas about contemporary issues like homelessness, class and the Labour Party.

I had been aware since the early 1980s, when I visited Pakistan for the first time, that extreme Islam, or 'fundamentalism' – Islam as a political ideology – was filling a space where Marxism and capitalism had failed to take hold. To me this kind of Islam resembled neo-fascism or even Nazism: an equality of oppression for the masses with a necessary enemy – in this case 'the West' – helping to keep everything in place. When I was researching *The Black Album* and *My Son The Fanatic* a young fundamentalist I met did compare his 'movement' to the IRA, to Hitler, and to the Bolsheviks. I guess he had in mind the idea that small groups of highly motivated people could make a powerful political impact.

This pre-Freudian puritanical ideology certainly provided meaning and authority for the helpless and dispossessed. As importantly, it worked too, for those in the West who identified with them; for those who felt guilty at having left their 'brothers' behind in the Third World. How many immigrant families are there who haven't done that? Most of my family, for instance, have long since fled to Canada, Germany, the US and Britain; but some members

refused to go. There can't have been a single middle-class family in
Pakistan who didn't always have a bank account in the First World,
'just in case'. Those left behind are usually the poor, uneducated,
weak, old and furious.

Fundamentalist Islam is an ideology that began to flourish in a
conspicuous age of plenty in the West, and in a time of media
expansion. Everyone could see via satellite and video not only how
wealthy the West was, but how sexualized it had become. (All 'sex
and secularity over there, yaar', as I heard it put). This was
particularly shocking for countries that were still feudal. If you were
in any sense a Third Worlder, you could either envy Western ideals
and aspire to them, or you could envy and reject them. Either way,
you could only make a life in relation to them. The new Islam is as
recent as postmodernism.

Until recently I had forgotten Saeed Jaffrey's fruity line in *My
Beautiful Laundrette*, 'Our country has been sodomized by religion,
it is beginning to interfere with the making of making of money.'
Jaffrey's lordly laundrette owner was contrasted with the
desiccated character played by Roshen Seth, for whom fraternity is
represented by rational socialism rather than Islam, the sort of
hopeful socialism he might have learned at the LSE in London in
the 1940s. It is a socialism that would have no hope of finding a base
in either 1980s Britain, or in Pakistan.

What Hussein, Omar and even his lover Johnny have in common
is the desire to be rich. Not only that: what they also want, which is
one of the West's other projects, is to flaunt and demonstrate to
others their wealth and prosperity. They want to show off. This will,
of course, induce violent envy in some of the poor and dispossessed,
and may even encourage their desire to kill the rich.

One of my favourite uncles, a disillusioned Marxist, and a
template for the character played by Shashi Kapoor in *Sammy and
Rosie Get Laid*, had, by the mid-80s, become a supporter of Reagan
and Thatcher. Every morning we'd knock around Karachi, going
from office to office, where he had friends, to be given tea. No one
ever seemed too busy to talk. My uncle claimed that economic
freedom was Pakistan's only hope. If this surprised me, it was
because I didn't grasp what intellectuals and liberals in the Third
World were up against. There was a mass of people for whom

alternative political ideologies either had no meaning or were tainted with colonialism, particularly when Islamic grass-roots organization was made so simple through the mosques. For my uncle the only possible contrast to revolutionary puritanism had to be acquisition; liberalism smuggled in via materialism. So if Islam represented a new puritanism, progress would be corruption, through the encouragement of desire. But it was probably too late for this already; American materialism, and the dependence and quasi-imperialism that accompanied it, was resented and despised.

In Karachi there were few books written, films made or theatre productions mounted. If it seemed dull to me, still I had never lived in a country where social collapse and murder were everyday possibilities. At least there was serious talk. My uncle's house, a version of which appears in *My Beautiful Laundrette*, was a good place to discuss politics and books, and read the papers and watch films. In the 1980s American businessmen used to come by. My uncle claimed they all said they were in 'tractors'. They worked for the CIA; they were tolerated if not patronized, not unlike the old-style British colonialists the Pakistani men still remembered. No one thought the 'tractor men' had any idea what was really going on, because they didn't understand the force of Islam.

But the Karachi middle-class had some idea, and they were worried. They were obsessed with their 'status' or their position. Were they wealthy, powerful leaders of the country, or were they a complacent parasitic class – oddballs, Western but not, Pakistani but not – about to become irrelevant in the coming chaos of disintegration?

A few years later, in 1989, the fatwah against Rushdie was announced and although I saw my family in London, I didn't return to Karachi. I was told by the Embassy that my safety 'could not be guaranteed'. Not long after, when I was writing *The Black Album*, a fundamentalist acquaintance told me that killing Rushdie had become irrelevant. The point was that this was 'the first time the community has worked together. It won't be the last. We know our strength now.'

I have often been asked how it's possible for someone like me to carry two quite different world-views within, of Islam and the West: not, of course, that I do. Once my uncle said to me with some suspicion, 'You're not a Christian are you?' 'No', I said. 'I'm an atheist'. 'So am I', he replied. 'But I am still Muslim'. 'A Muslim atheist?' I said, 'it sounds odd'. He said, 'Not as odd as being nothing, an unbeliever'.

Like a lot of queries put to writers, this question about how to put different things together is a representative one. We all have built-in and contrasting attitudes, represented by the different sexes of our parents, each of whom would have a different background and psychic history. Parents always disagree about which ideals they believe their children should pursue. A child is a cocktail of its parent's desires. Being a child at all involves resolving, or synthesising, at least two different worlds, outlooks and positions.

If it becomes too difficult to hold disparate material within, if this feels too 'mad' or becomes a 'clash', one way of coping would be to reject one part entirely, perhaps by forgetting it. Another way is to be at war with it internally, trying to evacuate it, but never succeeding, an attempt Farid makes in *My Son The Fanatic*. All he does is constantly reinstate an electric tension between differences – differences that his father can bear and even enjoy, as he listens to Louis Armstrong and speaks Urdu. My father, who had similar tastes to the character played by Om Puri, never lived in Pakistan. But like a lot of middle class Indians, he was educated by both mullahs and nuns, and developed an aversion to both. He came to love Nat King Cole and Louis Armstrong, the music of black American former slaves. It is this kind of complexity that the fundamentalist has to reject.

Like the racist, the fundamentalist works only with fantasy. For instance, there are those who like to consider the West to be only materialistic and the East only religious. The fundamentalist's idea of the West, like the racist's idea of his victim, is immune to argument or contact with reality. (Every self-confessed fundamentalist I have met was anti-Semitic.) This fantasy of the Other is always sexual, too. The West is re-created as a godless orgiastic stew of immoral copulation. If the black person has been demonised by the white, in turn the white is now being demonized by the militant Muslim. These fighting couples can't leave one another alone.

These disassociations are eternal human strategies and they are

banal. What a fiction writer can do is show the historical forms
they take at different times: how they are lived out day by day by
particular individuals. And if we cannot prevent individuals
believing whatever they like about others – putting their fantasies
into them – we can at least prevent these prejudices becoming
institutionalized or an acceptable part of the culture.

A few days after the September 11 attack on the World Trade
Centre, a film director friend said to me, 'What do we do now?
There's no point to us. It's all politics and survival. How do the
artists go on?'

I didn't know what to say; it had to be thought about.

Islamic fundamentalism is a mixture of slogans and resentment;
it works well as a system of authority that constrains desire, but it
strangles this source of human life too. But of course in the Islamic
states, as in the West, there are plenty of dissenters and quibblers,
and those hungry for mental and political freedom. These essential
debates can only take place within a culture; they are what a
culture is, and they demonstrate how culture opposes the
domination of either materialism or puritanism. If both racism
and fundamentalism are diminishers of life – reducing others to
abstractions – the effort of culture must be to keep others alive by
describing and celebrating their intricacy, by seeing that this is not
only of value but a necessity.

Hanif Kureishi, November 8 2001

My Beautiful Laundrette

CAST AND CREW

MAIN CAST

JOHNNY	Daniel Day Lewis
GENGHIS	Richard Graham
SALIM	Derrick Branche
OMAR	Gordon Warnecke
PAPA	Roshan Seth
NASSER	Saeed Jaffrey
RACHEL	Shirley Anne Field
BILQUIS	Charu Bala Choksi
CHERRY	Souad Faress
TANIA	Rita Wolf
ZAKI	Gurdial Sira
MOOSE	Stephen Marcus
GANG MEMBER ONE	Dawn Archibald
GANG MEMBER TWO	Jonathan Moore

MAIN CREW

Photography	Oliver Stapleton
Film Editor	Mick Audsley
Designer	Hugo Luczyc Wyhowski
Sound Recordist	Albert Bailey
Music	Ludus Tonalis
Casting	Debbie McWilliams
Costume Design	Lindy Hemming
Make-up	Elaine Carew
Screenplay	Hanif Kureishi
Producers	Sarah Radclyffe and Tim Bevan
Director	Stephen Frears

EXT. OUTSIDE A LARGE DETACHED HOUSE. DAY

CHERRY *and* SALIM *get out of their car. Behind them, the* FOUR
JAMAICANS *get out of their car.*

    CHERRY *and* SALIM *walk towards the house. It is a large falling-down
place, in South London. It's quiet at the moment – early morning – but
the ground floor windows are boarded up.*

    *On the boarded-up windows is painted: 'Your greed will be the death of
us all' and 'We will defeat the running wogs of capitalism' and 'Opium is
the opium of the unemployed'.*

    CHERRY *and* SALIM *look up at the house. The* FOUR JAMAICANS
stand behind them, at a respectful distance.

> CHERRY

I don't even remember buying this house at the auction. What
are we going to do with it?

> SALIM

Tomorrow we start to renovate it.

> CHERRY

How many people are living here?

> SALIM

There are no people living here. There are only squatters. And
they're going to be renovated – right now.
(*And* SALIM *pushes* CHERRY *forward, giving her the key.* CHERRY
goes to the front door of the house. SALIM, *with* TWO JAMAICANS
goes round the side of the house. TWO JAMAICANS *go round the
other side.*)

INT. A ROOM IN THE SQUAT. DAY

GENGHIS *and* JOHNNY *are living in a room in the squat. It is freezing
cold, with broken windows.* GENGHIS *is asleep on a mattress, wrapped up.
He has the flu.* JOHNNY *is lying frozen in a deck chair, with blankets over
him. He has just woken up.*

EXT. OUTSIDE THE HOUSE. DAY

CHERRY *tries to unlock the front door of the place. But the door has been barred. She looks in through the letter box. A barricade has been erected in the hall.*

EXT. THE SIDE OF THE HOUSE. DAY

The JAMAICANS *break into the house through side windows. They climb in.* SALIM *also climbs into the house.*

INT. INSIDE THE HOUSE. DAY

The JAMAICANS *and* SALIM *are in the house now.*
    The JAMAICANS *are kicking open the doors of the squatted rooms. The* SQUATTERS *are unprepared, asleep or half-awake, in disarray.*
    The JAMAICANS *are going from room to room, yelling for everyone to leave now or get thrown out of the windows with their belongings.*
    Some SQUATTERS *complain but they are shoved out of their rooms into the hall; or down the stairs.* SALIM *is eager about all of this.*

INT. GENGHIS AND JOHNNY'S ROOM. DAY

JOHNNY *looks up the corridor to see what's happening. He goes back into the room quickly and starts stuffing his things into a black plastic bag. He is shaking* GENGHIS *at the same time.*

                    GENGHIS
I'm ill.

                    JOHNNY
We're moving house.

                    GENGHIS
No, we've got to fight.

                    JOHNNY
Too early in the morning.
(*He rips the blankets off* GENGHIS, *who lies there fully dressed, coughing and shivering. A* JAMAICAN *bursts into the room.*)
All right, all right.

(*The* JAMAICAN *watches a moment as* GENGHIS, *too weak to resist, but cursing violently, takes the clothes* JOHNNY *shoves at him and follows* JOHNNY *to the window.* JOHNNY *opens the broken window.*)

EXT. OUTSIDE THE HOUSE. DAY

A wide shot of the house.

The SQUATTERS *are leaving through windows and the re-opened front door and gathering in the front garden, arranging their wretched belongings. Some of them are junkies. They look dishevelled and disheartened.*

From an upper room in the house come crashing a guitar, a TV and *some records. This is followed by the enquiring head of a* JAMAICAN, *looking to see these have hit no one.*

One SQUATTER, *in the front garden, is resisting and a* JAMAICAN *is holding him. The* SQUATTER *screams at* CHERRY: *you pig, you scum, you filthy rich shit, etc.*

As SALIM *goes to join* CHERRY, *she goes to the screaming* SQUATTER *and gives him a hard backhander across the face.*

EXT. THE BACK OF THE HOUSE. DAY

JOHNNY *and* GENGHIS *stumble down through the back garden of the house and over the wall at the end,* JOHNNY *pulling and helping the exhausted* GENGHIS.

At no time do they see CHERRY *or* SALIM.

INT. BATHROOM. DAY

OMAR *has been soaking Papa's clothes in the bath. He pulls them dripping from the bath and puts them in an old steel bucket, wringing them out. He picks up the bucket.*

EXT. BALCONY. DAY

OMAR *is hanging out Papa's dripping pyjamas on the washing line on the balcony, pulling them out of the bucket.*

The balcony overlooks several busy railway lines, commuter routes into Charing Cross and London Bridge, from the suburbs.

OMAR *turns and looks through the glass of the balcony door into the main room of the flat.* PAPA *is lying in bed. He pours himself some vodka. Water from the pyjamas drips down Omar's trousers and into his shoes.*

When he turns away, a train, huge, close, fast, crashes towards the camera and bangs and rattles its way past, a few feet from the exposed overhanging balcony. OMAR *is unperturbed.*

INT. PAPA'S ROOM. DAY

The flat OMAR *and his father,* PAPA, *share in South London. It's a small, damp and dirty place which hasn't been decorated for years.*

PAPA *is as thin as a medieval Christ: an unkempt alcoholic. His hair is long; his toenails uncut; he is unshaven and scratches his arse shamelessly. Yet he is not without dignity.*

His bed is in the living room. PAPA *never leaves the bed and watches TV most of the time.*

By the bed is a photograph of Papa's dead wife, Mary. And on the bed is an address book and the telephone.

PAPA *empties the last of a bottle of vodka into a filthy glass. He rolls the empty bottle under the bed.*

OMAR *is now pushing an old-fashioned and ineffective carpet sweeper across the floor.* PAPA *looks at* OMAR's *face. He indicates that* OMAR *should move his face closer, which* OMAR *reluctantly does. To amuse himself,* PAPA *squashes* OMAR's *nose and pulls his cheeks, shaking the boy's unamused face from side to side.*

> PAPA
>
> I'm fixing you with a job. With your uncle. Work now, till you go back to college. If your face gets any longer here you'll overbalance. Or I'll commit suicide.

INT. KITCHEN. DAY

OMAR *is in the kitchen of the flat, stirring a big saucepan of dall. He can see through the open door his* FATHER *speaking on the phone to* NASSER. PAPA *speaks in Urdu. 'How are you?' he says. 'And Bilquis? And Tania and the other girls?'*

PAPA

(*Into phone*)
Can't you give Omar some work in your garage for a few
weeks, yaar? The bugger's your nephew after all.

NASSER

(*VO on phone*)
Why do you want to punish me?

INT. PAPA'S ROOM. DAY

PAPA *is speaking to* NASSER *on the phone. He watches* OMAR *slowly
stirring dall in the kitchen.* OMAR *is, of course, listening.*

PAPA

He's on dole like everyone else in England. What's he doing
home? Just roaming and moaning.

NASSER

(*VO on phone*)
Haven't you trained him up to look after you, like I have with
my girls?

PAPA

He brushes the dust from one place to another. He squeezes
shirts and heats soup. But that hardly stretches him. Though
his food stretches me. It's only for a few months, yaar. I'll send
him to college in the autumn.

NASSER

(*VO*)
He failed once. He had this chronic laziness that runs in our
family except for me.

PAPA

If his arse gets lazy – kick it. I'll send a certificate giving
permission. And one thing more. Try and fix him with a nice
girl. I'm not sure if his penis is in full working order.

INT. FLAT. DAY

Later. OMAR *puts a full bottle of vodka on the table next to Papa's bed.*

PAPA

Go to your uncle's garage.

(*And* PAPA *pours himself a vodka.* OMAR *quickly thrusts a bottle of tomato juice towards* PAPA, *which* PAPA *ignores. Before* PAPA *can take a swig of the straight vodka,* OMAR *grabs the glass and adds tomato juice.* PAPA *takes it.*)

If Nasser wants to kick you – let him. I've given permission in two languages.

(*To the photograph.*)

The bloody's doing me a lot of good. Eh, bloody Mary?

EXT. STREET. DAY

OMAR *walks along a South London street, towards Nasser's garage. It's a rough area, beautiful in its own falling-down way.*

A youngish white BUSKER *is lying stoned in the doorway of a boarded-up shop, his guitar next to him.* OMAR *looks at him.*

Walking towards OMAR *from an amusement arcade across the street are* JOHNNY *and* GENGHIS *and* MOOSE. GENGHIS *is a well-built white man carrying a pile of right-wing newspapers, badges, etc.* MOOSE *is a big white man,* GENGHIS's *lieutenant.*

JOHNNY *is an attractive man in his early twenties, quick and funny.*

OMAR *doesn't see* JOHNNY *but* JOHNNY *sees him and is startled. To avoid* OMAR, *in the middle of the road,* JOHNNY *takes* GENGHIS's *arm a moment.*

GENGHIS *stops suddenly.* MOOSE *charges into the back of him.* GENGHIS *drops the newspapers.* GENGHIS *remonstrates with* MOOSE. JOHNNY *watches* OMAR *go. The traffic stops while* MOOSE *picks up the newspapers.* GENGHIS *starts to sneeze.* MOOSE *gives him a handkerchief.*

They walk across the road, laughing at the waiting traffic.

They know the collapsed BUSKER. *He could even be a member of the gang.* JOHNNY *still watches* OMAR's *disappearing back.*

GENGHIS *and* MOOSE *prepare the newspapers.*

JOHNNY

(*Indicating* OMAR)

That kid. We were like that.

GENGHIS
(*Sneezing over* MOOSE's *face*)
You don't believe in nothing.

INT. UNDERGROUND GARAGE. DAY

Uncle Nasser's garage. It's a small private place where wealthy businessmen keep their cars during the day. It's almost full and contains about fifty cars – all Volvos, Rolls-Royces, Mercedes, Rovers, etc.
    At the end of the garage is a small glassed-in office.
    OMAR *is walking down the ramp and into the garage.*

INT. GARAGE OFFICE. DAY

The glassed-in office contains a desk, a filing cabinet, a typewriter, phone, etc. With NASSER *is* SALIM.
    SALIM *is a Pakistani in his late thirties, well-dressed in an expensive, smooth and slightly vulgar way. He moves restlessly about the office. Then he notices* OMAR *wandering about the garage. He watches him.*
    Meanwhile, NASSER *is speaking on the phone in the background.*

NASSER
(*Into phone*)
We've got one parking space, yes. It's £25 a week. And from this afternoon we provide a special on the premises 'clean-the-car' service. New thing.
(*From Salim's POV in the office, through the glass, we see* OMAR *trying the door of one of the cars.* SALIM *goes quickly out of the office.*)

INT. GARAGE. DAY

SALIM *stands outside the office and shouts at* OMAR. *The sudden sharp voice in the echoing garage.*

SALIM
Hey! Is that your car? Why are you feeling it up then?
(OMAR *looks at him.*)
Come here. Here, I said.

INT. GARAGE OFFICE. DAY

NASSER *puts down the phone.*

INT. GARAGE OFFICE. DAY

NASSER *is embracing* OMAR *vigorously, squashing him to him and bashing him lovingly on the back.*

> NASSER
> (*Introducing him to* SALIM)
> This one who nearly beat you up is Salim. You'll see a lot of him.

> SALIM
> (*Shaking hands with* OMAR)
> I've heard many great things about your father.

> NASSER
> (*To* OMAR)
> I must see him. Oh God, how have I got time to do anything?

> SALIM
> You're too busy keeping this damn country in the black. Someone's got to do it.

> NASSER
> (*To* OMAR)
> Your papa, he got thrown out of that clerk's job I fixed him with? He was pissed?
> (OMAR *nods.* NASSER *looks regretfully at the boy.*)
> Can you wash a car?
> (OMAR *looks uncertain.*)

> SALIM
> Have you washed a car before?
> (OMAR *nods.*)
> Your uncle can't pay you much. But you'll be able to afford a decent shirt and you'll be with your own people. Not in a dole queue. Mrs Thatcher will be pleased with me.

INT. GARAGE. DAY

SALIM *and* OMAR *walk across the garage towards a big car.* OMAR *carries a full bucket of water and a cloth. He listens to* SALIM.

> SALIM
> It's easy to wash a car. You just wet a rag and rub. You know how to rub, don't you?
> (*The bucket is overfull.* OMAR *carelessly bangs it against his leg. Water slops out.* SALIM *dances away irritably.* OMAR *walks on.* SALIM *points to a car.* RACHEL *swings down the ramp and into the garage, gloriously.*)
> Hi, baby.

> RACHEL
> My love.
> (*And she goes into the garage office. We see her talking and laughing with* NASSER.)

> SALIM
> (*Indicating car*)
> And you do this one first. Carefully, as if you were restoring a Renaissance painting. It's my car.
> (OMAR *looks up and watches as* RACHEL *and* NASSER *go out through the back of the garage office into the room at the back.*)

INT. ROOM AT BACK OF GARAGE OFFICE. DAY

RACHEL *and* NASSER, *half-undressed, are drinking, laughing and screwing on a bulging sofa in the wrecked room behind the office, no bigger than a large cupboard.* RACHEL *is bouncing up and down on his huge stomach in her red corset and outrageous worn-for-a-joke underwear.*

> NASSER
> Rachel, fill my glass, darling.
> (RACHEL *does so, then she begins to move on him.*)

> RACHEL
> Fill mine.

> NASSER
> What am I, Rachel, your trampoline?

RACHEL

Yes, oh, je vous aime beaucoup, trampoline.

NASSER

Speak my language, dammit.

RACHEL

I do nothing else. Nasser, d'you think we'll ever part?

NASSER

Not at the moment.
(*Slapping her arse*)
Keep moving, I love you. You move . . . Christ . . . like a
liner . . .

RACHEL

And can't we go away somewhere?

NASSER

Yes, I'm taking you.

RACHEL

Where?

NASSER

Kempton Park, Saturday.

RACHEL

Great. We'll take the boy.

NASSER

No, I've got big plans for him.

RACHEL

You're going to make him work?

INT. GARAGE OFFICE. DAY

OMAR *has come into the garage office with his car-washing bucket and
sponge.* SALIM *has gone home.* OMAR *is listening at the door to his uncle*
NASSER *and* RACHEL *screwing. He hears:*

NASSER

Work? That boy? You'll think the word was invented for him!

INT. COCKTAIL BAR/CLUB. EVENING

RACHEL *and* NASSER *have taken* OMAR *to Anwar's club/bar.*
OMAR *watches Anwar's son* TARIQ *behind the bar.* TARIQ *is rather
contemptuous of* OMAR *and listens to their conversation.*
  OMAR *eats peanuts and olives off the bar.* TARIQ *removes the bowl.*

NASSER

By the way, Rachel is my old friend.
(*To her*)
Eh?

OMAR

(*To* NASSER)
How's Auntie Bilquis?

NASSER

(*Glancing at amused* RACHEL)
She's at home with the kids.

OMAR

Papa sends his love. Uncle, if I picked Papa up –

NASSER

(*Indicating the club*)
Have you been to a high-class place like this before? I suppose
you stay in that black-hole flat all the time.

OMAR

If I picked Papa up, uncle –

NASSER

(*To* RACHEL)
He's one of those underprivileged types.

OMAR

And squeezed him, squeezed Papa out, like that, Uncle, I often
imagine. I'd get–

NASSER

Two fat slaps.

OMAR

Two bottles of pure vodka. And a kind of flap of skin.
(*To* RACHEL)
Like a French letter.

NASSER

What are you talking, madman? I love my brother. And I love
you.

OMAR

I don't understand how you can . . . love me.

NASSER

Because you're such a prick?

OMAR

You can't be sure that I am.

RACHEL

Nasser.

NASSER

She's right. Don't deliberately egg me on to laugh at you when
I've brought you here to tell you one essential thing. Move
closer.
(OMAR *attempts to drag the stool he is sitting on near to* NASSER. *He
crashes off it.* RACHEL *helps him up, laughing.* TARIQ *also laughs.*
NASSER *is solicitous.*)
In this damn country which we hate and love, you can get
anything you want. It's all spread out and available. That's why
I believe in England. You just have to know how to squeeze the
tits of the system.

RACHEL

(*To* OMAR)
He's saying he wants to help you.

OMAR

What are you going to do with me?

NASSER

What am I going to do with you? Make you into something
damn good. Your father can't now, can he?

(RACHEL *nods at* NASSER *and he takes out his wallet. He gives* OMAR *money.* OMAR *doesn't want to take it.* NASSER *shoves it down Omar's jumper, then cuddles his confused nephew.*)
Damn fool, you're just like a son to me.
(*Looking at* RACHEL)
To both of us.

INT. GARAGE. DAY

OMAR *is vigorously washing down a car, the last to be cleaned in the garage. The others cars are gleaming.* NASSER *comes quickly out of the office and watches* OMAR *squeezing a cloth over a bucket.*

                    NASSER
You like this work?
(OMAR *shrugs.*)
Come on, for Christ's sake, take a look at these accounts for me.
(OMAR *follows him into the garage office.*)

INT. GARAGE OFFICE. NIGHT

OMAR *is sitting at the office desk in his shirt-sleeves. The desk is covered with papers. He's been sitting there some time and it is late. Most of the cars in the garage have gone.*

    NASSER *drives into the garage, wearing evening clothes.* RACHEL, *looking divine, is with him.* OMAR *goes out to them.*

INT. GARAGE. NIGHT

                    NASSER
(*From the car*)
Kiss Rachel.
(OMAR *kisses her.*)

                    OMAR
I'll finish the paperwork tonight, Uncle.

                    NASSER
(*To* RACHEL)
He's such a good worker I'm going to promote him.

RACHEL

What to?

NASSER

(*To* OMAR)
Come to my house next week and I'll tell you.

RACHEL

It's far. How will he get there?

NASSER

I'll give him a car, dammit.
(*He points to an old convertible parked in the garage. It has always looked out of place.*)
The keys are in the office. Anything he wants.
(*He moves the car off. To* OMAR.)
Oh yes, I've got a real challenge lined up for you.
(RACHEL *blows him a kiss as they drive off.*)

INT. PAPA'S FLAT. EVENING

PAPA *is lying on the bed drinking.* OMAR, *in new clothes, tie undone, comes into the room and puts a plate of steaming food next to* PAPA. *Stew and potatoes.* OMAR *turns away and looking in the mirror snips at the hair in his nostrils with a large pair of scissors.*

PAPA

You must be getting married. Why else would you be dressed like an undertaker on holiday?

OMAR

Going to Uncle's house, Papa. He's given me a car.

PAPA

What? The brakes must be faulty. Tell me one thing because there's something I don't understand, though it must be my fault. How is it that scrubbing cars can make a son of mine look so ecstatic?

OMAR

It gets me out of the house.

PAPA

Don't get too involved with that crook. You've got to study. We
are under siege by the white man. For us education is power.
(OMAR *shakes his head at his father.*)
Don't let me down.

EXT. COUNTRY LANE. EVENING

OMAR, *in the old convertible, speeds along a country lane in Kent. The
car has its roof down, although it's raining. Loud music playing on the
radio.*

*He turns into the drive of a large detached house. The house is brightly
lit. There are seven or eight cars in the drive.* OMAR *sits there a moment,
music blaring.*

INT. LIVING ROOM IN NASSER'S HOUSE. EVENING

A large living room furnished in the modern style. A shy OMAR *has been
led in by* BILQUIS, *Nasser's wife. She is a shy, middle-aged Pakistani
woman. She speaks and understands English, but is uncertain in the
language. But she is warm and friendly.*

OMAR *has already been introduced to most of the women in the room.*

*There are five women there: a selection of wives; plus Bilquis's three
daughters. The eldest,* TANIA, *is in her early twenties.*

CHERRY, *Salim's Anglo-Indian wife is there.*

*Some of the women are wearing saris or salwar kamiz, though not
necessarily only the Pakistani women.*

TANIA *wears jeans and T-shirt. She watches* OMAR *all through this
and* OMAR, *when he can, glances at her. She is attracted to him.*

BILQUIS

(*To* OMAR)
And this is Salim's wife, Cherry. And of course you remember
our three naughty daughters.

CHERRY

(*Ebulliently to* BILQUIS)
He has his family's cheekbones, Bilquis.
(*To* OMAR)
I know all your gorgeous family in Karachi.

OMAR

(*This is a faux pas*)
You've been there?

CHERRY

You stupid, what a stupid, it's my home. Could anyone in their
right mind call this silly little island off Europe their home?
Every day in Karachi, every day your other uncles and cousins
are at our house for bridge, booze and VCR.

BILQUIS

Cherry, my little nephew knows nothing of that life there.

CHERRY

Oh God, I'm so sick of hearing about these in-betweens.
People should make up their minds where they are.

TANIA

Uncle's next door.
(*Leading him away. Quietly.*)
Can you see me later? I'm so bored with these people.
(CHERRY *stares at* TANIA, *not approving of this whispering and
cousin-closeness.* TANIA *glares back defiantly at her.* BILQUIS *looks
warmly at* OMAR.)

INT. CORRIDOR OF NASSER'S HOUSE. DAY

TANIA *takes* OMAR *by the hand down the corridor to Nasser's room. She
opens the door and leads him in.*

INT. NASSER'S ROOM. EVENING

*Nasser's room is further down the corridor. It's his bedroom but where he
receives guests. And he has a VCR in the room, a fridge, small bar, etc.
Behind his bed a window which overlooks the garden.*

OMAR *goes into the smoke-filled room, led by* TANIA. *She goes.*

NASSER *is lying on his bed in the middle of the room like a fat king. His
cronies are gathered round the bed:* ZAKI, SALIM, *an* ENGLISHMAN *and
an American called* DICK O'DONNELL.

They're shouting and hooting and boozing and listening to NASSER's
story, which he tells with great energy. OMAR *stands inside the door shyly,
and takes in the scene.*

NASSER

There'd been some tappings on the window. But who would
stay in a hotel without tappings? My brother Hussein, the boy's
papa, in his usual way hadn't turned up and I was asleep. I
presumed he was screwing some barmaid somewhere. Then
when these tappings went on I got out of bed and opened the
door to the balcony and there he was, standing outside. With
some woman! They were completely without clothes! And
blue with cold! They looked like two bars of soap. This I refer
to as my brother's blue period.

DICK O'DONNELL

What happened to the woman?

NASSER

He married her.
(*When* NASSER *notices the boy, conversation ceases with a wave of
his hand. And* NASSER *unembarrassedly calls him over to be fondled
and patted.*)
Come along, come along. Your father's a good man.

DICK O'DONNELL

This is the famous Hussein's son?

NASSER

The exact bastard. My blue brother was also a famous
journalist in Bombay and great drinker. He was to the bottle
what Louis Armstrong is to the trumpet.

SALIM

But you are to the bookie what Mother Theresa is to the
children.

ZAKI

(*To* NASSER)
Your brother was the clever one. You used to carry his
typewriter.
(TANIA *appears at the window behind the bed, where no one sees her
but* OMAR *and then* ZAKI. *Later in the scene, laughing, and to
distract the serious-faced* OMAR, *she bares her breasts.* ZAKI *sees this
and cannot believe his swimming-in-drink eyes.*)

DICK O'DONNELL

Isn't he coming tonight?

SALIM

(*To* NASSER)
Whatever happened to him?

OMAR

Papa's lying down.

SALIM

I meant his career.

NASSER

That's lying down too. What chance would the Englishman
give a leftist communist Pakistani on newspapers?

OMAR

Socialist. Socialist.

NASSER

What chance would the Englishman give a leftist communist
socialist?

ZAKI

What chance has the racist Englishman given us that we
haven't torn from him with our hands? Let's face up to it.
(*And* ZAKI *has seen the breasts of* TANIA. *He goes white and
panics.*)

NASSER

Zaki, have another stiff drink for that good point!

ZAKI

Nasser, please God, I am on the verge already!

ENGLISHMAN

Maybe Omar's father didn't make chances for himself. Look at
you, Salim, five times richer and more powerful than me.

SALIM

Five times? Ten, at least.

ENGLISHMAN

In my country! The only prejudice in England is against the useless.

SALIM

It's rather tilted in favour of the useless I would think. The only positive discrimination they have here.
(*The* PAKISTANIS *in the room laugh at this. The* ENGLISHMAN *looks annoyed.* DICK O'DONNELL *smiles sympathetically at the* ENGLISHMAN.)

DICK O'DONNELL

(*To* NASSER)
Can I make this nice boy a drink?

NASSER

Make him a man first.

SALIM

(*To* ZAKI)
Give him a drink. I like him. He's our future.

INT. THE VERANDAH. NIGHT

OMAR *shuts the door of Nasser's room and walks down the hall, to a games room at the end. This is a verandah overlooking the garden. There's a table-tennis table, various kids' toys, an exercise cycle, some cane chairs and on the walls numerous photographs of India.*

TANIA *turns as he enters and goes eagerly to him, touching him warmly.*

TANIA

It's been years. And you're looking good now. I bet we understand each other, eh?
(*He can't easily respond to her enthusiasm. Unoffended, she swings away from him. He looks at photographs of his Papa and Bhutto on the wall.*)
Are they being cruel to you in their typical men's way?
(*He shrugs.*)
You don't mind?

OMAR

I think I should harden myself.

TANIA

(*Patting seat next to her*)
Wow, what are you into?

OMAR

Your father's done well.
(*He sits. She kisses him on the lips. They hold each other.*)

TANIA

Has he? He adores you. I expect he wants you to take over the
businesses. He wouldn't think of asking me. But he is too
vicious to people in his work. He doesn't want you to work in
that shitty laundrette, does he?

OMAR

What's wrong with it?

TANIA

And he has a mistress, doesn't he?
(OMAR *looks up and sees* AUNTI BILQUIS *standing at the door.*
TANIA *doesn't see her.*)
Rachel. Yes, I can tell from your face. Does he love her? Yes.
Families, I hate families.

BILQUIS

Please Tania, can you come and help.
(BILQUIS *goes.* TANIA *follows her.*)

INT. HALL OF NASSER'S HOUSE. DAY

OMAR *is standing in the hall of Nasser's house as the guests leave their
respective rooms and go out into the drive.* OMAR *stands there.*
NASSER *shouts to him from his bed.*

NASSER

Take my advice. There's money in muck.
(TANIA *signals and shakes her head.*)
What is it the gora Englishman always needs? Clean
clothes!

EXT. NASSER'S DRIVE. NIGHT

OMAR *has come out of the house and into the drive. A strange sight:*
SALIM *staggering about drunkenly. The* ENGLISHMAN, ZAKI *and*
CHERRY *try to get him into the car.* SALIM *screams at* ZAKI.

SALIM

Don't you owe me money? Why not? You usually owe me
money! Here, take this! Borrow it!
(*And he starts to scatter money about.*)
Pick it up!
(ZAKI *starts picking it up. He is afraid.*)

CHERRY

(*To* OMAR)
Drive us back, will you. Pick up your own car tomorrow. Salim
is not feeling well.
(*As* ZAKI *bends over,* SALIM *who is laughing, goes to kick him.*
BILQUIS *stands at the window watching all this.*)

INT. SALIM'S CAR, DRIVING INTO SOUTH LONDON. NIGHT

OMAR *driving* SALIM's *car enthusiastically into London.* CHERRY *and*
SALIM *are in the back. The car comes to a stop at traffic lights.*
   On the adjacent pavement outside a chip shop a group of LADS *are*
kicking cans about. The LADS *include* MOOSE *and* GENGHIS.
   A lively street of the illuminated shops, amusement arcades and late-
night shops of South London.
   MOOSE *notices that Pakistanis are in the car. And he indicates to the*
others.
   The LADS *gather round the car and bang on it and shout. From inside*
the car this noise is terrifying. CHERRY *starts to scream.*

SALIM

Drive, you bloody fool, drive!
(*But* MOOSE *climbs on the bonnet of the car and squashes his arse*
grotesquely against the windscreen. Faces squash against the other
windows.
   Looking out of the side window OMAR *sees* JOHNNY *standing to*
one side of the car, not really part of the car-climbing and banging.
   Impulsively, unafraid, OMAR *gets out of the car.*)

EXT. STREET. NIGHT

OMAR *walks past* GENGHIS *and* MOOSE *and the others to the embarrassed* JOHNNY. CHERRY *is yelling after him from inside the open-doored car.*

The LADS *are alert and ready for violence but are confused by* OMAR's *obvious friendship with* JOHNNY.

OMAR *sticks out his hand and* JOHNNY *takes it.*

> OMAR
>
> It's me.

> JOHNNY
>
> I know who it is.

> OMAR
>
> How are yer? Working? What you doing now then?

> JOHNNY
>
> Oh, this kinda thing.

> CHERRY
>
> (*Yelling from the car*)
> Come on, come on!
> (*The lads laugh at her.* SALIM *is hastily giving* MOOSE *cigarettes.*)

> JOHNNY
>
> What are you now, chauffeur?

> OMAR
>
> No. I'm on to something.

> JOHNNY
>
> What?

> OMAR
>
> I'll let you know. Still living in the same place?

> JOHNNY
>
> Na, don't get on with me mum and dad. You?

> OMAR
>
> She died last year, my mother. Jumped on to the railway line.

                    JOHNNY

Yeah. I heard. All the trains stopped.

                    OMAR

I'm still there. Got the number?

                    JOHNNY

(*Indicates the* LADS)
Like me friends?
(CHERRY *starts honking the car horn. The* LADS *cheer.*)

                    OMAR

Ring us then.

                    JOHNNY

I will.
(*Indicates car*)
Leave 'em there. We can do something. Now. Just us.

                    OMAR

Can't.
(OMAR *touches* JOHNNY's *arm and runs back to the car.*)

INT. CAR. NIGHT

They continue to drive. CHERRY *is screaming at* OMAR.

                    CHERRY

What the hell were you doing?
(SALIM *slaps her.*)

                    SALIM

He saved our bloody arses!
(*To* OMAR, *grabbing him round the neck and pressing his face close to his.*)
I'm going to see you're all right!

INT. PAPA'S ROOM. NIGHT

OMAR *has got home. He creeps into the flat. He goes carefully along the hall, fingertips on familiar wall.*
    He goes into Papa's room. No sign of PAPA. PAPA *is on the balcony. Just a shadow.*

EXT. BALCONY. NIGHT

PAPA *is swaying on the balcony like a little tree. Papa's pyjama bottoms have fallen down. And he's just about maintaining himself vertically. His hair has fallen across his terrible face. A train bangs towards him, rushing out of the darkness. And* PAPA *sways precariously towards it.*

>   OMAR
> (*Screams above the noise*)
> What are you doing?

>   PAPA
> I want to pee.

>   OMAR
> Can't you wait for me to take you?

>   PAPA
> My prick will drop off before you show up these days.

>   OMAR
> (*Pulling up Papa's bottoms*)
> You know who I met? Johnny. Johnny.

>   PAPA
> The boy who came here one day dressed as a fascist with a quarter inch of hair?

>   OMAR
> He was a friend once. For years.

>   PAPA
> There were days when he didn't deserve your admiration so much.

>   OMAR
> Christ, I've known him since I was five.

>   PAPA
> He went too far. They hate us in England. And all you do is kiss their arses and think of yourself as a little Britisher!

INT. PAPA'S ROOM. NIGHT

They are inside the room now, and OMAR *shuts the doors.*

> OMAR
> I'm being promoted. To Uncle's laundrette.
> (PAPA *pulls a pair of socks from his pyjama pockets and thrusts them
> at* OMAR.)

> PAPA
> Illustrate your washing methods!
> (OMAR *throws the socks across the room.*)

EXT. SOUTH LONDON STREET. DAY

NASSER *and* OMAR *get out of Nasser's car and walk over the road to the
laundrette. It's called 'Churchills'. It's broad and spacious and in bad
condition. It's situated in an area of run-down second-hand shops, betting
shops, grocers with their windows boarded-up, etc.*

> NASSER
> It's nothing but a toilet and a youth club now. A finger up my
> damn arse.

INT. LAUNDRETTE. DAY

*We are inside the laundrette. Some of the benches in the laundrette are
church pews.*

> OMAR
> Where did you get those?

> NASSER
> Church.
> (*Three or four rough-lookings* KIDS, *boys and girls, one of whom
> isn't wearing shoes, sitting on the pews. A character by the
> telephone. The thunderous sound of running-shoes in a spin-drier.
> The* KID *coolly opens the spin-drier and takes out his
> shoes.*)
> Punkey, that's how machines get buggered!
> (*The* KID *puts on his shoes. He offers his hot-dog to another* KID,
> *who declines it. So the* KID *flings it into a spin-drier.*

NASSER *moves to throttle him. He gets the* KID *by the throat. The other* KIDS *get up.* OMAR *pulls his eager* UNCLE *away. The* TELEPHONE CHARACTER *looks suspiciously at everyone. Then makes his call.*)

                    TELEPHONE CHARACTER
Hi, baby, it's number one here, baby. How's your foot
now?

INT. BACK ROOM OF LAUNDRETTE. DAY

NASSER *stands at the desk going through bills and papers.*

                         NASSER
(*To* OMAR)
Get started. There's the broom. Move it!

                         OMAR
I don't only want to sweep up.

                         NASSER
What are you now, Labour Party?

                         OMAR
I want to be manager of this place. I think I can do it.
(*Pause.*)
Please let me.
(NASSER *thinks.*)

                         NASSER
I'm just thinking how to tell your father that four punks
drowned you in a washing machine. On the other hand, some
water on the brain might clear your thoughts. Okay. Pay me a
basic rent. Above that – you keep.
(*He goes quickly, eager to get out. The* TELEPHONE CHARACTER *is
shouting into the phone.*)

                    TELEPHONE CHARACTER
(*Into phone*)
Was it my fault? But you're everything to me! More than
everything. I prefer you to Janice!
(*The* TELEPHONE CHARACTER *indicates to* NASSER *that a*

washing machine has overflowed all over the floor, with soap suds.
NASSER *gets out.* OMAR *looks on.*)

INT. BACK ROOM OF LAUNDRETTE. DAY

OMAR *sitting gloomily in the back room. The door to the main area open.*
KIDS *push each other about. Straight customers are intimidated.*
  From Omar's POV through the laundrette windows, we see SALIM
getting out of his car. SALIM *walks in through the laundrette, quickly.*
Comes into the back room, slamming the door behind him.

SALIM

Get up!
(OMAR *gets up.* SALIM *rams the back of a chair under the door
handle.*)
I've had trouble here.

OMAR

Salim, please. I don't know how to make this place work. I'm
afraid I've made a fool of myself.

SALIM

You'll never make a penny out of this. Your uncle's given
you a dead duck. That's why I've decided to help you
financially.
(*He gives him a piece of paper with an address on it. He also gives
him money.*)
Go to this house near the airport. Pick up some video cassettes
and bring them to my flat. That's all.

INT. SALIM'S FLAT. EVENING

The flat is large and beautiful. Some Sindi music playing. SALIM *comes
out of the bathroom wearing only a towel round his waist. And a plastic
shower cap. He is smoking a fat joint.*
  CHERRY *goes into another room.*
  OMAR *stands there with the cassettes in his arms.* SALIM *indicates
them.*

SALIM

Put them. Relax. No problems?

(SALIM *gives him the joint and* OMAR *takes a hit on it.* SALIM
points at the walls. Some erotic and some very good paintings.)
One of the best collections of recent Indian painting. I
patronize many painters. I won't be a minute. Watch
something if you like.
(SALIM *goes back into the bedroom.* OMAR *puts one of the cassettes
he has brought into the VCR. But there's nothing on the tape. Just a
screenful of static.*

   Meanwhile, OMAR *makes a call, taking the number off a piece of
paper.*)

OMAR

(*Into phone*)
Can I speak to Johnny? D'you know where he's staying? Are
you sure? Just wanted to help him. Please, if you see him, tell
him to ring Omo.

INT. SALIM'S FLAT. EVENING

Dressed now, and ready to go out, SALIM *comes quickly into the room. He
picks up the video cassettes and realizes one is being played.* SALIM
screams savagely at OMAR.

SALIM

Is that tape playing?
(OMAR *nods.*)
What the hell are you doing?
(*He pulls the tape out of the VCR and examines it.*)

OMAR

Just watching something, Salim.

SALIM

Not these! Who gave you permission to touch these?
(OMAR *grabs the tape from* SALIM'S *hand.*)

OMAR

It's just a tape!

SALIM

Not to me!

OMAR

What are you doing? What business, Salim?
(SALIM *pushes* OMAR *hard and* OMAR *crashes backwards across the room. As he gets up quickly to react* SALIM *is at him, shoving him back down, viciously. He puts his foot on* OMAR's *nose.*
      CHERRY *watches him coolly, leaning against a door jamb.*)

SALIM

Nasser tells me you're ambitious to do something. But twice
you failed your exams. You've done nothing with the
laundrette and now you bugger me up. You've got too much
white blood. It's made you weak like those pale-faced
adolescents that call us wog. You know what I do to them? I
take out this.
(*He takes out a pound note. He tears it to pieces.*)
I say: your English pound is worthless. It's worthless like you,
Omar, are worthless. Your whole great family – rich and
powerful over there – is let down by you.
(OMAR *gets up slowly.*)
Now fuck off.

OMAR

I'll do something to you for this.

SALIM

I'd be truly happy to see you try.

EXT. OUTSIDE LAUNDRETTE. EVENING

OMAR, *depressed after his humiliation at* SALIM's, *drives slowly past the laundrette. Music plays over this. It's raining and the laundrette looks grim and hopeless.*
      OMAR *sees* GENGHIS *and* MOOSE. *He drives up alongside them.*

OMAR

Seen Johnny?

GENGHIS

Get back to the jungle, wog boy.
(MOOSE *kicks the side of the car.*)

INT. PAPA'S ROOM. EVENING

OMAR *is cutting* PAPA's *long toenails with a large pair of scissors.* OMAR's *face is badly bruised.* PAPA *jerks about, pouring himself a drink. So* OMAR *has to keep grabbing at his feet. The skin on* PAPA's *legs is peeling through lack of vitamins.*

PAPA

Those people are too tough for you. I'll tell Nasser you're through with them.
(PAPA *dials. We hear it ringing in Nasser's house. He puts the receiver to one side to pick up his drink. He looks at* OMAR *who wells with anger and humiliation.* TANIA *answers.*)

TANIA

Hallo.
(OMAR *moves quickly and breaks the connection.*)

PAPA

(*Furious*)
Why do that, you useless fool?
(OMAR *grabs* PAPA's *foot and starts on the toe job again. The phone starts to ring.* PAPA *pulls away and* OMAR *jabs him with the scissors. And* PAPA *bleeds.* OMAR *answers the phone.*)

OMAR

Hallo.
(*Pause.*)
Johnny.

PAPA

(*Shouts over*)
I'll throw you out of this bloody flat, you're nothing but a bum liability!
(*But* OMAR *is smiling into the phone and talking to* JOHNNY, *a finger in one ear.*)

INT. THE LAUNDRETTE. DAY

OMAR *is showing* JOHNNY *round the laundrette.*

JOHNNY

I'm dead impressed by all this.

OMAR

You were the one at school. The one they liked.

JOHNNY

(*Sarcastic*)
All the Pakis liked me.

OMAR

I've been through it. With my parents and that. And with
people like you. But now there's some things I want to do.
Some pretty big things I've got in mind. I need to raise money
to make this place good. I want you to help me do that. And I
want you to work here with me.

JOHNNY

What kinda work is it?

OMAR

Variety. Variety of menial things.

JOHNNY

Cleaning windows kinda thing, yeah?

OMAR

Yeah. Sure. And clean out those bastards, will ya?
(OMAR *indicates the sitting* KIDS *playing about on the benches.*)

JOHNNY

Now?

OMAR

I'll want everything done now. That's the only attitude if you
want to do anything big.
(JOHNNY *goes to the* KIDS *and stands above them. Slowly he
removes his watch and puts it in his pocket. This is a strangely
threatening gesture. The* KIDS *rise and walk out one by one. One*
KID *resents this. He pushes* JOHNNY *suddenly.* JOHNNY *kicks him
hard.*)

EXT. OUTSIDE THE LAUNDRETTE. DAY

Continuous. The kicked KID *shoots across the pavement and crashes into* SALIM *who is getting out of his car.* SALIM *pushes away the frantic arms and legs and goes quickly into the laundrette.*

INT. LAUNDRETTE. DAY

SALIM *drags the reluctant* OMAR *by the arm into the back room of the laundrette.* JOHNNY *watches them, then follows.*

INT. BACK ROOM OF LAUNDRETTE. DAY

SALIM *lets go of* OMAR *and grabs a chair to stuff under the door handle as before.* OMAR *suddenly snatches the chair from him and puts it down slowly. And* JOHNNY, *taking* OMAR's *lead, sticks his big boot in the door as* SALIM *attempts to slam it.*

> SALIM
>
> Christ, Omar, sorry what happened before. Too much to drink. Just go on one little errand for me, eh?
> (*He opens* OMAR's *fingers and presses a piece of paper into his hand.*)
> Like before. For me.

> OMAR
>
> For fifty quid as well.

> SALIM
>
> You little bastard.
> (OMAR *turns away.* JOHNNY *turns away too, mocking* SALIM, *parodying* OMAR.)
> All right.

INT. HOTEL ROOM. DUSK

OMAR *is standing in a hotel room. A modern high building with a view over London. He is with a middle-aged Pakistani who is wearing salwar kamiz. Suitcases on the floor.*

   The MAN *has a long white beard. Suddenly he peels if off and hands it to* OMAR. OMAR *is astonished. The* MAN *laughs uproariously.*

INT. LAUNDRETTE. EVENNG

JOHNNY *is doing a service wash in the laundrette.* OMAR *comes in quickly, the beard in a plastic bag. He puts the beard on.*

> JOHNY
>
> You fool.
> (OMAR *pulls* JOHNNY *towards the back room.*)

> OMAR
>
> I've sussed Salim's game. This is going to finance our whole future.

INT. BACK ROOM OF LAUNDRETTE. DAY

JOHNNY *and* OMAR *sitting at the desk.* JOHNNY *is unpicking the back of the beard with a pair of scissors. The door to the laundrette is closed.*

JOHNNY *carefully pulls plastic bags out of the back of the beard. He looks enquiringly at* OMAR. OMAR *confidently indicates that he should open one of them.* OMAR *looks doubtfully at him.* OMAR *pulls the chair closer.* JOHNNY *snips a corner off the bag. He opens it and tastes the powder on his finger. He nods at* OMAR. JOHNNY *quickly starts stuffing the bags back in the beard.*

OMAR *gets up.*

> OMAR
>
> Take them out. You know where to sell this stuff. Yes? Don't you?

> JOHNNY
>
> I wouldn't be working for you now if I wanted to go on being a bad boy.

> OMAR
>
> This means more. Real work. Expansion.
> (JOHNNY *reluctantly removes the rest of the packets from the back of the beard.*)
> We'll re-sell it fast. Tonight.

> JOHNNY
>
> Salim'll kill us.

OMAR

Why should he find out it's us? Better get this back to him.
Come on. I couldn't be doing any of this without you.

INT. OUTSIDE SALIM'S FLAT. NIGHT

OMAR, *wearing the beard, is standing outside* SALIM's *flat, having rung
the bell.* CHERRY *answers the door. At first she doesn't recognize him.
Then he laughs. And she pulls him in.*

INT. SALIM'S FLAT. NIGHT

There are ten people sitting in SALIM's *flat. Well-off Pakistani friends
who have come round for dinner. They are chatting and drinking. At the
other end of the room the table has been laid for dinner.*
    SALIM *is fixing drinks, and talking to his friends over his shoulder.*

SALIM

We were all there, yaar, to see Ravi Shankar. But you all just
wanted to talk about my paintings. My collection. That's why I
said, why don't you all come round. I will turn my place into an
art gallery for the evening . . .
(*The friends are giggling at* OMAR, *who is wearing the beard.*
SALIM, *disturbed, turns suddenly.* SALIM *is appalled by* OMAR *in
the beard.*)
Let's have a little private chat, eh?

INT. SALIM'S BEDROOM. EVENING

SALIM *snatches the beard from* OMAR's *chin. He goes into the bathroom
with it.* OMAR *moves towards the bathroom and watches* SALIM
frantically examine the back of the beard. When SALIM *sees, in the
mirror,* OMAR *watching him, he kicks the door shut.*

INT. SALIM'S BEDROOM. NIGHT

SALIM *comes back into the bedroom from the bathroom. He throws down
the beard.*

SALIM

You can go.

OMAR

But you haven't paid me.

SALIM

I'm not in the mood. Nothing happened to you on the way
here?
(OMAR *shakes his head.*)
Well, something may happen to you on the way back.
(SALIM *is unsure at the moment what's happened.* OMAR *watches
him steadily. His nerve is holding out.*)
Get the hell out.

EXT. OUTSIDE SALIM'S FLAT. NIGHT

As OMAR *runs down the steps of the flats to* JOHNNY *waiting in the
revving car,* SALIM *stands at the window of his flat, watching them.
Music over. We go with the music into:*

INT. CLUB/BAR. NIGHT

OMAR *has taken* JOHNNY *to the club he visited with* NASSER *and*
RACHEL.
    *The club is more lively in the evening, with West Indian, English and
Pakistani customers. All affluent. In fact, a couple of the* JAMAICANS
from the opening scene are there.
    OMAR *and* JOHNNY *are sitting at a table.* TARIQ, *the young son of the
club's owner, stands beside them. He puts two menus down.*

TARIQ

(*To* OMAR)
Of course a table is always here for you. Your Uncle Nasser – a
great man. And Salim, of course. No one touches him. No one.
You want to eat?

OMAR

Tariq, later. Bring us champagne first.
(TARIQ *goes. To* JOHNNY)
Okay?

JOHNNY

I'm selling the stuff tonight. The bloke's coming here in an
hour. He's testing it now.

                              OMAR

Good.
(*Smiles at a girl.*)
She's nice.

                              JOHNNY

Yes.

INT. CLUB/BAR. NIGHT

OMAR *is sitting alone at the table, drinking.* TARIQ *clears the table and
goes.* JOHNNY *comes out of the toilet with the white* DEALER. *The*
DEALER *goes.* JOHNNY *goes and sits beside* OMAR.

                              JOHNNY

We're laughing.

INT. NASSER'S ROOM. EVENING

NASSER *is lying on his bed wearing salwar kamiz. One of the young*
DAUGHTERS *is pressing his legs and he groans with delight.* OMAR *is
sitting across the room from him, well-dressed and relaxed. He eats Indian
sweets. The other* DAUGHTER *comes in with more sweets, which she places
by* OMAR.

                              OMAR

Tell me about the beach at Bombay, Uncle. Juhu beach.
(*But* NASSER *is in a bad mood.* TANIA *comes into the room. She is
wearing salwar kamiz for the first time in the film. And she looks
stunning. She has dressed up for* OMAR.)
(*Playing to* TANIA)
Or the house in Lahore. When Auntie Nina put the garden
hose in the window of my father's bedroom because he
wouldn't get up. And Papa's bed started to float.
(TANIA *stands behind* OMAR *and touches him gently on the
shoulder. She is laughing at the story.*)

                              TANIA

Papa.
(*But he ignores her.*)

OMAR

(*To* TANIA)
You look beautiful.
(*She squeezes his arm.*)

NASSER

(*Sitting up suddenly*)
What about my damn laundrette? Damn these stories about a
place you've never been. What are you doing, boy!

OMAR

What am I doing?

INT. LAUNDRETTE. DAY

OMAR *and* JOHNNY *in the laundrette.* JOHNNY, *with an axe, is
smashing one of the broken-down benches off the wall while* OMAR *stands
there surveying the laundrette, pencil and pad in hand. Splinters, bits of
wood fly about as* JOHNNY, *athletically and enthusiastically singing at
the top of his voice, demolishes existing structures.*

OMAR

(*Voice over*)
It'll be going into profit any day now. Partly because I've hired
a bloke of outstanding competence and strength of body and
mind to look after it with me.

INT. NASSER'S ROOM. EVENING

NASSER

(*To young* DAUGHTER)
Jasmine, fiddle with my toes.
(*To* OMAR)
What bloke?

INT. LAUNDRETTE. DAY

JOHNNY *is up a ladder vigorously painting a wall and singing loudly.
The washing machines are covered with white sheets. Pots and paints and
brushes lie about.*
   OMAR *watches* JOHNNY.

OMAR

(*Voice over*)
He's called Johnny.

NASSER

(*Voice over*)
How will you pay him?

INT. NASSER'S ROOM. EVENING

SALIM *and* ZAKI *come into the room.* SALIM *carries a bottle of whisky.* ZAKI *looks nervously at* TANIA *who flutters her eyelashes at him.*
    SALIM *and* ZAKI *shake hands with* NASSER *and sit down in chairs round the bed.*

ZAKI

(*To* NASSER)
How are you, you old bastard?

NASSER

(*Pointing to drinks*)
Tania.
(TANIA *fixes drinks for everyone.* SALIM *looks suspiciously at* OMAR *through·this. But* OMAR *coolly ignores him.*)
Zaki, how's things now then?

ZAKI

Oh good, good, everything. But . . .
(*He begins to explain about his declining laundrette business and how bad his heart is, in Urdu.* NASSER *waves at* OMAR.)

NASSER

Speak in English, Zaki, so this boy can understand.

ZAKI

He doesn't understand his own language?

NASSER

(*With affectionate mock anger*)
Not only that. I've given him that pain-in-the-arse laundrette to run.

SALIM

I know.

NASSER

But this is the point. He's hired someone else to do the work!

ZAKI

Typically English, if I can say that.

SALIM

(*Harshly*)
Don't fuck your uncle's business, you little fool.

TANIA

I don't think you should talk to him like that, Uncle.

SALIM

Why, what is he, royalty?
(SALIM *and* NASSER *exchange amused looks.*)

ZAKI

(*To* NASSER)
She is a hot girl.

TANIA

I don't like it.

OMAR

(*To* SALIM)
In my small opinion, much good can come of fucking.
(TANIA *laughs.* ZAKI *is shocked.* SALIM *stares at* OMAR.)

NASSER

(*To* OMAR)
Your mouth is getting very big lately.

OMAR

Well.
(*And he gets up quickly, to walk out.*)

NASSER

All right, all right, let's all take it easy.

SALIM

Who is it sitting in the drive? It's bothering me.
(*To* TANIA.)
Some friend of yours?
(*She shakes her head.*)

NASSER

Zaki, go and check it for me please.

OMAR

It's only Johnny. My friend. He works for me.

NASSER

No one works without my permission.
(*To* TANIA.)
Bring him here now.
(*She goes.* OMAR *gets up and follows her.*)

EXT. NASSER'S FRONT DRIVE. EVENING

JOHNNY *is standing by the car, music coming from the car radio.*
TANIA *and* OMAR *walk over to him.* TANIA *takes* OMAR'S *arm.*

TANIA

I know why you put up with them. Because there's so much
you want. You're greedy like my father.
(*Nodding towards* JOHNNY.)
Why did you leave him out here?

OMAR

He's lower class. He won't come in without being asked.
Unless he's doing a burglary.
(*They get to* JOHNNY, OMAR *not minding if he overhears the last
remark.*)

TANIA

Come in, Johnny. My father's waiting for you.
(*She turns and walks away.* OMAR *and* JOHNNY *walk towards the
house.* BILQUIS *is standing in the window of the front room, looking
at them.* OMAR *smiles and waves at her.*)

JOHNNY

How's Salim today?

OMAR

Wearing too much perfume as usual.

(OMAR *stops* JOHNNY *a moment and brushes his face.*)

An eyelash.

(TANIA, *waiting at the door, watches this piece of affection and wonders.*)

INT. NASSER'S ROOM, EVENING

NASSER, SALIM, JOHNNY, ZAKI *and* OMAR *are laughing together at one of Nasser's stories.* JOHNNY *has been introduced and they are getting along well.* TANIA *hands* SALIM *another drink and checks that everyone else has drinks.*

NASSER

. . . So I said, in my street I am the law! You see, I make wealth, I create money.

(*There is a slight pause.* NASSER *indicates to* TANIA *that she should leave the room. She does so, irritably.* SALIM *tries to take her hand as she goes but she pulls away from him. She has gone now.*)

(*To* OMAR)

You like Tania?

OMAR

Oh yes.

NASSER

I'll see what I can do.

(ZAKI *laughs and slaps* OMAR *on the knee.* OMAR *is uncomprehending.*)

To business now. I went to see the laundrette. You boys will make a beautiful job of it, I know. You need nothing more from there.

(*To* JOHNNY)

But in exchange I want you to do something. You look like a tough chap. I've got some bastard tenants in one of my houses I can't get rid of.

JOHNNY

No, I don't do nothing rough no more.

NASSER

I'm not looking for a mass murderer, you bloody fool.

JOHNNY

What's it involve, please?

NASSER

I tell you. Unscrewing.
(*To* SALIM)
We're on your favourite subject.

SALIM

For Christ's sake!

JOHNNY

What is unscrewing?

ZAKI

You're getting into some family business, that's all.

SALIM

What the hell else is there for them in this country now?

NASSER

(*To* OMAR)
Send him to my garage. And call Tania to bring us champagne.
And we'll drink to Thatcher and your beautiful laundrette.

JOHNNY

Do they go together?

NASSER

Like dall and chipatis!

EXT. OUTSIDE THE LAUNDRETTE. NIGHT

JOHNNY *and* OMAR *have parked their car by the laundrette. They lean
against the car, close together, talking.*

JOHNNY

The timber's coming tomorrow morning. I'm getting it cheap.
(*They walk slowly towards the laundrette.*)

OMAR

I've had a vision. Of how this place could be. Why do people hate laundrettes? Because they're like toilets. This could be a Ritz among laundrettes.

JOHNNY

A laundrette as big as the Ritz. Yeah.

(JOHNNY *puts his arm round* OMAR. OMAR *turns to him and they kiss on the mouth. They kiss passionately and hold each other.*

On the other side of the laundrette, GENGHIS, MOOSE *and three other* LADS *are kicking the laundrette dustbins across the pavement. They can't see* OMAR *and* JOHNNY.

JOHNNY *detaches himself from* OMAR *and walks round the laundrette to the* LADS. OMAR *moves into a position from where he can see, but doesn't approach the* LADS.

MOOSE *sees* JOHNNY *and motions to* GENGHIS *who is engrossed with the kicking.* GENGHIS *faces* JOHNNY. JOHNNY *controls himself. He straightens the dustbin and starts banging the rubbish back in. He gestures to a couple of the* LADS *to help him. They move back, away from him.*

JOHNNY *grabs* MOOSE *by the hair and stuffs his head into a dustbin.* MOOSE, *suitably disciplined, then helps* JOHNNY *stuff the rubbish back in the bin, looking guiltily at* GENGHIS.)

GENGHIS

Why are you working for them? For these people? You were with us once. For England.

JOHNNY

It's work. I want to work. I'm fed up of hanging about.

GENGHIS

I'm angry. I don't like to see one of our men grovelling to Pakis. They came here to work for us. That's why we brought them over. OK?

(*And* GENGHIS *moves away. As he does so, he sees* OMAR. *The others see him at the same time.* MOOSE *takes out a knife.* GENGHIS *indicates for him to keep back. He wants to concentrate on* JOHNNY.)

Don't cut yourself off from your own people. Because there's
no one else who really wants you. Everyone has to belong.

EXT. SOUTH LONDON STREET. NIGHT

*They are in a street of desolate semi-detached houses in bad condition,
ready for demolition.* JOHNNY *kisses* OMAR *and opens the car door.*

JOHNNY
I can't ask you in. And you'd better get back to your father.

OMAR
I didn't think you'd ever mention my father.

JOHNNY
He helped me, didn't he? When I was at school.

OMAR
And what did you do but hurt him?

JOHNNY
I want to forget all of those things.
(*He gets out quickly and walks across the front of the car. He
turns the corner of the street.* OMAR *gets out of the car and follows
him.*)

EXT. STREET. NIGHT

OMAR *follows* JOHNNY, *making sure he isn't seen.*
    JOHNNY *turns into a boarded-up derelict house.* OMAR *watches him go
round the side of the house and climb in through a broken door.*
    OMAR *turns away.*

INT. PAPA'S FLAT. NIGHT

PAPA *is asleep in the room, dead drunk and snoring.* OMAR *has come in.
He stands by Papa's bed and strokes his head.*
    *He picks up an almost empty bottle of vodka and drinks from it,
finishing it. He goes to the balcony door with it.*

EXT. BALCONY. NIGHT

OMAR *stands on the balcony, looking over the silent railway line. Then, suddenly, he shouts joyfully into the distance. And throws the empty bottle as far as he can.*

EXT. OUTSIDE THE LAUNDRETTE. DAY

OMAR *and* JOHNNY *are working hard and with great concentration, painting the outside of the laundrette, the doors, etc. Although it's not finished, it's beginning to reach its final state. The new windows have been installed; but the neon sign isn't yet up.*

KIDS *play football nearby. And various cynical* LOCALS *watch, a couple of* OLD MEN *whom we see in the betting shop later. Also* MOOSE *and another* LAD *who are amused by all the effort. They lean against a wall opposite and drink from cans.*

Further up the street SALIM *is watching all this from his parked car.*

JOHNNY *is up a ladder. He gets down the ladder, nods goodbye to* OMAR *and puts his paint brush away.* SALIM *reverses his car.*

JOHNNY *walks away.* OMAR *looks nervously across at* MOOSE *who stares at him.*

INT. GARAGE OFFICE. DAY

NASSER *and* SALIM *in the glassed-in office of the garage.* NASSER *is going through various papers on his desk.* SALIM *watches him and is very persistent.*

SALIM

I passed by the laundrette. So you gave them money to do it up?
(NASSER *shakes his head.*)
Where did they get it from, I wonder?

NASSER

Government grant.
(SALIM *looks dubiously at* NASSER.)
Oh, Omo's like us, yaar. Doesn't he fit with us like a glove?
He's pure bloody family.
(*Looks knowingly at* SALIM.)
So, like you, God knows what he's doing for money.
(NASSER *looks up and sees* JOHNNY *squashing his face against the glass of the door of the office. He starts to laugh.*)

SALIM

That other joker's a bad influence on Omo. I'm sure of it.
There's some things between them I'm looking into.
(JOHNNY *comes in.*)
(*To* JOHNNY)
So they let you out of prison. Too crowded, are they?

JOHNNY

Unscrew.
(SALIM *reacts.* NASSER *quickly leads* JOHNNY *out of the office,
while speaking to* SALIM *through the open door.*)

NASSER

(*In Urdu*)
Don't worry, I'm just putting this bastard to work.

SALIM

(*In Urdu*)
The bastard, it's a job in itself.

NASSER

(*In Urdu*)
I'll have my foot up his arse at all times.

SALIM

(*In Urdu*)
That's exactly how they like it. And he'll steal your boot too.
(JOHNNY *looks amusedly at them both.*)

INT. HOUSE. DAY

*This is one of Nasser's properties. A falling-down four-storey place in
South London, the rooms of which he rents out to itinerants and
students.*

Peeling walls, faded carpets, cat piss. JOHNNY *and* NASSER *are on the
top landing of the house, standing by a door.* JOHNNY *is holding a tool kit,
which he starts to unpack.*

NASSER

He's changed the lock so you take off the whole door in case he
changes it again. He's only a poet with no money.

JOHNNY

I'm not hurting nobody, OK?

INT. TOP CORRIDOR OF HOUSE. DAY

Later. NASSER *has gone.* JOHNNY *has got through the lock and the door is open. He is unscrewing the hinges and singing to himself.*

At the end of the hall a Pakistani in his fifties watches him. JOHNNY *lifts the door off the frame and leans it against the wall.*

POET

Now that door you've just taken off. Hang it back.

(*With great grunting effort* JOHNNY *picks the door up. He tries hard to move past the* POET *with it. The* POET *shoves* JOHNNY *hard.* JOHNNY *almost balances himself again but not quite, does a kind of dance with the door before crashing over with it on top of him.*

JOHNNY *struggles to his feet. The* POET *advances towards him and* JOHNNY *retreats.*)

I'm a poor man. This is my room. Let's leave it that way.

(*And the* POET *shoves* JOHNNY *again.*

JOHNNY, *not wanting to resist, falls against the wall.*

At the end of the hall, at the top of the stairs, NASSER *appears. The* POET *turns to* NASSER *and moves towards him, abusing him in Punjabi.* NASSER *ignores him. As the* POET *goes for* NASSER, JOHNNY *grabs the* POET *from behind and twists his arm up behind him.*)

NASSER

Throw this bugger out!

(JOHNNY *shoves the struggling* POET *along the corridor to the top of the stairs and then bundles him downstairs.*)

INT. ROOM. DAY

The room from which JOHNNY *removed the door. A large badly furnished bedsit with a cooker, fridge, double-bed, wardrobe, etc.*

(NASSER *is giving* JOHNNY *money. Then* NASSER *opens the window and looks out down the street. The* POET *is walking away from the house.* NASSER *calls out after him in Punjabi. And he throws the poet's things out of the window. The* POET *scrabbles around down below, gathering his things.*)

JOHNNY

Aren't you giving ammunition to your enemies doing this kind
of . . . unscrewing? To people who say Pakis just come here to
hustle other people's lives and jobs and houses.

NASSER

But we're professional businessmen. Not professional
Pakistanis. There's no race question in the new enterprise
culture. Do you like the room? Omar said you had nowhere to
live. I won't charge.

JOHNNY

Why not?

NASSER

You can unscrew. That's confirmed beautifully. But can you
unblock and can you keep this zoo here under control? Eh?

EXT. LAUNDRETTE. EVENING

Music.

   JOHNNY *is working on the outside of the laundrette. He's fixing up the
neon sign, on his own, and having difficulty.* OMAR *stands down below,
expensively dressed, not willing to assist. Across the street* MOOSE *and a
couple of* LADS *are watching.*

OMAR

I wish Salim could see this.

JOHNNY

Why? He's on to us. Oh yeah, he's just biding his time. Then
he'll get us.
   (*He indicates to* MOOSE. MOOSE *comes over and helps him.*
   The OLD MEN *are watching wisely as* JOHNNY *and* MOOSE
*precariously sway on a board suspended across two ladders, while
holding the neon sign saying POWDERS.*)

OMAR

You taking the room in Nasser's place?
   (*A ball is kicked by the* KIDS *which whistles past* JOHNNY's *ear.*
MOOSE *reacts.*)

Make sure you pay the rent. Otherwise you'll have to chuck
yourself out of the window.
(GENGHIS *walks down the street towards the laundrette.* OMAR
turns and goes.

MOOSE *goes into a panic, knowing* GENGHIS *will be furious at
this act of collaboration.* JOHNNY *glances at* MOOSE.

GENGHIS *is coming. The ladders sway. And the* OLD MEN *watch.*
GENGHIS *stops.* MOOSE *looks at him.*)

INT. LAUNDRETTE. DAY

The day of the opening of the laundrette.

*The laundrette is finished. And the place looks terrific: pot plants; a TV
on which videos are showing; a sound system; and the place is brightly
painted and clean.*

OMAR *is splendidly dressed. He is walking round the place, drink in
hand, looking it over.*

*Outside, local people look in curiously and press their faces against the
glass. Two old ladies are patiently waiting to be let in. A queue of people
with washing gradually forms.*

In the open door of the back room JOHNNY *is changing into his new
clothes.*

JOHNNY
Let's open. The world's waiting.

OMAR
I've invited Nasser to the launch. And Papa's coming. They're
not here yet. Papa hasn't been out for months. We can't move
till he arrives.

JOHNNY
What time did they say they'd be here?

OMAR
An hour ago.

JOHNNY
They're not gonna come, then.
(OMAR *looks hurt.* JOHNNY *indicates that* OMAR *should go to him.
He goes to him.*)

INT. BACK ROOM OF LAUNDRETTE. DAY

The back room has also been done up, in a bright high-tech style. And a two-way mirror has been installed, through which they can see into the laundrette.

   OMAR *watches* JOHNNY, *sitting on the desk.*

> JOHNNY
>
> Shall I open the champagne then?
> (*He opens the bottle.*)

> OMAR
>
> Didn't I predict this?
> (*They look through the mirror and through the huge windows of the laundrette to the patient punters waiting outside.*)
> This whole stinking area's on its knees begging for clean clothes. Jesus Christ.
> (OMAR *touches his own shoulders.* JOHNNY *massages him.*)

> JOHNNY
>
> Let's open up.

> OMAR
>
> Not till Papa comes. Remember? He went out of his way with you. And with all my friends.
> (*Suddenly harsh.*)
> He did, didn't he!

> JOHNNY
>
> Omo. What are you on about, mate?

> OMAR
>
> About how years later he saw the same boys. And what were they doing?

> JOHNNY
>
> What?

> OMAR
>
> What were they doing on marches through Lewisham? It was bricks and bottles and Union Jacks. It was immigrants out. It was kill us. People we knew. And it was you. He saw you

marching. You saw his face, watching you. Don't deny it. We were there when you went past.

(OMAR *is being held by* JOHNNY, *in his arms.*)

Papa hated himself and his job. He was afraid on the street for me. And he took it out on her. And she couldn't bear it. Oh, such failure, such emptiness.

(JOHNNY *kisses* OMAR *then leaves him, sitting away from him slightly.* OMAR *touches him, asking him to hold him.*)

INT. LAUNDRETTE. DAY

NASSER *and* RACHEL *stride enthusiastically into the not yet open laundrette, carrying paper cups and a bottle of whisky. Modern music suitable for waltzing to is playing.*

NASSER

What a beautiful thing they've done with it! Isn't it? Oh, God and with music too!

RACHEL

It's like an incredible ship. I had no idea.

NASSER

He's a marvellous bloody boy, Rachel, I tell you.

RACHEL

You don't have to tell me.

NASSER

But I tell you everything five times.

RACHEL

At least.

NASSER

Am I a bad man to you then?

RACHEL

You are sometimes . . . careless.

NASSER

(*Moved*)
Yes.

RACHEL

Dance with me.
(*He goes to her.*)
But we are learning.

NASSER

Where are those two buggers?

INT. BACK ROOM OF LAUNDRETTE. DAY

OMAR *and* JOHNNY *are holding each other.*

JOHNNY

Nothing I can say, to make it up to you. There's only things I
can do to show that I am . . . with you.
(OMAR *starts to unbutton* JOHNNY*'s shirt.*)

INT. LAUNDRETTE. DAY

NASSER *and* RACHEL *are waltzing across the laundrette. Outside, the old
ladies are shifting about impatiently.*

NASSER

Of course, Johnny did all the physical work on this.

RACHEL

You're fond of him.

NASSER

I wish I could do something more to help the other deadbeat
children like him. They hang about the road like pigeons,
making a mess, doing nothing.

RACHEL

And you're tired of work.

NASSER

It's time I became a holy man.

RACHEL

A sadhu of South London.

> NASSER
> (*Surprised at her knowledge*)
> Yes. But first I must marry Omar off.

INT. BACK ROOM OF LAUNDRETTE. DAY

OMAR *and* JOHNNY *are making love vigorously, enjoying themselves thoroughly. Suddenly* OMAR *stops a moment, looks up, sees* NASSER *and* RACHEL *waltzing across the laundrette.* OMAR *jumps up.*

INT. LAUNDRETTE. DAY

NASSER *strides impatiently towards the door of the back room.*

INT. BACK ROOM OF LAUNDRETTE. DAY

OMAR *and* JOHNNY *are quickly getting dressed.* NASSER *bursts into the room.*

> NASSER
> What the hell are you doing? Sunbathing?

> OMAR
> Asleep, Uncle. We were shagged out. Where's Papa?
> (NASSER *just looks at* OMAR. RACHEL *appears at the door behind him.*)

INT. LAUNDRETTE. DAY

The laundrette is open now. The ladies and other locals are doing their washing. The machines are whirring, sheets are being folded, magazines read, music played, video games played, etc.
  SALIM *arrives with* ZAKI. *They talk as they come in.*

> ZAKI
> Laundrettes are impossible. I've got two laundrettes and two ulcers. Plus . . . piles!
> (GENGHIS, MOOSE *and the rest of the gang arrive.* MOOSE *goes into the laundrette, followed by* GENGHIS. GENGHIS *turns and forbids the rest of the* GANG *from entering. They wait restlessly outside.*
>   JOHNNY *is talking to* RACHEL.)

RACHEL

What's your surname?

JOHNNY

Burfoot.

RACHEL

That's it. I know your mother.
(*The* TELEPHONE CHARACTER *is on the phone, talking eagerly to his Angela.*

   Through the window, OMAR, *who is talking to* NASSER, *sees* TANIA. *She is crossing the road and carrying a bouquet of flowers.*)

OMAR

I thought Papa just might make it today, Uncle.

NASSER

He said he never visits laundrettes.
(TANIA *comes in through the door.*)

JOHNNY

(*To* RACHEL)
Oh good, it's Tania.

RACHEL

I've never met her. But she has a beautiful face.
(JOHNNY *leaves* RACHEL *and goes to* TANIA, *kissing her. He takes the flowers delightedly.*

   NASSER *is disturbed by the sudden unexpected appearance of his daughter, since he is with his mistress,* RACHEL.)

NASSER

(*To* OMAR)
Who invited Tania, dammit?
(GENGHIS *and* MOOSE *shout out as they play the video game.*)

OMAR

I did, Uncle.
(*They watch as* TANIA *goes to* RACHEL *with* JOHNNY. JOHNNY *has no choice but to introduce* TANIA *and* RACHEL.)

TANIA

(*Smiles at* RACHEL)
At last. After so many years in my family's life.

RACHEL

Tania, I do feel I know you.

TANIA

But you don't.

NASSER

(*Watching this*)
Bring Tania over here.

TANIA

(*To* RACHEL)
I don't mind my father having a mistress.

RACHEL

Good. I am so grateful.

NASSER

(*To* OMAR)
Then marry her.
(OMAR *looks at him.*)
What's wrong with her? If I say marry her then you damn well
do it!

TANIA

(*To* RACHEL)
I don't mind my father spending our money on you.

RACHEL

Why don't you mind?

NASSER

(*To* OMAR)
Start being nice to Tania. Take the pressure off my fucking
head.

TANIA

(*To* RACHEL)
Or my father being with you instead of with our mother.

NASSER

(*To* OMAR)
Your penis works, doesn't it?

TANIA

(*To* RACHEL)
But I don't like women who live off men.

NASSER

(*Shoving* OMAR *forward*)
Get going then!

TANIA

(*To* RACHEL)
That's a pretty disgusting parasitical thing, isn't it?

OMAR

(*To* TANIA)
Tania, come and look at the spin-driers. They are rather
interesting.

RACHEL

But tell me, who do you live off? And you must understand, we
are of different generations, and different classes. Everything is
waiting for you. The only thing that has ever waited for me is
your father.
(*Then, with great dignity,* NASSER *goes to* RACHEL.)

NASSER

We'd better get going. See you boys.
(*He shakes hands warmly with* OMAR *and* JOHNNY. *And goes out
with* RACHEL, *ignoring* TANIA.

   Outside in the street, RACHEL *and* NASSER *begin to argue bitterly.
They are watched by the rest of the* GANG. RACHEL *and* NASSER
finally walk away from each other, in different directions, sadly.)

INT. LAUNDRETTE. DAY

*The laundrette is full now, mostly with real punters doing their washing
and enjoying being there.*

   GENGHIS *and* MOOSE *are still drinking.* GENGHIS *talks across the
laundrette to* JOHNNY. JOHNNY *is doing a service wash, folding clothes.*

OMAR *is saying goodbye to* TANIA *at the door.*

SALIM *has hung back and is waiting for* OMAR, ZAKI *says goodbye to him and goes tentatively past the volatile breast-baring* TANIA.

TANIA

(*To* OMAR)
I want to leave home. I need to break away. You'll have to help me financially.
(OMAR *nods enthusiastically.*)

GENGHIS

(*To* JOHNNY)
Why don't you come out with us no more?

OMAR

(*To* TANIA)
I'm drunk.

JOHNNY

(*To* GENGHIS)
I'm busy here full-time, Genghis.

OMAR

(*To* TANIA)
Will you marry me, Tania?

TANIA

(*To* OMAR)
If you can get me some money.

GENGHIS

(*To* JOHNNY)
Don't the Paki give you time off?

MOOSE

(*To* JOHNNY)
I bet you ain't got the guts to ask him for time off.

SALIM

(*To* JOHHNY, *indicating* OMAR)
Omo's getting married.
(TANIA *goes.* SALIM *goes to* OMAR. *He puts his arm round him and*

takes him outside. OMAR *is reluctant to go at first, but* SALIM *is firm and strong and pulls him out.* JOHNNY *watches.*)

GENGHIS

(*To* JOHNNY)
You out with us tonight then?

EXT. STREET OUTSIDE LAUNDRETTE. DAY

It is starting to get dark. OMAR *and* SALIM *stand beside Salim's smart car.*

Eager and curious customers are still arriving. SALIM *nods approvingly at them.*

Above them the huge pink flashing neon sign saying 'POWDERS'.
Some kids are playing football in the street opposite the laundrette.
JOHNNY *rushes to the door of the laundrette. He shouts at the kids.*

JOHNNY

You mind these windows!
(SALIM, *being watched by* JOHNNY, *starts to lead* OMAR *up the street, away from the laundrette.*)

SALIM

(*To* OMAR)
I'm afraid you owe me a lot of money. The beard? Remember? Eh? Good. It's all coming back. I think I'd better have that money back, don't you?

OMAR

I haven't got money like that now.

SALIM

Because it's all in the laundrette?
(GENGHIS *and* MOOSE *have come out of the laundrette and walked up the street away from it, parallel with* OMAR *and* SALIM.
GENGHIS *stares contemptuously at* SALIM *and* MOOSE *spits on the pavement.* SALIM *ignores them.*)
I'd better have a decent down payment then, of about half.
(OMAR *nods.*)
By the time Nasser has his annual party, say. Or I'll instruct

him to get rid of the laundrette. You see, if anyone does
anything wrong with me, I always destroy them.
(JOHNNY *comes out of the laundrette and runs up behind* GENGHIS
and MOOSE, *jumping on* MOOSE'*s back. They turn the corner,
away from* SALIM *and* OMAR. OMAR *watches them go anxiously,
not understanding what* JOHNNY *could be doing with them.*)

OMAR

Took you a while to get on to us.

SALIM

Wanted to see what you'd do. How's your Papa?
(OMAR *shrugs.*)
So many books written and read. Politicians sought him out.
Bhutto was his close friend. But we're nothing in England
without money.

INT. BETTING SHOP. DAY

There are only five or six people in the betting shop, all of them men.
   *And the men are mostly old, in slippers and filthy suits; with bandaged
legs and stained shirts and unshaven milk-bottle-white faces and
National Health glasses.* NASSER *looks confident and powerful beside
them. He knows them. There's a good sense of camaraderie amongst
them.*
   When OMAR *goes into the betting shop* NASSER *is sitting on a stool, a
pile of betting slips in front of him, staring at one of the newspaper pages
pinned to the wall. An* OLD MAN *is sitting next to* NASSER, *giving him
advice.*
   OMAR *goes to* NASSER.

OMAR

(*Anxiously*)
Uncle.
(NASSER *ignores him.*)
Uncle.

NASSER

(*Scribbling on betting slip*)
Even royalty can't reach me in the afternoons.

OMAR

I've got to talk. About Salim.

NASSER

Is he squeezing your balls?

OMAR

Yes. I want your help, Uncle.

NASSER

(*Getting up*)

You do it all now. It's up to you, boy.

(NASSER *goes to the betting counter and hands over his betting slips.*
He also hands over a thick pile of money.

Over the shop PA we can hear that the race is beginning. It starts.

NASSER *listens as if hypnotized, staring wildly at the others in the*
shop, for sympathy, clenching his fists, stamping his feet and shouting
loudly as his horse, 'Elvis', is among the front runners.

OMAR *has never seen* NASSER *like this before.*)

(*To horse*)

Come on, Elvis, my son.

(*To* OMAR)

You'll just have to run the whole family yourself now.

(*To horse*)

Go on, boy!

(*To* OMAR)

You take control.

(*To horse and others in shop*)

Yes, yes, yes, he's going to take it, the little bastard black
beauty!

(*To* OMAR)

It's all yours. Salim too.

(*To horse*)

Do it, do it, do it, baby! No, no, no, no.

(NASSER *is rigid with self-loathing and disappointment as 'Elvis'*
loses the race. The betting slip falls from his hand. And he hangs his
head in despair.)

OMAR

Where's Rachel?

NASSER

You can't talk to her. She's busy pulling her hair out. If only your damn father were sober. I'd talk to him about her. He's the only one who knows anything.

(*Facetious.*)

I'd ask him about Salim if I were you.

(OMAR *stares at* NASSER *in fury and disgust. He storms out of the betting shop, just as the next race – a dog race – is about to start.*)

INT. LAUNDRETTE. EVENING

The laundrette is fully functional now, busy and packed with customers.
Music is playing – a soprano aria from Madam Butterfly.

Customers are reading magazines. They are talking, watching TV with the sound turned down and one white man is singing along with the Puccini which he knows word for word.

The TELEPHONE CHARACTER *is yelling into the bright new yellow phone.*

TELEPHONE CHARACTER

(*Into phone*)

'Course I'll look after it! I'll come round every other night. At least. Honest. I want children!

(OMAR *walks around the laundrette, watching over it, proud and stern. He helps people if the doors of the renovated machines are stiff.*
And he hands people baskets to move their washing about in.
Shots of people putting money into the machines.

But JOHNNY *isn't there.* OMAR *doesn't know where he is and looks outside anxiously for him. He is worried and upset about Salim's demand for money.*

Finally, OMAR *goes out into the street and asks a kid if he's seen* JOHNNY.)

INT. TOP HALL OF THE HOUSE JOHNNY'S MOVED INTO. NIGHT

A party is going on in one of the rooms on this floor. The noise is tremendous and people are falling about the hall.

A PAKISTANI STUDENT, *a man in his late twenties with an intelligent face, is bent over someone who has collapsed across the doorway between room and hall.*

> PAKISTANI STUDENT
> (*As* OMAR *goes past*)
> There's only one word for your uncle.
> (OMAR *walks on fastidiously, ignoring them, to Johnny's door. The* STUDENT *yells.*)
> Collaborator with the white man!
> (OMAR *knocks on Johnny's door.*)

INT. JOHNNY'S ROOM. NIGHT

OMAR *goes into Johnny's room.* JOHNNY *is lying on the bed, drinking, wearing a pair of boxer shorts.*
   OMAR *stands at the open door.*
   JOHNNY *runs to the door and screams up the hall to the* PAKISTANI STUDENT.

> JOHNNY
> Didn't I tell you, didn't I tell you 'bout that noise last night?
> (*Pause.*)
> Well, didn't I?
> (*The* PAKISTANI STUDENT *stares contemptuously at him. The drunks lie where they are.* JOHNNY *slams the door of his room. And* OMAR *starts on him.*)

> OMAR
> Where did you go? You just disappeared!

> JOHNNY
> Drinking, I went. With me old mates. It's not illegal.

> OMAR
> 'Course it is. Laundrettes are a big commitment. Why aren't you at work?

> JOHNNY
> It'll be closing time soon. You'll be locking the place up, and coming to bed.

OMAR

No, it never closes. And one of us has got to be there. That way we begin to make money.

JOHNNY

You're getting greedy.

OMAR

I want big money. I'm not gonna be beat down by this country. When we were at school, you and your lot kicked me all round the place. And what are you doing now? Washing my floor. That's how I like it. Now get to work. Get to work I said. Or you're fired!

(OMAR *grabs him and pulls him up.* JOHNNY *doesn't resist.* OMAR *throws his shirt and shoes at him.* JOHNNY *dresses.*)

JOHNNY

(*Touching him*)
What about you?

OMAR

I don't wanna see you for a little while. I got some big thinking to do.

(JOHNNY *looks regretfully at him.*)

JOHNNY

But today, it's been the best day!

OMAR

Yeah. Almost the best day.

INT. TOP HALL. NIGHT

JOHNNY, *dressed now, walks past the party room. The* PAKISTANI STUDENT *is now playing a tabla in the hall.* JOHNNY *ignores him, though the student looks ironically at him.*

INT. BOTTOM ENTRANCE HALL OF THE HOUSE, NIGHT

JOHNNY *stops by a wall box in the hall. He pulls a bunch of keys out of his pocket and unlocks the wall box.*
    He reaches in and pulls a switch.

INT. OUTSIDE THE HOUSE. NIGHT

JOHNNY *walks away from the house. He has plunged the party room into darkness. In the room people are screaming.*

The PAKISTANI STUDENT *yells out of the window at* JOHNNY.

PAKISTANI STUDENT

You are not human! You are cold people, you English, the big icebergs of Europe!

(OMAR *stands at the next window along, looking out. This room is lighted.*

JOHNNY *chuckles to himself as he walks jauntily away.*)

INT. LAUNDRETTE. NIGHT

Nina Simone's smooth 'Walk On By' playing in the laundrette.

And there are still plenty of people around.

The TELEPHONE CHARACTER *has turned to the wall, head down, to concentrate on his conversation.*

A MAN *is asleep on a bench.* JOHNNY *walks past him, notices he's asleep and suddenly pokes him. The* MAN *jumps awake.* JOHNNY *points at the man's washing.*

A young black COUPLE *are dancing, holding each other sleepily as they wait for their washing.*

A BUM *comes in through the door, slowly, with difficulty in walking. He's wearing a large black overcoat with the collar turned up.* JOHNNY *watches him.*

JOHNNY

Hey!

(*The* BUM *doesn't respond.* JOHNNY *goes to him and takes his arm, about to chuck him out. Then the* BUM *turns to* JOHNNY.)

PAPA

I recognize you at least. Let me sit.

(JOHNNY *leads* PAPA *up the laundrette.*

The TELEPHONE CHARACTER *throws down the receiver and walks out.*)

JOHNNY

(*Deferential now*)

We were expecting you today.

PAPA

I've come.

JOHNNY

The invitation was for two o'clock, Mr Ali.

PAPA

(*Looking at his watch*)
It's only ten past now. I thought I'd come to the wrong place.
That I was suddenly in the ladies' hairdressing salon in Pinner,
where one might get a pink rinse. Do you do a pink rinse,
Johnny? Or are you still a fascist?

JOHNNY

You used to give me a lot of good advice, sir. When I was
little.

PAPA

When you were little. What's it made of you? Are you a
politician? Journalist? A trade unionist? No, you are an
underpants cleaner.
(*Self-mocking*)
Oh dear, the working class are such a great disappointment to
me.

JOHNNY

I haven't made much of myself.

PAPA

You'd better get on and do something.

JOHNNY

Yes. Here, we can do something.

PAPA

Help me. I want my son out of this underpants cleaning
condition. I want him reading in college. You tell him: you go
to college. He must have knowledge. We all must, now. In order
to see clearly what's being done and to whom in this country.
Right?

JOHNNY

I don't know. It depends on what he wants.

PAPA

No.
(*Strongly*)
You must use your influence.
(PAPA *gets up and walks out slowly.* JOHNNY *watches him go, sadly.*
PAPA *turns.*)
Not a bad dump you got here.

EXT. OUTSIDE THE LAUNDRETTE. NIGHT

PAPA *walks away from the laundrette.*

EXT. THE DRIVE OF NASSER'S HOUSE. DAY

JOHNNY *has come by bus to Nasser's house. And* OMAR *opens the front
door to him.* JOHNNY *is about to step into the house.* OMAR *takes him out
into the drive.*

JOHNNY

What you make me come all this way for?

OMAR

Gotta talk.

JOHNNY

You bloody arse.
(*At the side of the house a strange sight.* TANIA *is climbing a tree.*
BILQUIS *is at the bottom of the tree yelling instructions to her in
Urdu.* JOHNNY *and* OMAR *watch.*)
What's going on?

OMAR

It's heavy, man. Bilquis is making magical potions from leaves
and bird beaks and stuff. She's putting them on Rachel.
(JOHNNY *watches* TANIA *groping for leaves in amazement.*)

JOHNNY

Is it working?

OMAR

Rachel rang me. She's got the vicar round. He's performing an exorcism right now. The furniture's shaking. Her trousers are walking by themselves.

INT. NASSER'S ROOM. DAY

OMAR *and* JOHNNY *and* NASSER *are sitting at a table in Nasser's room, playing cards.* TANIA *is sulky. He puts his cards down.*

NASSER

I'm out.
(*He gets up and goes and lies down on the bed, his arm over his face.*
    OMAR *and* JOHNNY *continue playing. They put their cards down.*
JOHNNY *wins. He collects the money.*)

OMAR

Salim's gotta have money. Soon. A lot of money. He threatened me.
(*They get up and walk out of the room, talking in low voices.*
NASSER *lies there on the bed, not listening but brooding.*)
I didn't wanna tell you before. I thought I could raise the money on the profits from the laundrette. But it's impossible in the time.

INT. HALL OUTSIDE NASSER'S ROOM. DAY

They walk down the hall to the verandah.

JOHNNY

This city's chock-full of money. When I used to want money –

OMAR

You'd steal it.

JOHNNY

Yeah. Decide now if you want it to be like that again.

INT. VERANDAH. DAY

They reach the verandah. Outside, in the garden, the two younger DAUGHTERS *are playing.*

At the other end of the verandah BILQUIS *and* TANIA *are sitting on the sofa, a table in front of them.* BILQUIS *is mixing various ingredients in a big bowl – vegetables, bits of bird, leaves, some dog urine, the squeezed eyeball of a newt, half a goldfish, etc. We see her slicing the goldfish.*

At the same time she is dictating a letter to TANIA, *which* TANIA *takes down on a blue airletter.* TANIA *looks pretty fed-up.*

OMAR *and* JOHNNY *sit down and watch them.*

OMAR

She's illiterate. Tania's writing to her sister for her. Bilquis is thinking of going back, after she's hospitalized Rachel.
(BILQUIS *looks up at them, her eyes dark and her face humourless.*)
Nasser's embarked on a marathon sulk. He's going for the world record.
(*Pause.* JOHNNY *changes the subject back when* TANIA – *suspecting them of laughing at her – gives them a sharp look.*)

JOHNNY

We'll just have to do a job to get the money.

OMAR

I don't want you going back to all that.

JOHNNY

Just to get us through, Omo. It's for both of us. If we're going to go on. You want that, don't you?

OMAR

Yes. I want you.
(*Suddenly* NASSER *appears at the door and starts abusing* BILQUIS *in loud Urdu, telling her that the magic business is stupid, etc. But* BILQUIS *has a rougher, louder tongue. She says, among other things, in Urdu, that* NASSER *is a big fat black man who should get out of her sight for ever.*

TANIA *is very distressed by this, hands over face. Suddenly she gets up. The magic potion bowl is knocked over, the evil ingredients spilling over Bilquis's feet.* BILQUIS *screams.* JOHNNY *starts laughing.* BILQUIS *picks up the rest of the bowl and throws the remainder of the potion over* NASSER.)

INT. OUTSIDE A SMART HOUSE. NIGHT

A semi-detached house. A hedge around the front of the house.
   JOHNNY *is forcing the front window. He knows what he's doing. He climbs in. He indicates to* OMAR *that he should follow. And* OMAR *follows.*

INT. FRONT ROOM OF THE HOUSE. NIGHT

They're removing the video and TV and going out the front door with them. Their car is parked outside.
   Suddenly a tiny KID *of about eight is standing behind them at the bottom of the stairs. He is an* INDIAN KID. OMAR *looks at him, the* KID *opens his mouth to yell.* OMAR *grabs the* KID *and slams his hand over his mouth. While he holds the* KID, JOHNNY *goes out with the stereo. Then the compact disc player.*
   OMAR *leaves the stunned* KID *and makes a run for it.*

INT. BACK ROOM OF LAUNDRETTE. NIGHT

There are televisions, stereos, radios, videos, etc. stacked up in the back room. OMAR *stands there looking at them.*
   JOHNNY *comes in struggling with a video.* OMAR *smiles at him.* JOHNNY *doesn't respond.*

INT. HALL. DAY

   The top hall of the house JOHNNY *lives in.* JOHNNY, *wearing jeans and T-shirt, barefoot, only recently having woken up, is banging on the door of the Pakistani student's room.*
   OMAR *is standing beside him, smartly dressed and carrying a briefcase. He's spent the night with* JOHNNY. *And now he's going to the laundrette.*

                    JOHNNY
      (*To door*)
      Rent day! Rent up, man!
      (OMAR *watches him.* JOHNNY *looks unhappy.*)

                    OMAR
      I said it would bring you down, stealing again. It's no good for
      you. You need a brand new life.

(*The* PAKISTANI STUDENT *opens the door.* OMAR *moves away. To*
JOHNNY)
Party tonight. then we'll be in the clear.

PAKISTANI STUDENT
Unblock the toilet, yes, Johnny?

JOHNNY
(*Looking into the room*)
Tonight. You're not doing nothing political in there, are you,
man? I've gotta take a look.
(OMAR, *laughing, moves away.* JOHNNY *shoves the door hard and
the* PAKISTANI STUDENT *relents.*)

INT. PAKISTANI STUDENT'S ROOM. DAY

JOHNNY *goes into the room. A young* PAKISTANI STUDENT *is sitting on
the bed with a* CHILD.
  A younger PAKISTANI BOY *of about fourteen is standing behind her.
And across the room a* PAKISTANI GIRL *of seventeen.*

PAKISTANI STUDENT
My family, escaping persecution.
(JOHNNY *looks at him.*)
Are you a good man or are you a bad man?

EXT. COUNTRY LANE AND DRIVE OF NASSER'S HOUSE. EVENING

OMAR *and* JOHNNY *are sitting in the back of a mini-cab.*
  JOHNNY *is as dressed up as is* OMAR, *but in fashionable street clothes
rather than an expensive dark suit.* JOHNNY *will be out of keeping
sartorially with the rest of the party.*
  The young ASIAN DRIVER *moves the car towards Nasser's house.*
  The house is a blaze of light and noise. And the drive is full of cars and
PAKISTANIS *and* INDIANS *getting noisily out of them. Looking at the
house, the lights, the extravagance,* JOHNNY *laughs sarcastically.*
  OMAR, *paying the driver, looks irritably at* JOHNNY.

JOHNNY
What does he reckon he is, your uncle? Some kinda big Gatsby
geezer?

(OMAR *gives him a cutting look.*)
Maybe this just isn't my world. You're right. Still getting
married?
(*They both get out of the car.* OMAR *walks towards the house.*
JOHNNY *stands there a moment, not wanting to face it all.*

When OMAR *has almost reached the front door and* TANIA *has
come out to hug him,* JOHNNY *moves towards the house.*

TANIA *hugs* JOHNNY.

OMAR *looks into the house and sees* SALIM *and* CHERRY *in the
crowd in the front room. He waves at* SALIM *but* SALIM *ignores him.*
CHERRY *is starting to look pregnant.*

BILQUIS *is standing at the end of the hall. She greets* OMAR *in
Urdu. And he replies in rudimentary Urdu.*

JOHNNY *feels rather odd since he's the only white person in sight.*)

INT./EXT. THE VERANDAH, PATIO AND GARDEN. EVENING

*The house, patio and garden are full of well-off, well-dressed, well-pissed,
middle-class* PAKISTANIS *and* INDIANS.

The American, DICK, *and the* ENGLISHMAN *are talking together.*

DICK

England needs more young men like Omar and Johnny, from
what I can see.

ENGLISHMAN

(*Slightly camp*)
The more boys like that the better.
(*We see* OMAR *on the verandah talking confidently to various
people. Occasionally he glances at* SALIM *who is engrossed in
conversation with* ZAKI *and Zaki's* WIFE. *A snatch of their
conversation.*)

SALIM

Now Cherry is pregnant I will be buying a house. I am going to
have many children . . .
(BILQUIS *is there. She is alone but there is a fierceness and
cheerfulness about her that we haven't noticed before.*

JOHNNY *doesn't know who to talk to.* CHERRY *goes up to him.*)

CHERRY

Please, can you take charge of the music for us?
(JOHNNY *looks at her. Then he shakes his head.*

  NASSER, *in drunken, ebullient mood, takes* OMAR *across the room to* ZAKI, *who is with* SALIM.)

ZAKI

(*Shaking hands with* OMAR)
Omar, my boy.
(SALIM *moves away.*)

NASSER

(*To* OMAR, *of* ZAKI)
Help him
(*To* ZAKI)
Now tell him, please.

ZAKI

Oh God, Omo, I've got these two damn laundrettes in your area. I need big advice on them.
(*We hear Omar's voice as we look at the party.*)

OMAR

I won't advise you. If the laundrettes are a trouble to you I'll pay you rent for them plus a percentage of the profits.

NASSER

How about it, Zaki? He'll run them with Johnny.
(*We see* TANIA *talking to two interested* PAKISTANI MEN *in their middle twenties who see her as marriageable and laugh at everything she says. But* TANIA *is looking at* JOHNNY *who is on his own, drinking. He also dances, bending his knees and doing an inconspicuous handjive. He smiles at* TANIA.

  TANIA *goes across to* JOHNNY. *He whispers something in her ear. She leads* JOHNNY *by the hand out into the garden.*

  BILQUIS *looks in fury at* NASSER, *blaming him for this. He turns away from her.*

  ZAKI *is happily explaining to his wife about the deal with* OMAR.)

EXT. GARDEN. EVENING

TANIA *leads* JOHNNY *across the garden, towards the little garden house at the end. A bicycle is leaning against it. She takes off her shoes. And they hold each other and dance.*

INT. THE HOUSE. EVENING

SALIM *is on his own a moment.* OMAR *moves towards him.* SALIM *walks out and across the garden.*

EXT. GARDEN. EVENING

OMAR *follows* SALIM *across the lawn.*

> OMAR
>
> I've got it.
> (SALIM *turns to him.*)
> The instalment. It's hefty, Salim. More than you wanted.
> (OMAR *fumbles for the money in his jacket pocket. At the end of the garden* JOHNNY *and* TANIA *are playing around with a bicycle.* OMAR, *shaking, drops some of the money.* SALIM *raises his hand in smiling rejection.*)
>
> SALIM
>
> Don't ever offer me money. It was an educational test I put on you. To make you see you did a wrong thing.
> (TANIA *and* JOHNNY *are now riding the bicycle on the lawn.*)
> Don't in future bite the family hand when you can eat out of it. If you need money just ask me. Years ago your uncles lifted me up. And I will do the same for you.
> (*Through this* OMAR *has become increasingly concerned as* TANIA, *with* JOHNNY *on the back of the bicycle, is riding at Salim's back.* OMAR *shouts out*)
>
> OMAR
>
> Tania!
> (*And he tries to pull* SALIM *out of the way. But* TANIA *crashes into* SALIM, *knocking him flying flat on his face.* NASSER *comes rushing down the lawn.*
>   TANIA *and* JOHNNY *lie laughing on their backs.*

SALIM *gets up quickly, furiously, and goes to punch* JOHNNY.
OMAR *and* NASSER *grab an arm of* SALIM'*s each.* JOHNNY *laughs
in* SALIM'*s face.*)

OMAR

(*To* SALIM)
All right, all right, he's no one.
(SALIM *calms down quickly and just raises a warning finger at*
JOHNNY. *The confrontation is mainly diverted by* NASSER *going for*
TANIA.)

NASSER

(*To* TANIA)
You little bitch!
(*He grabs at* TANIA *to hit her.* JOHNNY *pulls her away.*)
What the hell d'you think you're doing?

SALIM

(*To* NASSER)
Can't you control your bloody people?
(*And he abuses* NASSER *in Urdu.* NASSER *curses and scowls in
English*)
Why should you be able to? You've gambled most of your
money down the toilet!
(SALIM *turns and walks away.*)

TANIA

(*Pointing after him*)
That smooth suppository owns us! Everything! Our education,
your businesses, Rachel's stockings. It's his!

NASSER

(*To* OMAR)
Aren't you two getting married?

OMAR

Yes, yes, any day now.

TANIA

I'd rather drink my own urine.

OMAR

I hear it can be quite tasty, with a slice of lemon.

NASSER

Get out of my sight, Tania!

TANIA

I'm going further than that.
(NASSER *turns and storms away. As he walks up the lawn we see that* BILQUIS *has been standing a quarter of the way down the lawn, witnessing all this.*

NASSER *stops for a moment beside her, not looking at her. He walks on.*)

OMAR

(*To* JOHNNY)
Let's get out of here.

TANIA

(*To* JOHNNY)
Take me.
(OMAR *shakes his head and takes* JOHNNY's *hand.*)

OMAR

Salim'll give us a lift.

JOHNNY

What?

OMAR

I need him for something I've got in mind.

INT. SALIM'S CAR. NIGHT

SALIM *is driving* JOHNNY *and* OMAR *along a country lane, fast, away from Nasser's house.*

JOHNNY *is sitting in the back, looking out of the window.*

OMAR *is sarcastic for* JOHNNY's *unheeding benefit and undetected by the humourless* SALIM.

OMAR

Well, thanks, Salim, you know. For saving the laundrette and everything. And for giving us a lift. Our car's bust.

SALIM

(*Accelerating*)
Got to get to a little liaison.

(*To* JOHNNY.) He doesn't have to thank me. Eh, Johnny?
What's your problem with me, Johnny?

JOHNNY

(*Eventually, and tough*)
Salim, we know what you sell, man. Know the kids you sell it
to. It's shit, man. Shit.

SALIM

Haven't you noticed? People are shit. I give them what they
want. I don't criticize. I supply. The laws of business apply.

JOHNNY

Christ, what a view of people. Eh, Omo? You think that's a
filthy shit thing, don't you, Omo?
(*Suddenly* SALIM *steps on the brakes. They skid to a stop on the edge
of a steep drop away from the road.*)

SALIM

Get out!
(JOHNNY *opens the car door. He looks down the steep hill and across
the windy Kent landscape. He leans back in his seat, closing the car
door.*)

JOHNNY

I don't like the country. The snakes make me nervous.
(SALIM *laughs and drives off.*)

INT. SALIM'S CAR. NIGHT

They've reached South London, near the laundrette.
   OMAR'*s been explaining to* SALIM *about his new scheme.*

OMAR

. . . So I was talking to Zaki about it. I want to take over his two
laundrettes. He's got no idea.

SALIM

None.

OMAR

Do them up. With this money.
(*He pats his pocket.*)

SALIM

Yeah. Is it enough?

OMAR

I thought maybe you could come in with me . . . financially.

SALIM

Yeah. I'm looking for some straight outlets.
(*Pause.*)
You're a smart bastard.
(*Suddenly*)
Hey, hey, hey . . .
(*And he sees, in the semi-darkness near the football ground, a group
of roaming, laughing* LADS. *They are walking into a narrow lane.*
SALIM *slows the car down and enters the street behind them,
following them now, watching them and explaining. To* JOHNNY)
These people. What a waste of life. They're filthy and ignorant.
They're just nothing. But they abuse people.
(*To* OMAR)
Our people.
(*To* JOHNNY)
All over England, Asians, as you call us, are beaten, burnt to
death. Always we are intimidated. What these scum need –
(*and he slams the car into gear and starts to drive forward fast*)
is a taste of their own piss.
(*He accelerates fast, and mounting the pavement, drives at the* LADS
ahead of him. MOOSE *turns and sees the car. They scatter and run.
Another of the* LADS *is* GENGHIS. *Some of the others we will
recognize as mates of his.*

GENGHIS *gets in close against the wall, picking up a lump of
wood to smash through the car windscreen. But he doesn't have time
to fling it and drops it as* SALIM *drives at him, turning away at the
last minute.* GENGHIS *sees clearly who is in the front of the car.*

As SALIM *turns the car away from* GENGHIS, MOOSE *is
suddenly standing stranded in the centre of the road.* SALIM *can't
avoid him.* MOOSE *jumps aside but* SALIM *drives over his foot.*
MOOSE *screams.*

SALIM *drives on.*)

INT. JOHNNY'S ROOM. NIGHT

OMAR *and* JOHNNY *have made love.* OMAR *appears to be asleep, lying across the bed.*

JOHNNY *gets up, walks across the room and picks up a bottle of whisky. He drinks.*

INT. ANOTHER LAUNDRETTE. DAY

This is a much smaller and less splendid laundrette than Omar's.

OMAR *is looking it over 'expertly'.* ZAKI *is awaiting Omar's verdict. This is Zaki's problem laundrette.*

SALIM *is also there, striding moodily about.*

> OMAR
>
> I think I can do something with this. Me and my partner.

> ZAKI
>
> Take it. I trust you and your family.

> OMAR
>
> Salim?

> SALIM
>
> I'd happily put money into it.

> OMAR
>
> All right. Wait a minute.

EXT. OUTSIDE THIS SMALLER LAUNDRETTE. DAY

JOHNNY *is morosely sitting in the car, examining himself in the car mirror. In the mirror, at the far end of the street, he sees a figure on crutches watching them. This is* MOOSE.

OMAR *comes out of the laundrette and talks to* JOHNNY *through the car window.*

> OMAR
>
> You wanna look at this place? Think we could do something with it?

> JOHNNY
>
> Can't tell without seeing it.

OMAR

Come on, then.

JOHNNY

Not if that scum Salim's there.
(OMAR *turns away angrily and walks back into the laundrette.*)

EXT. OUTSIDE OMAR AND JOHNNY'S BEAUTIFUL
LAUNDRETTE. DAY

GENGHIS *is standing on the roof of the laundrette, a plank of wood
studded with nails in his hand.*

Across the street, in the alley and behind cars, the LADS *are waiting and
watching the laundrette.* MOOSE *is with them, hobbling. Inside,* JOHNNY
washes the floor. TANIA, *not seeing* GENGHIS *or the* LADS, *walks down
the street towards the laundrette.*

INT. LAUNDRETTE. DAY

JOHNNY *is washing the floor of the laundrette. A white* MAN *opens a
washing machine and starts picking prawns out of it, putting them in a
black plastic bag.* JOHNNY *watches in amazement.*

TANIA *comes into the laundrette to say goodbye to* JOHNNY. *She is
carrying a bag.*

TANIA

(*Excited*)
I'm going.

JOHNNY

Where?

TANIA

London. Away.
(*Some* KIDS *are playing football outside, dangerously near the
laundrette windows.* JOHNNY *goes to the window and bangs on it.
He spots a* LAD *and* MOOSE *watching the laundrette from across the
street.* JOHNNY *waves at them. They ignore him.*)
I'm going, to live my life. You can come.

JOHNNY

No good jobs like this in London.

TANIA

Omo just runs you around everywhere like a servant.

JOHNNY

Well. I'll stay here with my friend and fight it out.

TANIA

My family, Salim and all, they'll swallow you up like a little
kebab.

JOHNNY

I couldn't just leave him now. Don't ask me to. You ever
touched him?
(*She shakes her head.*)
I wouldn't trust him, though.

TANIA

Better go.
(*She kisses him and turns and goes. He stands at the door and
watches her go.*)

EXT. OUTSIDE THE LAUNDRETTE. DAY

From the roof GENGHIS *watches* TANIA *walk away from the laundrette.*
   At the end of the street, Salim's car turns the corner. A LAD *standing
on the corner signals to* GENGHIS. GENGHIS *nods at the* LADS *in the
alley opposite and holds his piece of wood ready.*

INT. CLUB/BAR. DAY

NASSER *and* RACHEL *are sitting at a table in the club/bar. They have
been having an intense, terrible, sad conversation. Now they are staring
at each other.* NASSER *holds her hand. She withdraws her hand.*
   TARIQ *comes over to the table with two drinks. He puts them down. He
wants to talk to* NASSER. NASSER *touches his arm, without looking up.
And* TARIQ *goes.*

RACHEL

So . . . so . . . so that's it.

NASSER

Why? Why d'you have to leave me now?
(*She shrugs.*)
After all these days.

RACHEL

Years.

NASSER

Why say you're taking from my family?

RACHEL

Their love and money. Yes, apparently I am.

NASSER

No.

RACHEL

And it's not possible to enjoy being so hated.

NASSER

It'll stop.

RACHEL

Her work.
(*She pulls up her jumper to reveal her blotched, marked stomach. If possible we should suspect for a moment that she is pregnant.*)
And I am being cruel to her. It is impossible.

NASSER

Let me kiss you.
(*She gets up.*)
Oh, Christ.
(*She turns to go.*)
Oh, love. Don't go. Don't, Rachel. Don't go.

EXT. OUTSIDE LAUNDRETTE. DAY

SALIM *is sitting in his car outside the laundrette.* GENGHIS *stands above him on the roof, watching. Across the street the* LADS *wait in the alley, alert.*

    SALIM *gets out of his car.*

EXT. OUTSIDE ANWAR'S CLUB. DAY

RACHEL *walks away from the club.* NASSER *stands at the door and watches her go.*

EXT. OUTSIDE PAPA'S HOUSE. DAY

NASSER *gets out of his car and walks towards Papa's house. The door is broken and he pushes it, going into the hall, to the bottom of the stairs.*

EXT. OUTSIDE THE LAUNDRETTE. DAY

SALIM *walks into the laundrette.*

INT. PAPA'S HOUSE. DAY

NASSER *sadly climbs the filthy stairs of the house in which Papa's flat is.*

INT. LAUNDRETTE. DAY

SALIM *has come into the busy laundrette.* JOHNNY *is working.*

> SALIM
> I want to talk to Omo about business.

> JOHNNY
> I dunno where he is.

> SALIM
> Is it worth waiting?

> JOHNNY
> In my experience it's always worth waiting for Omo.
> (*The* TELEPHONE CHARACTER *is yelling into the receiver.*)

> TELEPHONE CHARACTER
> No, no, I promise I'll look after it. I want a child, don't I? Right, I'm coming round now!
> (*He slams the receiver down. Then he starts to dial again.*)

INT. PAPA'S HOUSE. DAY

NASSER *has reached the top of the stairs and the door to Papa's flat. He opens the door with his key. He walks along the hall to Papa's room. He stops at the open door to Papa's room.* PAPA *is lying in bed completely still.* NASSER *looks at him, worried.*

EXT. OUTSIDE THE LAUNDRETTE. DAY

The LADS *are waiting in the alley opposite.* GENGHIS *gives them a signal from the roof.*

The LADS *run across the street and start to smash up Salim's car with big sticks, laying into the headlights, the windscreen, the roof, etc.*

INT. LAUNDRETTE. DAY

We are looking at the TELEPHONE CHARACTER. *He is holding the receiver in one hand. His other hand over his mouth.* SALIM *sees him and then turns to see, out of the laundrette window, his car being demolished.*

INT. PAPA'S ROOM. DAY

NASSER *walks into Papa's room.* PAPA *hears him and looks up.* PAPA *struggles to get to the edge of the bed, and thrusts himself into the air.*

NASSER *goes towards him and they embrace warmly, fervently. Then* NASSER *sits down on the bed next to his brother.*

EXT. OUTSIDE THE LAUNDRETTE. DAY

SALIM *runs out of the laundrette towards his car. He grabs one of the* LADS *and smashes the* LAD's *head on the side of the car.*

GENGHIS *is standing above them, on the edge of the roof.*

GENGHIS
(*Yells*)
Hey! Paki! Hey! Paki!

INT. PAPA'S ROOM. DAY

PAPA *and* NASSER *sit side by side on the bed.*

PAPA
This damn country has done us in. That's why I am like this. We should be there. Home.

NASSER

But that country has been sodomized by religion. It is
beginning to interfere with the making of money. Compared
with everywhere, it is a little heaven here.

EXT. OUTSIDE THE LAUNDRETTE. DAY

SALIM *looks up at* GENGHIS *standing on the edge of the roof. Suddenly*
GENGHIS *jumps down, on top of* SALIM, *pulling* SALIM *to the ground
with him.*

GENGHIS *quickly gets to his feet. And as* SALIM *gets up,* GENGHIS *hits
him across the face with the studded piece of wood, tearing* SALIM*'s face.*

JOHNNY *is watching from inside the laundrette.*

INT. PAPA'S ROOM. DAY

PAPA *and* NASSER *are sitting on the bed.*

PAPA

Why are you unhappy?

NASSER

Rachel has left me. I don't know what I'm going to do.
(*He gets up and goes to the door of the balcony.*)

EXT. OUTSIDE THE LAUNDRETTE. DAY

SALIM, *streaming blood, rushes at* GENGHIS. GENGHIS *smashes him in
the stomach with the piece of wood.*

EXT. SOUTH LONDON STREET. DAY

OMAR *and* ZAKI *are walking along a South London street, away from
Zaki's small laundrette.*

Across the street is the club/bar. TARIQ *is just coming out. He waves at*
OMAR.

ZAKI

So you're planning an armada of laundrettes?

OMAR

What do you think of the dry-cleaners?

ZAKI

They are the past. But then they are the present also. Mostly
they are the past. But they are going to be the future too, don't
you think?

EXT. OUTSIDE THE LAUNDRETTE. DAY

SALIM *is on the ground.* MOOSE *goes to him and whacks him with his
crutch.* SALIM *lies still.* GENGHIS *kicks* SALIM *in the back. He is about to
kick him again.*

JOHNNY *is standing at the door of the laundrette. He moves towards*
GENGHIS.

JOHNNY

He'll die.
(GENGHIS *kicks* SALIM *again.* JOHNNY *loses his temper, rushes at*
GENGHIS *and pushes him up against the car.*)
I said: leave it out!
(*One of the* LADS *moves towards* JOHNNY. GENGHIS *shakes his
head at the* LAD. SALIM *starts to pull himself up off the floor.*
JOHNNY *holds* GENGHIS *like a lover. To* SALIM)
Get out of here!
(GENGHIS *punches* JOHNNY *in the stomach.* GENGHIS *and*
JOHNNY *start to fight.* GENGHIS *is strong but* JOHNNY *is
quick.* JOHNNY *tries twice to stop the fight, pulling away from*
GENGHIS.)
All right, let's leave it out now, eh?
(SALIM *crawls away,* GENGHIS *hits* JOHNNY *very hard and*
JOHNNY *goes down.*)

EXT. STREET. DAY

ZAKI *and* OMAR *turn the corner, into the street where the fight is taking
place.* ZAKI *sees* SALIM *staggering up the other side of the street.* ZAKI *goes
to him.*

OMAR *runs towards the fight.* JOHNNY *is being badly beaten now. A*
LAD *grabs* OMAR. OMAR *struggles.*

*Suddenly the sound of police sirens. The fight scatters. As it
does,* GENGHIS *throws his lump of wood through the laundrette*

*window, showering glass over the punters gathered round
the window.*

    OMAR *goes to* JOHNNY, *who is barely conscious.*

EXT. BALCONY OF PAPA'S FLAT. DAY

NASSER *is standing leaning over the balcony, looking across the railway
track.* PAPA *comes through the balcony door and stands behind him, in his
pyjamas.*

> NASSER
>
> You still look after me, eh? But I'm finished.

> PAPA
>
> Only Omo matters.

> NASSER
>
> I'll make sure he's fixed up with a good business future.

> PAPA
>
> And marriage? Tania is a possibility?
> (NASSER *nods confidently, perhaps over-confidently.*)

INT. BACK ROOM OF LAUNDRETTE. DAY

OMAR *is bathing* JOHNNY'*s badly bashed-up face at the sink in the back
room of the laundrette.*

> OMAR
>
> All right?

> JOHNNY
>
> What d'you mean all right? How can I be all right? I'm in the
> state I'm in.
> (*Pause.*)
> I'll be handsome. But where exactly am I?

> OMAR
>
> Where you should be. With me.

> JOHNNY
>
> No. Where does all this leave me?

OMAR

Are you crying?

JOHNNY

Where does it? Kiss me then.

OMAR

Don't cry. Your hand hurts too. That's why.

JOHNNY

Hey.

OMAR

What?

JOHNNY

I better go. I think I had, yeah.

OMAR

You were always going, at school. Always running about, you. Your hand is bad. I couldn't pin you down then.

JOHNNY

And now I'm going again. Give me my hand back.

OMAR

You're dirty. You're beautiful.

JOHNNY

I'm serious. Don't keep touching me.

OMAR

I'm going to give you a wash.

JOHNNY

You don't listen to anything.

OMAR

I'm filling this sink.

JOHNNY

Don't.

OMAR

Get over here!

(OMAR *fills the sink.* JOHNNY *turns and goes out of the room.*)
Johnny.
(*We follow* JOHNNY *out through the laundrette.*)

EXT. THE BALCONY. DAY

PAPA *turns away from* NASSER.
  A train is approaching, rushing towards NASSER. *Suddenly it is passing him and for a moment, if this is technically possible, he sees* TANIA *sitting reading in the train, her bag beside her. He cries out, but he is drowned out by the train.*
  If it is not possible for him to see her, then we go into the train with her and perhaps from her POV in the train look at the balcony, the two figures, at the back view of the flat passing by.

INT. LAUNDRETTE. DAY

JOHNNY *has got to the door of the laundrette.* OMAR *has rushed to the door of the back room.*
  The shattered glass from the window is still all over the floor. A cold wind blows through the half-lit laundrette.
  JOHNNY *stops at the door of the laundrette. He turns towards* OMAR.

INT. BACK ROOM OF LAUNDRETTE. DAY

As the film finishes, as the credits roll, OMAR *and* JOHNNY *are washing and splashing each other in the sink in the back room of the laundrette, both stripped to the waist. Music over this.*

Sammy and Rosie Get Laid

CAST AND CREW

MAIN CAST

RAFI	Shashi Kapoor
ALICE	Claire Bloom
SAMMY	Ayub Khan Din
ROSIE	Frances Barber
DANNY	Roland Gift
ANNA	Wendy Gazelle
VIVIA	Suzette Llewellyn
RANI	Meera Syal
CABBIE/GHOST	Badl Uzzaman

MAIN CREW

Producers	Tim Bevan and Sarah Radclyffe
Director	Stephen Frears
Screenplay	Hanif Kureishi
Lighting cameraman	Oliver Stapleton
Production designer	Hugo Luczyc Wyhowski
Editor	Mick Audsley
Music	Stanley Myers

INT. TUBE STATION. DAY

A young black man, DANNY, *stands in the open doors of a tube train. The doors are shutting. He holds them apart for an old woman to get through, yells up at the train guard, slips out himself, and runs up the platform. The tube platform is filled with music from a large straggly band of kids who play in a tunnel off the platform.*

EXT. STREET. DAY

A South London street. It is a residential area, foul, rundown. The police are tying off the street with white tape. A number of people have gathered to look on – some to protest. A mixture of black and white. But people are taken by surprise. Outside a house in the street are two police vans. The police are running about. The police are armed.

EXT. YARD. DAY

The yard of a poor house in the South London street. A high wall surrounds the yard. A dog runs round and round the yard, barking, chasing its tail. We hold on this wretched dog for as long as possible or bearable – maybe intercutting it with incidents from the previous scene.

INT. KITCHEN. DAY

The kitchen looks out on the yard. A middle-aged black woman is cooking in the kitchen. A frying pan full of bacon and tomatoes. Also a full chip pan bubbling away. The woman talks and laughs with her son, a young black man sitting at the kitchen table playing the trumpet.

EXT. YARD. DAY

And now the police, armed, jump over the wall into the yard. The dog goes berserk.

Cut to: Now the police are breaking into the front of the house.

Cut to: At the tied-off section of the street we see DANNY. *He presses against the tape, looking anxiously towards the house.*

Cut to: In the kitchen, the young man sees the police coming over the wall. He stands up and sits down. Then runs to the door of the kitchen. This door leads to a hall.

Cut to: DANNY, *at the tape, takes out a pair of scissors or a knife and cuts through the tape. People surge forward now, past the police.*

Cut to: The woman's hall is full of police. They are trying to grab the young man. The woman runs screaming into the hall. She carries the chip pan. She hurls it at the police, spraying them with boiling fat. A young hysterical cop at the end of the hall, frightened and confused, blasts two bullets into the woman's body. She falls to the ground.

Cut to: Outside, DANNY *has got to the house now. He hears the shots. There is chaos.*

TITLES

INT. ANNA'S STUDIO. DAY

We see a woman's naked back. She has a 'W' tattooed on each buttock. Behind it the sound of a man and woman in bed together. The woman is on top of the man. They are not copulating but playing. Numerous official papers are spread everywhere. SAMMY *then tries to write something down but* ANNA *bites him. She is American.* SAMMY, *in his late twenties, wears an open black shirt. We are in Anna's photographic studio. It is a huge room, in a converted warehouse, rather like a New York loft. Video and photographic equipment. Also many Indian things: fabrics, carvings, carpets, pictures of plump gurus, etc. On the table next to them is a cat. Through the open window trees are visible and the sound of kids playing is heard. A dog barks in the distance. The sound of an aeroplane.*

INT. AEROPLANE. DAY

Cross-fade on to each buttock of the swaying arse two seats in the plane. One seat is empty. In the other sits RAFI, *a suave old man with an angelic face. He is always exquisitely dressed in English suits.* RAFI *takes a large sherbet out of a paper bag and pops it into his mouth, sucking contentedly, with white sherbet on the end of his nose. The captain addresses the*

aircraft: 'We are approaching London, Heathrow, and will be landing
shortly . . . the temperature in London is . . .'

INT. ANNA'S STUDIO. DAY

SAMMY *and* ANNA *are in bed.* ANNA *laughs as* SAMMY *tries to get up,*
against her wishes.

> SAMMY
>
> As your accountant, Anna, I think we should look for some
> offshore investments for you.
> (*Pause.*)
> Now I've gotta go, baby. Meet someone at the airport.

> ANNA
>
> You'll get pimples on your tongue for telling lies, you couch
> potato. You mean your wife's got the dinner on and you gotta
> get home.

> SAMMY
>
> My wife. It's funny, Anna, the more Rosie hears about you, the
> more she's knocked out by you.

> ANNA
> (*Pulling his outstretched tongue*)
> That's another one – right there.

> SAMMY
>
> She's especially intrigued and totally knocked out by you
> having a 'W' tattooed on each buttock. Rosie wants to know if
> it's some kind of New York code.

> ANNA
>
> You know what it is, you couch potato. It's just so that if I bend
> over it spells 'wow'!

INT. COUNCIL FLAT. DAY

ROSIE, *beautiful and well dressed, about thirty, a social worker, walks*
through an old man's filthy falling-down council flat. There are
many photographs of his children and grandchildren. ROSIE *looks*
for him.

ROSIE

Mr Weaver, Mr Weaver! It's Rosie Hobbs!
(*She sits down in the middle of the room for a moment and we hold on her face. We hear* SAMMY's *voice.*)

SAMMY

(*Voice over*)
There's two things my main squeeze Rosie doesn't believe in. Getting the dinner on and sexual fidelity. She says jealousy is wickeder than adultery.
(*Cut to: now* ROSIE *pushes open the door of the old man's bathroom.*)
(*Voice over*)
Rosie doesn't want to possess anyone. If she could see us now doing your accounts she'd feel so unpossessive she'd open a bottle of champagne.

EXT. HEATHROW AIRPORT. DAY

Surrounded by suitcases RAFI *stands, waiting for his son* SAMMY *outside the airport terminal. He is getting very impatient. Finally he waves at the nearest cab and picks up his suitcases.*

INT. ANNA'S STUDIO. DAY

SAMMY *lies there, greedily cracking another beer. Meanwhile* ANNA *has got up and is adjusting photographic screens around the bed.*

SAMMY

I haven't seen my old man for five years. When he was young and poor he lived in England. Then he went home to get powerful. He dumped me with my mother when they split up. He never wanted me. He left me here. I think I must have been the result of a premature ejaculation.

EXT. AIRPORT. DAY

We see RAFI *getting into the cab. The cab drives away. The* CABBIE *is an Asian man in a brown suit. One eye is bandaged and part of his skull has been smashed in.* RAFI *doesn't notice this but it's important we see and remember the* CABBIE's *face.*

SAMMY

(*Voice over*)

Rosie and I visited him there. He's a great patriarch and a little king, surrounded by servants.

(*Cut to: In the studio* ANNA *is ready to photograph* SAMMY.)

ANNA

You worship him, don't you? Does he have any kids from his other wife?

SAMMY

Not really. Only daughters.

(*They laugh.*)

Give me a comb, will ya, Anna?

INT. COUNCIL FLAT. DAY

SAMMY

(*Voice over*)

Anna, he's got to see me at my best tonight – plenty of dough, decent flat, Rosie not looking too tired.

(ROSIE *has pushed the bathroom door. She goes into the bathroom. The walls are peeling. Water drips from the walls. The old man is dead in the bath, his thin body under the water. His head is jaundice yellow. The water steams. She stares at him and pulls out the plug, accidentally touching his leg.*)

INT./EXT. CAB. DAY

It is dusk now. RAFI *in the cab is well into London, heading towards the grimmer stretches of South London.*

RAFI

(*To* CABBIE)

For me England is hot buttered toast on a fork in front of an open fire. And cunty fingers.

(*The cab stops in the traffic.* RAFI *pulls down the window and sticks his old grey head out. The cab accelerates. Above* RAFI, *and around him, he sees criss-crossed motorways, flyovers, huge direction indicators and a swirl of fast-moving traffic, dreamlike, noisy,*

*strange. We see it through his eyes as if for the first time. This isn't
the England he remembers.*)

EXT. BALCONY OF TOWER BLOCK. DAY

ROSIE *stands on the balcony of the tower block where the old man lives. It
is on one of those estates that look as if they have been transplanted from
the outskirts of Warsaw. She is waiting for the ambulance. She looks out
over London, towards the concrete sledge of the motorway in the distance.
Then she looks down. A group of youngish kids knock on the door of the
flat opposite. They push the owner aside and steam into the flat, wearing
masks and scarves tied around their faces. Down on the ground, in the
centre of the courtyard, there is a huge bonfire burning. Black and white
kids stoke it, throwing things on. The ambulance, its siren going, lights
flashing, screams into the courtyard.*

INT. SAMMY'S AND ROSIE'S BATHROOM. DAY

ROSIE *is now washing her hair in their 'Victorian' bathroom. She plunges
her hair into the water. She pulls her head out. We hold on her face and see
her hair full of water. This could be shot, perhaps using a mirror, so that
we can see through into the large, long, living room. There are several of*
ROSIE*'s women friends gathered here, plus one white and one black boy,
both deaf and dumb, who dance to music. Then one of the women,* RANI,
appears behind ROSIE, *banging the door shut.*

> RANI
> Rosie, there's trouble outside. I think there will be fires tonight.
> (ROSIE *turns and looks at her. Then they look into the bathroom
> mirror. They do not see themselves but instead a derelict shed in a
> green wood. It is pouring with rain. In the shed a young man is
> painting a portrait of* ROSIE.)

> ROSIE
> That's my lover, Walter. I'm seeing him later.

> RANI
> What will Sammy say about that?

> ROSIE
> Though a forest fire will have broken out in his heart, lungs

and liver, his tongue will try to say: 'What an interesting life you have, Rosie.'

RANI

How damaging for him.

EXT. STREETS. DUSK

Now RAFI's *cab enters the South London street where* SAMMY *and* ROSIE *live.*

RAFI

(*To* CABBIE)
My son Sammy is a very successful accountant.

CABBIE

And he lives here?
(*Halfway up, the street is blocked by police cars, police vans and an ambulance. This is the street from scene 2. The cab stops. It cannot go any further. We see puzzled* RAFI *taking in the chaotic scene. Now* RAFI, *with his suitcases, walks past the police cars and ambulance. The exteriors at night have a heightened, unreal feel. As* RAFI *passes by the terraced house from scene 3, two ambulance men carry out a body on a stretcher. A crowd of black people and some whites have gathered outside, many truculent, others weeping.* DANNY *stands apart from it all. His young black girlfriend and their kid are there now, with him.* RAFI *walks past, taking it all in. We hold fully and carefully on the faces.* RAFI *walks past some larger houses. The* CABBIE *watches him. On the steps of these houses* ROSIE *and* VIVIA *are standing, anxiously watching the ambulance incident.* RAFI *pushes his way through the crowd,* DANNY *watching him.* ROSIE *spots* RAFI *in the crowd and rushes down into the midst of it all to get him, pushing her way through.*)

ROSIE

Rafi! Rafi!
(*She finds him and embraces him.* DANNY *is watching.*)
What's wrong? Didn't Sammy pick you up?

RAFI

The only thing that boy's picking up at the moment is a sexually transmitted disease!

INT. SAMMY'S AND ROSIE'S FLAT. EVENING

A spacious flat, plenty of books stacked up, a jungle of plants, some decent prints, music playing. The flat is wild and untidy, not yuppie. Charts and maps on the walls, pictures of flowers, old Buddhas, lots of junk furniture, home-made sculpture, bidets full of books, velvet curtains on the walls, huge wrecked armchairs, layers of Turkish carpets, hookahs, brass pots, high-tech accoutrements . . . a hammock strung across the window, red silk billowing down from the ceiling. Four of Rosie's friends are drinking wine: EVA, RANI, BRIDGET and MARGY. EVA is a Jewish intellectual. BRIDGET has her head shaved at the sides, the rest of her hair is long. MARGY is very committed politically. BRIDGET and EVA massage each other.

> MARGY
>
> (*Ironic*)
> Sammy may be an accountant, but he's a radical
> accountant . . .

> RANI
>
> (*To* BRIDGET)
> Won't you massage me? Don't I need support too? Where's
> Rosie and Vivia gone?

> BRIDGET
>
> (*Part of a continuing conversation*)
> I've always been on the pill. Better cancer than pregnant. I've
> never even seen a rubber. I'm not that generation. Margy?
> (*Meanwhile the white boy is rubbing himself off on the carpet.*
> RANI *pulls him up and he stares panting at the women. They ignore him.*)

> MARGY
>
> I always carry half a dozen with me. In case I meet a tall dark,
> hard stranger.
> (*She pulls a packet of rubbers out of her pocket.*)

INT. STAIRS. EVENING

ROSIE *and* VIVIA *struggle up the stairs with Rafi's suitcases. This area of the flats is also spacious and open.* RAFI *climbs up the broad stone steps in front of them, with immaculate dignity as usual.*

RAFI

Is this world war typical of your streets?

ROSIE

(*To* RAFI)

The police shot a woman by mistake. They were looking for her son. It's easy enough to mistake a fifty-year-old office cleaner for a twenty-year-old jazz trumpeter.

(*When* RAFI *and* VIVIA *come into the room they see and hear.*)

MARGY

You hold the condom there and pull down.

(MARGY *pulls the condom down over a large knobbly carrot. The women have gathered round to look and laugh.*)

EVA

Carrots are certainly more attractive than ding-dongs. And more prolific in vitamins, I'd imagine.

(*Now* RAFI *stands there slightly bewildered. He also sees the deaf and dumb boys, one of whom tries to dance with him.* RANI *watches* RAFI *carefully. She recognizes him.*)

ROSIE

Rafi, these are my friends.

RAFI

(*Under his breath*)

Good God, are they really?

(MARGY *is hastily rolling the condom off the carrot.*)

BRIDGET

(*To* VIVIA)

Everything all right outside?

VIVIA

Not at all. Let's go, Margy. Eva. Everyone.

(MARGY *bites into the carrot. They get up.* ROSIE *takes* RAFI'*s arm and leads him away from the women to show him the flat.* VIVIA, *who is in the early stages of seducing* RANI, *looks expectantly at her.*)

RANI

(*To* VIVIA)
I'll see you later. I'll stay for a while.

VIVIA

Will you ring me?

RANI

Yes, yes.
(*They take each other's hands and kiss goodbye, a longish tonguey kiss, which* RAFI *sees and is rather thrown by.* RANI *looks up defiantly at him.* VIVIA, *laughing at this, leads the women out.* RANI *joins* ROSIE, *who is showing* RAFI *the flat. The deaf and dumb boys peer through the foliage at* RAFI.)

ROSIE

How d'you like our place, Rafi?

RANI

Aren't they just in clover?

RAFI

Well, 50 per cent clover, 50 per cent synthetic materials.

RANI

Have you entirely retired from politics, Mr Rahman?

RAFI

Oh yes, yes.

RANI

Asians in Britain have followed your political career with absolute fascination. I'd love to interview you for a paper I'm involved with.
(RAFI *shakes his head and puts his arms around* ROSIE.)

RAFI

I'm here as a purely private person.

RANI

Mr Rahman, someone like you could never be a purely private person.

INT. FRONT DOOR OF FLAT. EVENING

ROSIE *is saying goodbye to* RANI *and kissing her.* RAFI, *not seen by them, is walking towards the kitchen. When he hears* RANI *and* ROSIE *talking about him he stops in a place where he can overhear them.*
     RANI *has the deaf and dumb boys with her.*

                    ROSIE
Why are you so interested in Rafi?

                    RANI
How much d'you know about him?

                    ROSIE
Only that he was something in the government over there.
He's always claiming to be a friend of Mao Tse-tung.

                    RANI
Not that that'll get him into any nightclubs. I'll dig out some
stuff about him. I think it'll interest you.

INT. LIVING ROOM. EVENING

RAFI *sits at the table. Everyone has gone now.* RAFI *steadily eats his main course, having finished the avocado.* ROSIE *shouts through to him.*

                    ROSIE
I expect Sammy's got stuck with a client. He's got a lot of
freelance work – actors, disc jockeys, photographers. The
cream of the scum use Sammy.

EXT. MOTORWAY. DUSK

We are on the motorway through London. A high shot of sunset over London town. We close in to see SAMMY *in his car, shirt open to the waist, driving frantically at high speed, loud music playing in the car. A straggly band of kids, about twelve or fifteen of them, strangely dressed, some carrying musical instruments, have just crossed the motorway. Now they are climbing the rim of it and down, throwing a long rope over the side. One plays the trumpet, another a drum, one more the violin, etc. They are white and black, men and women.*

                              RAFI

(*Voice over*)
My boy is very well respected?

                              ROSIE

(*Voice over*)
For an accountant.

INT. LIVING ROOM. EVENING

Now ROSIE *is sitting down for her food. She takes a long gulp of wine.*
RAFI *watches her censoriously.*

                              RAFI

(*Eating*)
I hear the food in the West is a tribute to chemistry rather than
nature.

                              ROSIE

(*Drinking quickly*)
What do you want to do in London, Rafi?

                              RAFI

I want to see you both, because I love you. Plus there's an old
friend I have here, Alice. And before I die I must know my
beloved London again: for me it is the centre of civilization –
tolerant, intelligent and completely out of control now, I hear.

                              ROSIE

That depends on which newspaper you read.

EXT. STREET. EVENING

Having necessarily dumped his car nearby, SAMMY *is running along the
street towards the house. But he can't get through the crowd. The ambulance
has gone. There are several police vans instead. Black and white kids have
gathered in the street. The atmosphere is very heavy.* DANNY *stands there. A
white kid of about thirteen on a bicycle rides after* SAMMY.

                              KID

Hey, dude. Dude. Wanna buy some black hash? Coke?
(SAMMY *is now with the* KID. *As the* KID *sells him some stuff:*)

SAMMY

What the fuck's going on here, man?

KID

Shooting. Bad murder, man. Big trouble.

INT. SAMMY'S AND ROSIE'S LIVING ROOM. EVENING

ROSIE *and* RAFI *talk at the table.*

RAFI

There has been a strong hand on this country, yes?

ROSIE

The working class have not been completely beaten down by it but –

RAFI

Exactly. In my country the English not-working class we call them. In my factory people really work. That is how wealth is created.
(*He helps himself to food. She grinds pepper over it.*)
Luckily black is my favourite colour.

ROSIE

Rafi, you are still wicked.

RAFI

And you are still my favourite daughter-in-law. Look. To prove it I'll give you something.
(*Pulls a rather wretched cap out of a brown bag.*)
Put it on!
(*She puts it on.*)
Who do you think gave it to me! Mao Tse-tung, that's who!
(*A sound behind them. Through the foliage they turn to see*
SAMMY *at the door, looking exhausted, terrible.*)

SAMMY

Hallo, Dad. Rosie. Sorry I'm late. I was just looking into one or two important avenues.
(*To* ROSIE)
What have you got on your head?

ROSIE

The Chinese revolution.
(*Cut to: The meal is over and* ROSIE *and* SAMMY *are now clearing the table.* SAMMY *has a beer in each hand, sandwich in gob.*)

RAFI

Of course Auntie Rani's dog bites everyone, including her husband, the children –

ROSIE

(*Coldly*)
I'm going out soon, Samir.

RAFI

– and the servants . . .

SAMMY

(*To* ROSIE)
Where? Tonight? Tonight?

RAFI

But she won't have the dog destroyed. I'd put a bullet through his balls myself. Wouldn't you, Sammy?

SAMMY

(*To* ROSIE)
Don't go anywhere tonight. Something's happening out there. It'll be bloody, you know.

ROSIE

When black people were attacked before and defended themselves, you didn't used to stay in and have your supper.

SAMMY

My father's here, Rosie.

ROSIE

One of my cases died today. An old man. You wonder what your own life means. I hate my job, picking up the smashed pieces of people's lives. Everyone despises you for it: the people

whose lives you're poking into, and the others who think you're
pretending to be a fucking saint.
(RAFI *watches them. He gets up.*)

                    RAFI
I will recover. Am I in your own room?

                    SAMMY
(*Perfunctory*)
We're putting you in Rosie's study.
(RAFI *goes.*)

                    ROSIE
Don't hurt him.

                    SAMMY
He did abandon me years ago. He's a stranger to me.

                    ROSIE
I think he wants to know you again.

INT. ROSIE'S STUDY. EVENING

*A huge dark wood desk. A large framed photo of Virginia Woolf and a
photograph of Rodin's* The Kiss. *Many books. A bed has been installed
for* RAFI. *He unpacks his numerous medicines: ointments, pills,
suppositories.*

                    SAMMY
(*Voice over*)
Stay with us tonight, Rosie.

                    ROSIE
(*Voice over*)
I've arranged to see Walter.
(*Cut back to living room.*)

                    SAMMY
Your boyfriend. Lover.

                    ROSIE
I said I would. But I am honest with you at least.
(*Pause.*)

Sammy. Freedom plus commitment. Those were our words.
They were to be the two pillars of our love and life together.
(*Cut back to the study:* RAFI *unwraps a suppository. As he does so he
pulls aside the curtain and looks out of the window. He sees
aggressive people running about. And in the distance a car burns –
the flames strangely shooting straight up in the air. Nearer, a group
of kids, black and white, some of them masked, are kicking down a
wall, gathering the bricks up and running off with them.*)
(*Voice over*)
Didn't we agree? I'll tell you what I want. I don't want
deadness or order.
(*Cut to living room.*)
(*Putting her coat on*)
Sometimes I want a little passion.

SAMMY

Don't let me stand in your way.

ROSIE

(*Kindly*)
I can't always mother you, baby.

EXT. STREET. EVENING

ROSIE *runs up the street past the kids kicking the wall down. She runs
towards the burning car. Firemen are now trying to reach it, but the kids,
joyfully, are succeeding in keeping them back. One kid has a ghetto-
blaster with him.* ANNA *is there photographing everything, posing
people by the car.* ROSIE *watches her, laughing at her charming cheek.*

INT. ROSIE'S STUDY. EVENING

SAMMY *tucks* RAFI *up in bed. He pulls the curtains on the wild street.*

SAMMY

We thought we'd give you a room with a view. And here's some
cotton-wool for your earholes.
(*Outside someone screams and there's an explosion. A petrol bomb.*)
I expect it's a wild street party.

RAFI

Where's Rosie?

SAMMY

Just popped out for some fresh air.

RAFI

How's married life? Good? Bad?

SAMMY

Married life? It's a scream.

RAFI

(*Taking* SAMMY's *hand*)
Son, I am in great danger. I am here in London partly because
my life is threatened there.

SAMMY

Who from?
(*Pause.*)
Can't you tell me?

RAFI

Does it matter? Let's just say that from now on I am in your
hands.

EXT. STREET. NIGHT

ROSIE *runs into a shopping street. Chaos. A black man, accompanied by a
white man and large crowd of assorted others, black and white, men and
women, is about to smash a sledgehammer into the window of a hi-fi shop.
The glass shatters. A cheer goes up. The crowd rushes into the shop. A
young black man falls into the glass, getting up with his hands and face
streaming blood. A TV crew films it all. The others grab electrical goods
and flee with their loot through noise and chaos.* DANNY *stands there
looking at* ROSIE, *with some of the straggly kids.* ROSIE *runs on. A little
old white woman, with a shopping basket on wheels, rushes into the
electrical shop and loots a transistor radio. She rushes out as fast as
she can.*

INT. ROSIE'S STUDY. NIGHT

RAFI *lies in bed in the half-lit room. He's asleep, having a nightmare. He cries out, then awakes. He lies there being stared at by Virginia Woolf, which becomes more horrible the more she looks at him. The noise from outside rises around him. It could be in his head or for real: he doesn't know. He sits up. On the edge of the bed he pulls cotton wool out of his ears. He covers his face with his hands.*

INT. LIVING ROOM. NIGHT

SAMMY *is swigging a beer. An unnaturally large half-eaten hamburger and milkshake are on the table next to an open porn magazine.* SAMMY's *trousers are round his ankles. He's listening to a CD of something loud and noble – Shostakovich, for example. With half a straw stuck up his nose he leans over a line of coke he's laid out on the glass-topped table. Now* RAFI *is at the door. He yells but cannot be heard above the music and* SAMMY *sits with his back to him, having snorted the coke, bitten into the giant hamburger and eagerly turned over a page of the magazine. Disturbed,* SAMMY *turns to see, over the back of the sofa, his father gesticulating at him. Determinedly* RAFI *goes to the door of the flat, picking up his overcoat as he goes.* SAMMY *stands up, trousers round his ankles, and falls over, the rest of his coke flying everywhere. He could try to snort it out of the carpet.*

Cut to: SAMMY *stands at the top of the stairs pulling up his trousers as* RAFI *runs downstairs.*

                         SAMMY
     (*Yelling after him*)
     Haven't you got jet-lag, Dad?

                         RAFI
     I have seen wars, you know!

                         SAMMY
     Don't go out there, Dad!

EXT. STREET. NIGHT

RAFI *is now in the street and heading full-tilt towards the riot area.* SAMMY *comes out of the house, hamburger and shake in hand, and down the street after him. There is much running about in the street. The street is covered with debris. RAFI stops by the car that ROSIE saw in flames. It is burnt out now but little flames unnaturally flicker all over it.*

RAFI

My God, I can't understand it, why ever do you live here?

SAMMY

It's cosmopolitan, Pop. And cheap. Come on. Let's go, eh? Please.

RAFI

No, I want to see this.

(RAFI *pulls away from him. A young black man comes out of his house and runs down the street pursued by his father trying to stop him going out. His mother stands at the door. Father and son struggle.*)

SAMMY

Leonardo da Vinci would have lived in the inner city.

RAFI

You know that for certain, do you?

SAMMY

Yes, because the city is a mass of fascination.

(*Now we see* RANI, VIVIA, EVA, MARGY, BRIDGET, *taking care of each other, watching the riot.* RANI *screams abuse at the violence of the police in dealing with people.* MARGY *is disgusted with the violence of the entire thing and by the sympathy of the other women for the rioters.*)

MARGY

But it's just men, rotten men, being men!

(EVA *is sympathetic to the rioters and carries an iron bar threateningly. Suddenly a brick comes from somewhere and smashes* VIVIA *on the side of the head. She goes down. The women gather round her. They pick her up and rush her away as a phalanx of police with riot shields makes towards them.* EVA *throws her iron bar at the police. As* SAMMY *and* RAFI *flee, we see injured people lying in the rubble, some attended by friends and ambulance people. A young white man squats under a hedge crying.*)

SAMMY

Rosie says –

RAFI

What does the great Rosie say?

SAMMY

Rosie says these revolts are an affirmation of the human spirit.
A kind of justice is being done.
(*Pause. The situation becomes more dangerous. But* SAMMY *is
excited.*)
Let's get the hell out of here!
(RAFI *stumbles. Now* ANNA *runs towards them, taking pictures. A
bunch of white and black kids run past* RAFI.)
(*To* ANNA)
What are you doing here, Anna? This isn't your part of town!

RAFI

These are fools and madmen!

SAMMY

(*As she photographs*)
Anna, cut it out! This is my father!

ANNA

(*Shaking his hand*)
Pleased to meet you, sir. Welcome to England. I hope you
enjoy your stay!
(*Kisses* SAMMY.)
I'll give you a ring.
(*She goes. Cut to: Later.* SAMMY *is now hurrying* RAFI *back.
Suddenly they turn a corner and stop beside a car. The windows have
been smashed, the radio and speakers ripped out, etc. In the distance
we see the backs of a line of police, as they charge the screaming mob.*
SAMMY *is more concerned about the car and he kicks it wildly.*)

SAMMY

For fuck's fucking fuck sake, fuck it!

RAFI

Boy, didn't they teach you more than one word at the school I
paid through the arse for you to attend?

> SAMMY

But this is my fucking car!

> RAFI

Surely an affirmation of the human spirit?
(*Cut to:* SAMMY *and* RAFI *walk through gloomy reverberating alleys back to the house.* RAFI *has his arm around* SAMMY *now.*)
I don't want anything any more. The things I own are a burden to me. So I've given the factory to your cousins.

> SAMMY

What, those idiots?

> RAFI

They are going into air-conditioners. I think making heaters in one of the world's hottest countries was not good business sense.
(*Cut to: The steps of the house. On the steps an injured white kid is with his black girlfriend.*)
The money I've managed to get out of the country, and it's a lot of money –

> SAMMY

Which total prick have you thrown that at, Pop?

> RAFI

One of my main purposes in coming here is to transfer that money to your account, son.
(*Cut to: Now they are in the comparative silence of the stone hallway.*)
You can have the money provided you buy yourself a house in a part of England that hasn't been twinned with Beirut! Is there anywhere like that left? I would also like some grandchildren. Please. There is money for them too.

> SAMMY

How much?

INT. OFFICE. MORNING

The office of an organization rather like Amnesty. VIVIA *and* RANI *sitting across the desk from a young Japanese woman.*

JAPANESE WOMAN

Rafi Rahman.

RANI

Yes, I rang you yesterday to ask for information.
(*The* JAPANESE WOMAN *rises, smiles.*)

JAPANESE WOMAN

I remember. Let me get the file to show you what we've got.
(*She goes.* VIVIA *and* RANI *hold hands nervously.*)

VIVIA

(*To* RANI)
Suppose we find out some stuff about Rafi that you wouldn't
want to hear while you were eating your breakfast? What do we
do then – just tell Rosie and let her get on with it?

RANI

Wouldn't it be worse to conceal something we knew?

VIVIA

I know, I know, but we'll be putting her in a difficult position.
(*The* JAPANESE WOMAN *returns with a thick file and puts it down
on the desk.* RANI *and* VIVIA *lean forward to look at it.*)

JAPANESE WOMAN

That's volume one.

INT. LIVING ROOM. MORNING

RAFI *eats breakfast in his silk pyjamas. In front of him is his chequebook.
He has written the cheque and it lies on the table. Now he writes a
postcard. It is a few days later. He looks across the flat, fascinated by the
sight of* ROSIE *who, in a T-shirt and shorts, is doing muscle-bursting
vigorous weight-training and body-building exercises to the sound of
Mozart's Requiem.*

Cut to: A little later. ROSIE *is dressed for work now.*

RAFI, *walking about the flat, drops the postcard and bends over stiffly
to retrieve it.* ROSIE *picks it up for him.*

ROSIE

Writing home already? But you've only been here a few days, Rafi. And you've hardly been out.

RAFI

Sweetie, read it. It's to my fondest relatives.

ROSIE

(*Reads*)
'Streets on fire – wish you were here!'

RAFI

(*Pats her arse as she laughs.*)
Rosie, one thing more. What about the sound of little footsteps, eh? Isn't it about time?

ROSIE

(*Having to control herself*)
Rafi . . .

RAFI

Eh? I know you're a kind of feminist, but you're not a lesbian too, are you?

ROSIE

I'm thinking about having a child.

RAFI

(*Taking her hand*)
It would give me so much happiness.

ROSIE

And that's exactly what I want, Rafi.

RAFI

You've cheered me up. I may even have the nerve to go out today.
(*Cut to: A little later.* ROSIE *is leaving for work.* VIVIA *has called round. She stands at the door with* ROSIE. VIVIA *gives* ROSIE *a brown envelope.*)

VIVIA

This is from Rani.

ROSIE

Great. Thanks.
(*Calls to* RAFI)
See you later, Rafi.
(*Cut to: On the stairs down* ROSIE *opens the envelope.* VIVIA
looks over ROSIE*'s shoulder.* RANI *has sent* ROSIE *material about*
RAFI: *press cuttings from the Subcontinent and Britain: we can see*
his picture; photocopies of articles, Amnesty reports, etc.)

VIVIA

Does Sammy know about all of it?

ROSIE

He's always tried to cut his father out of his mind.
(*Pause.*)
Poor Sammy.

EXT. STREET. MORNING

RAFI *is out for a walk. In his natty hat he passes through an alley with
high walls and emerges into a run-down housing estate. One of those
estates that looks a little like Soweto – no shops, no nothing.* RAFI *walks
across the open area between graffiti-sprayed tower blocks. Kids roam
around, some with scarves over their faces. Others wear crash helmets.*

Cut to: RAFI *has left the estate and turned the corner into another street,
a main street. Here shops have been looted, burned out, the wrecked hulks
of cars litter the place, paving stones discarded, etc. Plenty of onlookers,
journalists, disconsolate shopkeepers, a film crew, street cleaners, etc.*
RAFI *looks on. Now a white kid runs across the street carrying a hi-fi deck
in his arms. He's followed by three cops. They all run incredibly fast. The
kid drops the deck. The police grab him. A fight breaks out. Other people,
both black and white, men and women, appear suddenly and pile in.*
DANNY *stands watching on the edge of this. Someone is thrown against*
DANNY *and he crashes back into the doorway. More police charge down
the street.* DANNY *gets up and prepares to flee. As others run,* RAFI *can't
get out of the way quickly enough, and gets knocked down. He falls to the
ground.* DANNY *is tearing past him.* DANNY *stops though, picks* RAFI *up,
and his natty hat, and pulls him away.*

Cut to: Breathless, DANNY *and* RAFI *have made it to an alleyway.*
RAFI*'s hands and knees are cut and grazed. He pulls up his trouser leg to*

examine the bloodied skin. DANNY *takes* RAFI'*s handkerchief, spits into it and rubs* RAFI '*s knee. There is noise all around them.* RAFI *is concerned about the state of his suit.*

DANNY

Where d'you live? Take you back home?

RAFI

Riot or no riot –

DANNY

Revolt. It's a revolt.

RAFI

Yes. Good. This society may be on its last legs but I am expected in Cockfosters. Please point me north and say a prayer in my favour.
(*A* TORY MP *and the* PROPERTY DEVELOPER *walk past the end of the alley at this moment.* RAFI *and* DANNY *hear this.*)

TORY MP

You're a wealthy, intelligent businessman.
(DANNY *spits.*)
You've got to invest in this area – for your sake and ours. You can do whatever you like.

PROPERTY DEVELOPER

I want that open space under the motorway – then we can talk.
(*When they've gone* DANNY *pulls* RAFI.)

DANNY

Come on. I'll take you.

RAFI

Where?

DANNY

Come on.

INT. TUBE TRAIN. DAY

DANNY *and* RAFI *sit down,* DANNY *whipping away a newspaper from the*

seat before RAFI *sits down. Opposite them sits a huge white man in a
tracksuit. He is doing various finger-strengthening exercises.* RAFI *watches
him warily. Next to the* FINGER MAN *sits a woman, middle-aged, off-
white, with a wretched dog that eats a sandwich off the floor. The woman
has a cigarette in her mouth. And as she scratches her ear the fag jumps
from left to right in her mouth.*

RAFI

Do we have to change trains?
(*Suddenly the* FINGER MAN *rises up on the arm-rests of the seat.
And there he suspends himself like a fat bat. This is obviously some
kind of tube-train callisthenic.*)

FINGER MAN

(*To* DANNY)
Time me, man!
(RAFI *practically has a heart attack as* DANNY *grabs his arm and
pulls his sleeve up to look at Rafi's watch. Meanwhile:*)

DANNY

(*To* RAFI)
Danny, my name is. But people who like me call me Victoria.
People who don't like me call me jerk-off.
(*Pause.*)
I know these tube lines. Sometimes I ride the tubes all day. It's
my office, the Victoria Line. It's where I do my paperwork.
Paperwork overwhelms me.
(*He glances over at the* FINGER MAN *whose face is about to explode.
He collapses back in his seat.*
　　Cut to: DANNY *and* RAFI *now walk together down a long tube
tunnel. As an expert, I suggest the tunnel that connects the Piccadilly
with the Victoria Line at Green Park – a superb sensation you get
here of endless walking in both directions. The acoustics are
excellent.*)

RAFI

I'm going to meet a woman – Alice – who I haven't seen for
over twenty years. I stayed in her house when I left university.
In those days before you were born there was a colour bar in
England. They gave me shelter, she and her husband. Then I

went back home to marry. But I . . . I loved her terribly.
(*In the tunnel the straggly band of musicians are playing. We last
saw them crossing the motorway. They play the theme song of the
movie – there are trumpeters, saxophonists, a hurdy-gurdy player,
bassoon groovers, etc. Rappers. The dog from scene 2 is with them. As
DANNY and RAFI walk past, everyone in the band says
simultaneously, 'Wotcha, Danny boy.' DANNY nods regally. Also, a
couple of girls and boys are dancing to the music. If we could film
them from the front for a moment, we could easily see for a second
the whole tube tunnel dancing, like in a Cliff Richard film.*)

DANNY

Why didn't you get it on with her?

RAFI

My father wanted me to marry someone else. And Alice's
husband was watching me like a hawk. When I die and go to
heaven, I will marry her there.

DANNY

You don't know what she's like now.
(*The Asian* CABBIE, *in the brown suit, with the bandage over one
eye, walks towards them and on past them quickly.*)

EXT. STREET. DAY

A leafy North London suburb, tree-lined, sedate, quiet. RAFI *and* DANNY
*walk towards Alice's house – a detached four-bedroom place with a front
and back garden.* RAFI *has bought a large bunch of flowers, a box of chocs
and a bottle of champagne which* DANNY *carries. Whites in the street
stop and stare at* RAFI *and* DANNY. RAFI *smiles politely at them.*

RAFI

Why are they looking at us like that?

DANNY

They think we're gonna rob their houses.

RAFI

God, things have changed to little! Poor Alice – she was born
and brought up in India, you know.

DANNY

She's black then?

RAFI

No, extremely white. But her family were in India for
generations. I think I probably threw anti-colonial stones at her
father's house in Bombay.
(*They arrive at the house.*)
This is it.
(RAFI *tries to get rid of* DANNY.)
OK then, Victoria. Be seeing you. Thanks.
(RAFI *pats him patronizingly on the shoulder and goes up the front
path and rings the bell. He turns and sees* DANNY *standing halfway
up the path.*)

DANNY

You won't make it alone out here in the country.

RAFI

This isn't the country, you damn fool. It's just respectable.
(DANNY *sees that* ALICE *has opened the door. He indicates to* RAFI.
RAFI *turns, sees* ALICE, *and goes towards her. It is* DANNY *who is
moved.* ALICE *and* RAFI *go into the house.* DANNY *stands there a
moment, then goes round the side of the house.*

   Cut to: Now DANNY *is in the back garden. An old white man and
a mentally defective boy are doing Alice's gardening.*

   Cut to: In Alice's living room RAFI *and* ALICE *sit on the sofa
drinking tea. As they put their cups to their old lips we see their faces
are streaming with tears although they talk normally. Alice's house
is full of Indian memorabilia from the twenties and thirties. The
walls are crumbling, everything is falling apart, it is a much stranger
and darker place than it seems at first.*)
I'll never forget the kindness you showed me.

ALICE

But you did forget, Rafi. You forgot all about me.
(*Cut to: In the garden* DANNY *is walking about. He finds an old
gardening hat on a bench which looks as if it's made from crushed
budgie.*)
Sometimes when you were in the government there, I'd see

you on the TV, talking about some crisis or other. You were impressive, though I did come to associate you exclusively with aeroplane hijackings.
(*Pause.*)
I thought you would come and see me before, you know.
(ALICE *has got up to put on a record, something romantic from the forties. When she sits beside him once more, they move into each other's arms.* RAFI *looks up to see* DANNY, *with the hat on, gazing through the window.* RAFI *becomes agitated, as you would. With his spare stroking hand he indicates that* DANNY *should disappear immediately. Just as* ALICE *looks up,* DANNY'*s face moves away.*)
Shall I make some more Earl Grey tea? Don't be distressed, Rafi. For me, you are still a charming and delightful man. What about a piece of Jamaica rum cake?

RAFI

Alice, there's someone I think you should meet.
(*Cut to: The garden.* DANNY *stands there.* ALICE *and* RAFI *outside.* ALICE *looks at* DANNY.)
(*To* ALICE)
This is my map-reader and guide, Victoria. We owe this visit to his ingenuity and kindness.
(*She greets him graciously.*)

EXT. SOUTH LONDON STREET. DUSK

A police car careers up the street. RAFI *and* DANNY *are crossing the road on their way home.* DANNY *pulls* RAFI *out of the way of the screaming police car.*

RAFI

(*To* DANNY)
You nearly gave me a fucking heart attack when I saw you outside Alice's window.
(*Pause.*)
What are you doing now? Haven't you got anywhere to go?

DANNY

Yeah. I'm going with you.

INT. SAMMY'S AND ROSIE'S LIVING ROOM. DUSK

RAFI *and* DANNY *enter the flat.* DANNY *looks around.*
  Cut to: We see DANNY *standing alone in the flat. He is clenching and unclenching his fists, obviously distressed about something, unable to get it out of his mind.* RAFI *comes up behind him.*

> RAFI

Victoria, what's wrong?

> DANNY

For a long time, right, I've been for non-violence. Never gone for burning things down. I can see the attraction but not the achievement. OK. After all, you guys ended colonialism non-violently. You'd sit down all over the place, right? We have a kind of domestic colonialism to deal with here, because they don't allow us to run our own communities. But if full-scale civil war breaks out we can only lose. And what's going to happen to all the beauty?

> RAFI

If I lived here . . . I would be on your side. All over the world the colonized people are fighting back. It's the necessity of the age. It gives me hope.

> DANNY

But how should we fight? That's what I want to know.

EXT. SOUTH LONDON STREET. DUSK

SAMMY *waiting in the street.* ROSIE *walks through the crowd towards him.* SAMMY *stands drinking from a can of beer. Scenes of patched-up desolation around them. People are reconstructing their shops. Gangs roam about, watching. A heavy police presence. A* TORY MP *and the* PROPERTY DEVELOPER *stand in the street talking with their advisers.* ROSIE *goes to* SAMMY *and they kiss and greet each other warmly.*

> ROSIE

Good day at the office, dear? I had only one suicide today.
(*Cut to: Later. They are walking through the shopping area.*)

SAMMY

How's that dreary untalented prick?

ROSIE

Cut it out. Walter's got an exhibition.

SAMMY

Christ, a Renaissance man. Rosie, I think we should have a kid,
you know. My seed's pretty rich at the moment – I've
examined it. I'm well hot to trot in that respect.

ROSIE

But you wouldn't be a responsible father. The unfair sex has so
far to go.
(*Pause.*)
Aren't you interested in politics any more? You were always out
improving society, Sammy.

SAMMY

I find more and more that the worst thing about being on the
left is the other people you've got on your side.
(*She kisses him, holding him, laughing.*)

INT. ASIAN SHOP. DUSK

Now SAMMY *and* ROSIE *are in a wretched dark Asian shop on the front
line. The Asian* SHOPKEEPER *is familiar to them. The shop was looted
during the revolt. A white woman customer in the shop has a Siamese cat
on her shoulder, on a lead.*

SAMMY

(*To* ROSIE)
I can't see my old man staying too long, can you?
(*To* SHOPKEEPER)
Any noodles, Ajeeb?

ROSIE

You kissed your father on the nose and said he could stay
forever.

SAMMY

You have to do that. It's a well-known lie.

SHOPKEEPER

The noodles are looking right at you.

SAMMY

So they are. Any Indian sweets?
(SHOPKEEPER *shakes his head.*)
You're joking. You're not joking? Ajeeb, it's a terrible disgrace.

SHOPKEEPER

Samir, I tell you, the trash took everything in the looting.
They're jealous of us. But why? In this country aren't we all in
the same position?

ROSIE

(*To* SAMMY)
Your father announced how long he wants to stay with us.
(*Pause.*)
One or two years, he said.

SAMMY

What?

INT. SAMMY'S AND ROSIE'S FLAT. EVENING

DANNY *has Sammy's huge TV in his arms and is staggering around
under the weight of it. The TV is on and* RAFI *watches it with his feet in a
bowl of water as* DANNY *perilously manoeuvres it into position for* RAFI.
This is to prevent RAFI *from having to move.* RAFI *is watching footage of
the riots on TV. He is wearing pyjamas and eating sherbets from a paper
bag.*

INT. THE STAIRS UP TO THE FLAT. EVENING

SAMMY *and* ROSIE *walk up drinking, stop at the landing for an
altercation and finally reach the door to their flat. They are getting on
really well, despite everything.*

ROSIE

And did you see him filing his fingernails and –

SAMMY

Putting powder between his toes!

ROSIE

Or cutting the hair in his ears! D'you know he handed me his washing and said, 'Be sure not to use too hot an iron on the silk shirts!'

(ROSIE *and* SAMMY *crack up, leaning against the wall, laughing and slapping each other exaggeratedly.* SAMMY *stops abruptly.*)

SAMMY

Stop badmouthing my father, you silly bitch!

ROSIE

Oh fuck off.

SAMMY

I better tell you, Rosie. He's pretty keen to unload some dough on us. It's a lotta dough I'm on about here, darling. So we better get fucking respectful right now!

(*Cut to: Seconds later. They walk up,* SAMMY *behind, his hand up her skirt playfully.*)

ROSIE

We went to that factory where Rafi made his money, remember? I know Dante based the Inferno on it. You don't have to be radical to see that to accept one penny from him is to get into bed with all kinds of evil.

(*At the top of the stairs* ROSIE *fumbles for her keys but* SAMMY *leans lazily on the bell.*)

SAMMY

I don't think they come any more against inherited wealth than me, Rosie. But didn't Engels have a factory?

(*She nods.*)

Right, let's take the money.

ROSIE

Sammy, I think you should know, your father was probably guilty of some other things too.

SAMMY

What things, beside paternalism, greed, general dissipation, mistreatment of my mother and vicious exploitation?

ROSIE

Well, he –
(DANNY *opens the door. He's holding a bottle of whisky and a glass.*
DANNY *indicates for them to come into the flat. He pours a drink,*
which he gives to ROSIE. SAMMY, *convinced they're being burgled,*
drops some of his shopping in fear. Through the open door ROSIE *sees*
RAFI *sitting there with his tired feet in the bowl.* ROSIE *smiles at*
DANNY. DANNY *is now picking up* SAMMY's *dropped shopping.*
SAMMY *walks into the room and stares at* RAFI.)

RAFI

What's the matter, boy?

SAMMY

What the hell's going on?
(*Cut to:* DANNY *and* ROSIE, *bending down to pick up the shopping,*
look at each other with great interest.)

ROSIE

(*To* DANNY)
Live nearby?

DANNY

Not far. You?

ROSIE

Right here.

DANNY

What a thing.

INT. LIVING ROOM. EVENING

Later. The washing-up bowl has been removed. DANNY *and* RAFI *sit there*
watching TV. SAMMY *walks uncomfortably around the room, drinking,*
trying to get rid of them.

SAMMY

(*To* RAFI)
I've gotta finish some accounts right now. And Rosie's got to
get on with her writing.

RAFI

And what is Rosie writing?

(*By mistake* SAMMY *stands in front of the TV.* DANNY *stares affrontedly at him.*)

SAMMY

Oh sorry.

(*To* RAFI)

Yeah, she's doing a major article.

RAFI

On body-building?

SAMMY

Yeah. Kind of. It's on the ins and outs, the types, qualities and varieties of . . . It's a kind of historical socio-political investigation. Into kissing.

RAFI

Kissing? Speak up, son. Did you say kissing?

SAMMY

Yeah. 'The Intelligent Woman's Guide to Kissing in History.'

RAFI

Oh my God!

(DANNY *and* RAFI *catch each other's eye and laugh. Meanwhile* SAMMY *picks up the cheque his father wrote in the morning. He is impressed. He goes to his father and kisses him tenderly.*)

SAMMY

Thanks a double-bundle for this, Pop.

RAFI

(*To* SAMMY)

I want to give you and my grandchildren everything I possess. Everything that is me.

(*To* DANNY)

And you, have you got any money?

(*To* SAMMY, *indicating* DANNY)

Give him some damn dough.

(ROSIE *walks into the room, having showered and changed. She looks stunning.*)
Rosie, what is all this I hear?

ROSIE

About what, Rafi?

RAFI

Kissing. 'The Intelligent Woman's Approach'?

ROSIE

Snogging as a socio-economic, political-psychological-physical event sunk in a profound complex of determinations? Don't tell me that for you a kiss is just a kiss?

RAFI

Just a kiss.
(*She goes to* SAMMY *and kisses him on the mouth.*)

ROSIE

My husband. Our married mouths. That is one thing. It's meaning is clear. Now this –
(*She goes to* DANNY *and kisses him on the mouth. A long kiss. He almost falls off the chair.* SAMMY *and* RAFI *watch wide-eyed.*)
Now that's a different kind of kiss, with a different social and political meaning.
(*She takes a step towards* RAFI. *He cowers. She kisses him lightly on the mouth.*)
So as you all can see, there's so much to say on the subject of snogging you don't know where to begin.
(RAFI *laughs loudly in pleasure at her charm.*)
(*To* RAFI)
Let's go out to dinner, eh? And how have you been today?

RAFI

Pretty well, in myself, despite the fact that several large people walked up and down on my head. Victoria saved me. Presumably this form of social exercise is an English custom now – a sort of Trooping of the Colour?

ROSIE

Yes, but less exciting for the working class.

(ROSIE *sees* SAMMY *glance again at the cheque before folding it and sliding it in his pocket.*)

SAMMY

Well, Victoria, won't your mother be wanting to know where you are?
(DANNY *gets up. He starts to walk towards the door.*)

RAFI

(*Quickly to* SAMMY *indicating* DANNY)
Help him out. Please do what I say for once.
(SAMMY *reluctantly gives* DANNY *a fiver.* RAFI *nods at* SAMMY *again and he gives him, painfully, another fiver.* RAFI *nods once more.* ROSIE *is laughing, egging* RAFI *on.*)
(*To* ROSIE)
But this is capitalism, Rosie. Redistribution once capitalism has created wealth, eh?
(DANNY *turns to go.* ROSIE *holds out her hands to him. He goes to her, shakes her hand, dropping the money in her lap. They look at each other.*)

SAMMY

Now, let's celebrate!

EXT. THE STEPS OF THE HOUSE. EVENING

The three of them stand on the steps looking out on the street. RAFI *has his arm round* SAMMY*'s shoulder.* SAMMY – *more or less unconsciously – pulls away from his father and takes* ROSIE*'s arm.* RAFI *is offended by this. They all walk down.*

INT. RESTAURANT. EVENING

ROSIE, SAMMY *and* RAFI *are eating in a smart expensive London restaurant. This is affluent, attractive London for a change. A string quartet of beautiful punks plays Mozart at the far end of the restaurant.* SAMMY *leaves the table a moment, excusing himself.*

RAFI

He hardly speaks to me, Rosie. Why doesn't he look after me and spoil his only father? Has he no feeling for me at all?

ROSIE

Why doesn't he carve miniatures?

RAFI

Perhaps he should. But why doesn't he?

ROSIE

Rafi, he doesn't know how to love you.

RAFI

Perhaps being ignorant of feelings helps him in his career.

ROSIE

He isn't completely ignorant of feelings. You did reject him.

RAFI

It was his ugly mother I rejected. I was made to marry her.
So I sent her to London and married again. You are very loyal
to Samir.
(SAMMY *rejoins them.*)
(*To* SAMMY)
She is a decent woman.
(*Pause. To* SAMMY)
So you got the nice cheque I gave you?

SAMMY

(*Nervous*)
In my pocket, Daddio.

ROSIE

(*To* SAMMY)
Let me have a look at it.

SAMMY

You know what a cheque looks like, don't you?
(*She nods.*)
Well, it's just one of those.

ROSIE

I want to know if you're going to return it to your father as you
said you would.

SAMMY

Why should I? Rosie, we're all set up now.

RAFI

(*To* ROSIE)
Yes. Your principles annoy me and will pull down my son.
(*There is a pause.* ROSIE *is furious with both of them.*)
Cheers to you all.
(ROSIE *admires a drag queen in the restaurant.*)

ROSIE

That woman is a real star.

RAFI

Now you're talking like a damn dyke.

ROSIE

(*To* RAFI)
More wine?
(*Pause.*)
By the way –

RAFI

Yes –

ROSIE

Didn't a journalist who once described you as balding have his
teeth smashed in?

RAFI

(*Careful*)
If his face had a mishap it improved his appearance.
(*To* SAMMY)
Besides, his wife stole underwear from Marks and Spencer's
and lowered the reputation of my country.

ROSIE

(*To* RAFI)
When you were in the government there, people – opposition
people sometimes – were tortured and murdered, weren't
they?

SAMMY

Rosie, let's enjoy our meal.

ROSIE

I want him to answer. It's important.

RAFI

(*To* ROSIE)
Sometimes. A little bit. It happens in the world. It is necessary
at times, everyone will admit that.
(RAFI, *finishing his meal, jabs his fork into a piece of meat on his
plate. As he raises it to his mouth we can see that it is a dead and
bloody finger with a long fingernail. We are aware of the people at
the next table, very straight yuppies in striped shirts and pearls, close
enough to hear* ROSIE. RAFI *places the indigestible fingernail on the
side of his plate, delicately.*)

ROSIE

Didn't they have to drink the urine of their gaolers?
(SAMMY *splutters into his drink.*)
Didn't you hang mullahs – religious people – upside down on
skewers and weren't red chillis stuck up their arses?
(*The yuppies call over the waiters.*)

RAFI

If they were, it was a waste of food. Let's have more wine.
Waiter!

SAMMY

(*To* ROSIE)
I think Rosie wants to say that charm is no substitute for virtue.

RAFI

(*Exploding*)
Our government awoke the down-trodden and expelled
Western imperialists! I nationalized the banks! I forged links
with the Palestinians! Remember that!
(*Irony.*)
Comrade. Khrushchev and I –

ROSIE

I just want to know –
(*The* MANAGER *hurries towards them.*)

RAFI

You know nothing but self-righteousness!

ROSIE

What does it feel like to kill, to torture, to maim, and what did you do in the evenings?

MANAGER

Please, could you keep the noise down?

SAMMY

Yes, I'm terribly sorry.

RAFI

I was imprisoned myself, you know! For ninety days, ill with malaria, I didn't see sunshine! In the next cell lunatics screamed. Their voices were even more irritating than yours!

ROSIE

You have increased the amount of evil in the universe.

RAFI

(*Furious*)
You've never suffered! Never had to make hard political decisions!

ROSIE

Yes, every day in my work!

RAFI

You are only concerned with homosexuals and women! A luxury that rich oppressors can afford! We were concerned with poverty, imperialism, feudalism! Real issues that burn people!

ROSIE

We're only asking what it is like to destroy another life.
(*The* MANAGER *stands there beside them, angry himself.*)

MANAGER

Please –

ROSIE

(*To him*)
All right, we're going!

RAFI

(*Pulling her towards him*)
A man who hasn't killed is a virgin and doesn't understand the
importance of love! The man who sacrifices others to benefit
the whole is in a terrible position. But he is essential! Even you
know that. I come from a land ground into dust by 200 years of
imperialism. We are still dominated by the West and you
reproach us for using the methods you taught us. I helped
people for their own good and damaged others for the same
reason – just like you in your feeble profession!

EXT. SOUTH KENSINGTON. NIGHT

They walk through South Kensington, from the restaurant to the car.

RAFI

(*Threatening*)
Be careful what you say to me in the future, little girl.
Remember who I am and have respect.

ROSIE

Who are you, Rafi? Who?

SAMMY

Rosie, he's my father.

EXT. SOUTH KENSINGTON. NIGHT

They have reached the car now. ROSIE *goes to the driver's side.*

RAFI

(*To* SAMMY)
You'll be able to buy a new car for yourself now, eh? Rosie's car
is good, but small.

EXT./INT. OVER THE RIVER. NIGHT

ROSIE *and* RAFI *in the front of the car,* SAMMY *in the back. They look at the Thames.*

> RAFI
>
> The river is ravishing tonight. But it must always be depressing to go back to that ghetto.

> SAMMY
>
> We try to entertain ourselves. And Rosie suggested the other day that we have a little party for you, Dad.
> (ROSIE *swerves the car dangerously.*)
> Yes, just a few friends, our and yours. Would you like that?

> RAFI
>
> That would be delightful. I must say, you have both been very kind to me – most of the time.

INT. LIVING ROOM. NIGHT

RAFI *stands on his head in a yoga position in his pyjamas.* SAMMY, *only a towel around his waist, carries two beers. He watches* RAFI *and walks across the room.*

> RAFI
>
> Nothing matters as long as you and I respect each other.

> SAMMY
>
> I know that.

> RAFI
>
> God bless you.

INT. SAMMY'S AND ROSIE'S BEDROOM. NIGHT

Continuous. ROSIE *doing stretching exercises in the bedroom, wearing a pair of blue silk pyjamas.* SAMMY *comes in.*

> ROSIE
>
> It was Rani and Vivia that got the information about your father.

SAMMY

There's all kinds of rumours about him! Some people say he
gave hundreds of pounds to beggars in the street. Others say
their relatives were bumped off! No one knows a thing for sure,
Rosie, least of all you!

ROSIE

Sammy, you've got to face up to it and –

SAMMY

(*Cutting in*)
Despite everything, Rosie, just admit it, he's a cheerful bastard
with great spirit and –

ROSIE

(*Cutting in*)
Sammy, listen to me –

SAMMY

Great generosity and optimism! He did miracles for that
country. He was a freedom fighter.

ROSIE

(*Cutting in*)
No, no, no!

SAMMY

We're just soft middle-class people who know nothing and
have everything!

ROSIE

Just shut up and let me read this. Will you let me?

SAMMY

What is it?

ROSIE

You'll see.
(*Finally he nods and gets into bed.* ROSIE *picks up the brown
envelope and reads from a testimonial given by a victim.*)
(*Reads*)
'I will tell the truth of what prison was like there. On the first

day they began to hit me on the back of my neck. Then they tied a wire around my testicles. A thin tube was pushed into my penis while someone forced a gun up into my arse, ripping the walls of my rectum until I was bleeding badly. I wanted to kill myself. Another man sat on my chest and stuck two fingers into each of my nostrils, tearing upwards until I thought I was going to choke. There were people I would willingly have betrayed. But I couldn't speak.'

(SAMMY *gets out of bed and goes to the door. He opens it and looks across the flat.* RAFI *sits at the table, reading a newspaper, listening to Wagner and drinking a glass of milk. He raises his glass to* SAMMY.)
(*Reads, as* SAMMY *looks at* RAFI)
'Two soldiers would ask me a question and then push my head into a toilet overflowing with human excrement. Later they taped adhesive over the end of my penis so I didn't pee for five days. The pain got worse and worse. I began to . . .'
(SAMMY *slams the door.*)

SAMMY

All right, all right!
(*He tears the paper from her hands.*

Cut to: Later that night. The living room. SAMMY *can't sleep. He listens to his father's contented snores at the door of his room. He goes to the window and looks out on the street. The man in the brown suit with the smashed head, the* CABBIE, *lights a cigarette under a street lamp.* SAMMY *turns and* ROSIE *is at the door to their room.*)
What am I going to do? We did say we'd have a little do, get some people round to meet him. We can't let a bit of torture interfere with a party. But who will we invite?

ROSIE

We'll just have to round up the usual social deviants, communists, lesbians and blacks, with a sprinkling of the mentally sub-normal –

SAMMY

Yeah –

ROSIE

To start the dancing. And Victoria, yes?

SAMMY

I do love you more than anyone else I've known.

ROSIE

Me too, stupid. But we're both looking for a way out. Aren't we, eh?

INT. LIVING ROOM. EVENING

SAMMY *is getting the flat ready for the little party. Furniture has been pushed back.* SAMMY *is putting out food.* RAFI *stands there moving things away. He takes the key to the drawer out of the fruit bowl.* RAFI *opens the drawer, revealing a number of nasty-looking weapons: lumps of woods with nails in them, big spanners, etc.*

SAMMY

We're gonna need more booze, Pop. You wouldn't mind popping out, would you?
(SAMMY *notices the table drawer is open.*)

RAFI

I can feel that you've turned against me in the last few days, even though your ignorance about me is profound. But there's something you must hear me say.
(*Indicates the weapons.*)
Look at this.

SAMMY

They're for self-protection. We're always getting burgled. Those depraved deprived are right out of control.

RAFI

Yes, London has become a cesspit. You'd better come home, Samir.

SAMMY

I am home, Pop. This is the bosom.

RAFI

What a sullen young man you are. I mean, home to your own country where you will be valued, where you will be rich and powerful. What can you possibly like about this city now?

SAMMY

Well . . .

(*Now we see a number of London scenes that* SAMMY *and* ROSIE *like:* SAMMY *and* ROSIE *are walking along the towpath towards Hammersmith Bridge.*)

(*Voice over*)

On Saturdays we like to walk along the towpath at Hammersmith and kiss and argue.

(*Next we see* SAMMY *and* ROSIE *in 'Any Amount of Books'.*)

(*Voice over*)

Then we go to the bookshop and buy novels written by women.

(*Next,* SAMMY *and* ROSIE *outside the Albert Hall.*)

(*Voice over*)

Or we trot past the Albert Hall and up through Hyde Park. On Saturday nights things really hot up.

(*Cut to: outside the Royal Court Theatre in Sloane Square.*)

(*Voice over*)

If we can get cheap seats we go to a play at the Royal Court. But if there's nothing on that hasn't been well reviewed by the *Guardian* –

(*Now we are in the small amused audience of a cabaret above a pub. This is the Finborough in Earl's Court. A man wearing a huge fat man's outfit, head disappeared into the neck, is dancing to an old French tune. (This is* ALOO BALOO.*)* SAMMY *and* ROSIE *sit in the audience laughing and drinking.*)

(*Voice over*)

We go to an Alternative Cabaret in Earl's Court in the hope of seeing our government abused. Or if we're really desperate for entertainment –

(*We are now in the seminar room at the ICA.* COLIN MCCABE *is talking to an enthralled audience about Derrida. A member of the audience has her hand up.*)

(*Voice over*)

We go to a seminar on semiotics at the ICA which Rosie especially enjoys.

(ROSIE *also has her hand up. But* MCCABE *points to someone else.* ROSIE *looks at* SAMMY, *disgusted with* MCCABE*'s indifference to her.*)

AUDIENCE MEMBER

What, would you say, is the relation between a bag of crisps
and the self-enclosed unity of the linguistic sign?
(COLIN MCCABE *starts to laugh.*)

SAMMY

(*Voice over*)
We love our city and we belong to it. Neither of us are English,
we're Londoners you see.

INT. SAMMY'S AND ROSIE'S BEDROOM. EVENING

Minutes later. In the bedroom ROSIE *is now getting changed for the party.*
SAMMY, *agitated and upset by* RAFI *, watches her sexually.*

ROSIE

Did you give him the money back?

SAMMY

(*Wanting her*)
Before I do anything, I need something to relax me.

ROSIE

(*Deliberately misunderstanding*)
OK. Here's a couple of Valium.

EXT. STREET. EVENING

RAFI, *now out to buy booze, strolls across the street in his natty hat.*

INT. ROSIE'S AND SAMMY'S LIVING ROOM/BEDROOM.
EVENING

ROSIE *continues to dress. During this* SAMMY *combs her hair and puts
her shoes on. Through the open door of the bedroom we can see that* RANI
and VIVIA *have arrived. They have their arms around each other. They
sit and snog on the sofa opposite the bedroom. They've brought the deaf
and dumb boys with them.*

SAMMY

(*To* ROSIE)
Why d'you think we don't want to screw now?

ROSIE

The usual reasons. Boredom. Indifference. Repulsion.
(*Cut to:*)

VIVIA

Are they rowing?

RANI

Just talking each other to death.

VIVIA

No, listen, they're talking about sex.

RANI

Yes, but it's only heterosexual sex. You know, that stuff when
the woman spends the whole time trying to come, but can't.
And the man spends the whole time trying to stop himself
coming, but can't.
(*Cut to:*)

SAMMY

(*To* ROSIE)
I wonder if it matters, us lying there night after night as if the
Berlin Wall had been built down the middle of the bed.

ROSIE

Don't ask me about sex. I know more about carrots. But I
expect it's an acquired taste that one could do without.

SAMMY

You? Not you.
(*Cut to:*)

RANI

(*To* VIVIA)
I'm always suspicious of those relationships where the couple
have read about Simone de Beauvoir and Jean-Paul Sartre at
too early an age. I want my partner to be on the rack or
nowhere at all.

VIVIA

Kiss me, darling.
(*Cut to:*)

ROSIE

I've just started to enjoy screwing.

SAMMY

Christ, how can things become so strange between a common
couple?
(*Cut to:*)

RANI

(*To* VIVIA)
Rosie calls this household 'the hedgehogs'.
(VIVIA *looks at her.*)
Because there are so many pricks around.
(SAMMY *and* ROSIE *come out of their bedroom,* SAMMY
overhearing the last bit. They have their arms around each other.)

SAMMY

Yeah but not all pricks are men.

INT./EXT. OFF-LICENCE. EVENING

RAFI *is in an off-licence across the street. The counter of the off-licence is
separated from the shop by chicken wire, with a small gap for the money.
Two Alsatians run up and down barking behind the counter. A huge
white man, the* FINGER MAN *that we met in the Tube, sits in the shop, a
baseball bat beside him.* RAFI *buys booze and is pretty disturbed by the
shop. The* FINGER MAN *fingers his bat, craning to watch* RAFI *as* RAFI
shops.

   Cut to: Outside the off-licence we see DANNY *looking through the
window at him.* DANNY *is with his girlfriend, the kid and the dog.*
DANNY *indicates to his girlfriend to come and have a look. They peer
through the glass at him. This makes* RAFI *rather uncomfortable.*

   Cut to: RAFI *coming out of the off-licence.* DANNY *takes the booze
from him.*

RAFI

Come on. You'd better come to a party.

INT. SAMMY'S AND ROSIE'S FLAT. EVENING

Now some guests have arrived. SAMMY *and* ROSIE *are together,* RANI *and* VIVIA *with them.* RAFI, *now elegantly dressed, goes to* SAMMY *and* ROSIE.

RAFI

Now you are together, tell me quickly: have you decided to buy a house in Hatfield with the money I've given you?
(ROSIE, *irritated by him, just looks across the room and sees that* DANNY *has arrived, among other guests.* DANNY *has the kid and the dog with him,* OMAR *and* JOHNNY *are there too,* JOHNNY *and* DANNY *talking. And then* ALICE *arrives.* RAFI *goes to her.*
    Cut to: Later on. The party swings. DANNY *stands by a sofa on which sit* RAFI *and* ANNA. *Bits of conversation as we move across the room.* RANI *and* BRIDGET *dance together, cheek to cheek.* VIVIA *watches jealously.*)

RANI

I said to her, it's love this time, I want to be with you.

BRIDGET

I couldn't imagine being with anyone for more than two weeks.
(ROSIE *watches* DANNY. SAMMY *watches* ROSIE. ANNA *watches* SAMMY. OMAR *and an* ASIAN ACCOUNTANT *watch* RAFI.)

OMAR

Sammy's our accountant. He never said his father was Rafi Fahman. He kept that quiet.

ASIAN ACCOUNTANT

I was in Dacca when their army came in. How d'you think my father was killed – falling out of bed?
(RAFI , *slightly drunk now – jacket off – has pulled up his polo-necked shirt and is showing* ANNA *his scars.*)

RAFI

I'll show you my life!
(ANNA *peers interestedly at them.* RAFI'S *stomach, chest and back are criss-crossed with long scars.*)
(*Indicating*)
The geography of suffering. Open-heart surgery, gall-bladder, appendix, lung removal. It's a miracle I am alive. Touch them.

                              ANNA

Are you sure?

                              RAFI

Treat yourself – the Kennedy children used to stay in my
house.

                              ANNA

I like men who try to impress me. They make me laugh.
(RAFI *looks up nervously and sees the white deaf and dumb boy
staring at him. Cut to:*)

                             JOHNNY

(*To* OMAR)
If you had to sleep with anyone in this room who would you
choose?

                              OMAR

(*Pause, looks around.*)
Er . . . You.
(*Cut to:* ALICE *is talking to* VIVIA . *She also glances at* RAFI *and*
ANNA, *a little disconcerted.*)

                              ALICE

Although I was curious about –

                              VIVIA

Other bodies –
(RANI *goes to* VIVIA *and kisses her warmly, looking at* ALICE.)

                              ALICE

Other men – and one is curious. And although I loved someone
else – I loved Rafi – I was faithful to my husband. For no other
reason than that we believed in not lying to each other. Loyalty
and honesty were the important things for us. Not attraction.
Not something called pleasure.
(*Cut to: Now* ROSIE *is with* DANNY.)

                              ROSIE

You look cool.
(*Pause.*)
Is it your kid? What's he called?

DANNY

Rosie, I missed you.

ROSIE

You don't know me.

DANNY

If I knew you it would have been worse.
(*Cut to:*)

ALICE

(*To* VIVIA)
In that old world of certainty and stability you didn't take it for
granted that a marriage would smash up in ten years. It was
your entire life you gave to someone else.
(*Cut to:*)

ANNA

(*To* RAFI)
I do Gestalt therapy, an hour of Indian yoga, followed by
Buddhist chanting. Do you chant?

RAFI

Chant what, my dear?

ANNA

Mantras, to calm yourself.

RAFI

I am calm. It is agitation I seek. You young international people
mystify me. For you the world and culture is a kind of
department store. You go in and take something you like from
each floor. But you're attached to nothing. Your lives are
incoherent, shallow.

ANNA

I am for self-development above all. The individual reaching
her fullest potential through a wide range of challenging
experience.

RAFI

Ah yes. The kind of thing I used to call bourgeois indulgence in

the days when I believed in reason and the struggle. My ideal
evening then was a dialogue by Plato followed by women
wrestling in mud.
(*Cut to:*)

ALICE

(*To* VIVIA)
We didn't have exaggerated expectations of what sex and love
could offer so we didn't throw each other over at the first
unhappiness.

VIVIA

You didn't have your own lives. You lived through men. The
penis was your life-line.
(ROSIE *and* DANNY *go off together, watched by* RAFI *and* ALICE.)
(*To* ALICE)
Let's keep in touch anyway. Can we exchange phone numbers?
(*Cut to:* ROSIE's *study.* ROSIE *shows* DANNY *her books, drawings,
etc. Now they hold each other. Their faces move closer together.
Incredible sensuality, their hands in each other's mouths.*)

DANNY

Why don't we get out of this lonely place? And go to a lonelier
one?
(*Cut to:* SAMMY *is with* RAFI *now.* ANNA *is photographing him.*
RAFI *holds up his jumper, having a wonderful time.*)

RAFI

(*To* SAMMY)
And where is Lady Chatterley?

SAMMY

Piss off.
(*To* ANNA)
What are you doing, please?

RAFI

I think I'm becoming a very free and liberated person.
(*Cut to:* SAMMY *stands disconsolately outside Rosie's study.* ANNA,
from the end of the hall, photographs him. VIVIA *and* RANI *stand
behind* ANNA *with their arms around each other.*)

SAMMY

Let's go, Anna!
(*We see* VIVIA *and* RANI *slip away.*)

INT. ROSIE'S STUDY. NIGHT

Seconds later. RAFI *is in his room, under the picture of Virginia Woolf.*
He's taking a couple of pills with a glass of whisky. He looks up – and the
room is dark – and sees VIVIA *and* RANI *standing there. They are not*
threatening him directly, but he is frightened.

RANI

We wanted to talk to you, Mr Rahman.

VIVIA

Yes, if you don't mind.

RANI

About politics and things.

VIVIA

About some things that happened to some people.

RAFI

If I were you two girls, I'd –

VIVIA

Yeah?
(*Suddenly the door opens and* ROSIE *is standing there. The*
atmosphere is broken. ROSIE *clocks the situation immediately and*
ensures that RAFI *gets out.*)

ROSIE

Rafi, Alice is looking for you.
(RAFI *goes.*)

ROSIE

(*To* RANI *and* VIVIA)
Please, not now.

RANI

But you do know who you having living in your flat?

ROSIE

I don't hate him.

RANI

Typically of your class and background. Your politics are just surface.

ROSIE

What do you want to do?

RANI

We want to drive him out of the country.
(*To* VIVIA)
This is liberalism gone mad!
(VIVIA *and* RANI *look pityingly at* ROSIE . *A hand appears on* ROSIE*'s head. She looks up to see* DANNY *there.*)

ROSIE

(*To* DANNY)
Ready?

DANNY

(*To* ROSIE)
For anything.

INT./EXT. CAR OUTSIDE ALICE'S HOUSE. NIGHT

ALICE *is in the front of* SAMMY*'s new car, next to him.* ANNA *and* RAFI *sit in the back, the electric windows going up and down. The suburbs are silent.*

SAMMY

Anna, how d'you like me new car?

RAFI

(*To* ANNA)
I bought it for him.

ANNA

And what does he have to do for you in return?

RAFI

Only care for me a little.

(ANNA *kisses* RAFI *goodbye, affectionately. He slides his hand up her skirt.*)

ANNA

You're quite an entertainment.
(*Cut to:* ALICE *walks towards her house, through the beams of the headlights.* SAMMY *and* RAFI *stand beside the car,* ANNA *inside. The car door is open and the music spills out into the street.* ANNA *can sing along with it.*)

RAFI

I'm staying here tonight because I want to be with Alice.

SAMMY

Now? At night?

RAFI

At all hours.

SAMMY

And on all-fours?

RAFI

The English waste their women. There's a good ten years' wear in Alice. You don't know what a good woman she is. In fact you don't know anything about women full stop.

SAMMY

What d'you mean, for God's sake?

RAFI

Where is your wife, for instance?

EXT. RAILWAY BRIDGE. NIGHT

ROSIE, DANNY, *the kid and the dog are crossing the railway bridge towards the waste ground. The kid and the dog run on, leaving* ROSIE *and* DANNY. *They stop and look over the bridge;* ROSIE, *never having seen the waste ground before, is startled and amazed. She watches the kids play chess on a huge iron-sculpted chess set. The players sit above the game like tennis umpires and order eager minions to move their pieces for them.* DANNY *is behind her, with his face in her hair. She tells him about herself.*

ROSIE

My father has a small furniture store and used to be the Mayor
of Bromley! My mother was having an affair with the official
chauffeur. I haven't spoken to Dad for five years. He's crude,
vicious, racist and ignorant. I'd happily die without seeing his
face again. I changed my name and became myself.
(*She turns. They kiss a little.*)

DANNY

Are you going to come in for some hot chocolate?
(*She nods. He takes her hand.*)
Come on then, follow me up the yellow brick road.

INT./EXT. STREET. NIGHT

SAMMY *stops the car outside* ANNA's *studio. She is still sitting in the back
seat of the car, her arms around him, her hands over him. Her studio is in
a working-class area of London now being taken over by the rich and the
smooth.*

ANNA

Wouldn't you like to be with me tonight?

SAMMY

I'm trying to get on to a whole new regime.

ANNA

What for?

SAMMY

My prick keeps leading me into trouble. I'm like a little man
being pulled around by a big dog.
(*She touches him. He groans. He goes to get out of the car.*)
Desire is pretty addictive though.

EXT. UNDER THE MOTORWAY. NIGHT

Here, on a large area of waste ground, is DANNY's *caravan. This is where
he lives. There are many other caravans and shacks for the straggly kids.
Some of them – maybe* DANNY's *– are decorated with flashing Christmas
lights. The traffic thunders overhead.* ROSIE, DANNY *waving a stick, the*

kid and the dog, walk towards the caravan. Kids in their teens and twenties, black and white, girls and boys, stand around open fires or sit in old car seats, dragged out into the open. Next to one fire, on a crate, is a huge TV which the kids watch. On TV a headless man reads the news. On another part of the waste ground, the straggly kids are playing a variety of instruments, the stranger and more home-made the better, of course. Nearby, two cars are half-buried in mud, as if they plunged over the rim of the motorway and nose-dived into the ground. A huge Red Indian totem pole sticks up into the sky. A swing hangs down from under the motorway. A kid swings in it.

ROSIE

My father would smash me across the room. Then he'd put on his mayor's chain and open church bazaars. Since then I've had difficulty in coming to terms with men's minds. Their bodes are all right.

DANNY

The neighbourhood's busy tonight.
(DANNY *and* ROSIE *walk up the steps into* DANNY*'s caravan.*)

INT. ANNA'S STUDIO. NIGHT

The light is strange and gloomy in the studio tonight. A lot of clothes – lace, silk, velvet, leather – lying about from a photography session. SAMMY *is very anxious, drinking, pacing about. She watches him, while putting various things in a bag: rugs, candles, cushions.*

ANNA

You've got some bad anxiety, man. There are two types of people – or combinations of both at different times. Toxic and nourishing types. T and N. You're more T than N right now. It'll take more than that to stop me loving you. You better come with me.

EXT. FIRE ESCAPE. NIGHT

ANNA *is leading* SAMMY *up a fire escape at the back of the building. He stops. She pulls him on. She carries a bag.*

INT. CARAVAN. NIGHT

In the large caravan, full of plants, pictures of Gandhi, Tolstoy, Martin
Luther King. DANNY *lies naked on the bed, reading a paperback. He*
looks desperately attractive. ROSIE *walks towards the bed and sees him.*
She stands and watches him, swigging from a bottle of cider, dancing a
little. He throws the book aside. She is fully dressed. The dog stretches on
the floor.

                            ROSIE

Danny, God, you are gorgeous. Your legs. Head. Chest. You
excite me. You're really doing it to me. Can you . . . would you
do something? Just turn over.
(*Unselfconsciously he turns over on to his stomach.* ROSIE *moves*
down towards him. And she touches him, moving her lips lightly over
him.
    Cut to: Outside, the band plays for the lovers and fires can be seen
from the caravan windows. And of course inside the music can be
heard.)

INT. ALICE'S BEDROOM. NIGHT

ALICE, *who has several Jane Austen novels beside her bed, is untying her*
hair in the crumbling eerie bedroom. Also, in this room, some Indian
memorabilia. She wears a dressing-gown. ALICE *looks at* RAFI.

                            RAFI

I like you in that dressing-gown.
(*Pause.*)
I'd like you out of it too.
(*Pause.*)
Do your kids come to see you?

                            ALICE

Once or twice a year.

                            RAFI

Is that more or less times than they go to the dentist?

                            ALICE

One works in the City. The other is in property.

RAFI

Rich?

ALICE

Of course, Rafi.

RAFI

The natural bonds are severed, though. And love is sought everywhere but at home. What is wrong with the home?

ALICE

Generally the people who live there.
(*Pause.*)
It's years since I've done this. And for you?

RAFI

(*Removing his trousers*)
When I can . . . I like to.

ALICE

Like most women my life has been based on denial, on the acknowledgement of limits.

RAFI

Christ, Alice, let's just enjoy ourselves, eh?
(RAFI , *cheerfully naked, is about to hang his clothes in the wardrobe. He catches sight of his own squat, hairy, wrinkled body in the wardrobe mirror. He jumps with shock. She laughs.*)

ALICE

Never look in a mirror you don't know.
(*But he continues looking in the mirror. Standing behind him for a moment, he sees the* CABBIE *with the caved-head.* RAFI *turns away and collects himself.*)

RAFI

Perhaps you're right. Right that we must contain and limit ourselves and learn to be content. The West has become very decadent, sex-mad and diseased since I came back. In my country you know what I did?

ALICE

Was it terrible?

RAFI

I shut all the night-clubs and casinos. The women have gone
back in their place. There is restriction. There is order. There
is identity through religion and a strict way of life.

ALICE

It is tyrannical no doubt.

RAFI

While here there is moral vertigo and constant change.

INT. CARAVAN. NIGHT

ROSIE *and* DANNY *lie on the bed in the caravan.* ROSIE *is half-undressed
now. Music from around the caravan. Their tongues dance over the
other's face.*

ROSIE

In my kissing research I've learned that some people have hard
tongues. Others, tongues that are too soft. You feel like sticking
a fork in them. Others kiss so much like vacuum cleaners you
fear for your fillings. But this is a kiss.

DANNY

I can't stop touching you.

ROSIE

Would you rather be writing a letter?

DANNY

I'm tell you something, Rosie.

ROSIE

I'm biting your neck. I love necks. Necks are mine.
(*And they wrestle a little.*)

DANNY

The woman who brought me up – because my mum was out at
work all day – lived right near you. That's why I've watched
you so often in the street.

ROSIE

Why didn't you say anything?

DANNY

I felt, well, that's quite a woman. But I thought: Victoria, you're well outclassed here. Until I realized that you're downwardly mobile!

ROSIE

What about the woman who brought you up?

DANNY

Paulette. The police just went into her house and shot her up. That was the start of the rebellion. Nobody knows the shit black people have to go through in this country.
(*We pull back to see, at the partition between the bed and the rest of the caravan, the kid standing there looking on.*)

INT. ALICE'S BEDROOM. NIGHT

An old record plays on the gramophone in the room. ALICE *and* RAFI *are in bed. She kisses him. She is releasing her hair, which until now has been tied at the top of the head. He pulls away from her and her hair tumbles free, all of it perfectly white, which shocks* RAFI. *Now she reaches down to pull up her nightdress.*

ALICE

Women like Vivia are unnatural and odious, of course, but there's something I've noticed about men that she would understand. One is constantly having to forgive men. Always they're wanting their women to see into them, understand them, absolve them. Is there anything in that line you'd like me to help you with, Rafi dear?

EXT. ROOF OF ANNA'S STUDIO. NIGHT

Here, overlooking London, the motorway nearby, are SAMMY *and* ANNA. ANNA *is dancing for* SAMMY *, energetic, balletic, fluid, soundless.* SAMMY *watches her. A helicopter passes over their heads, the thick beam of its light illuminating them, the hurricane wind of its propellers driving them into each other's arms.*

ANNA

You must be thinking about Rosie right now.
(*He nods.*)
How completely odd and freakish for a husband to think about
his wife when he is with his lover.
(*Suddenly she grabs him and pushes him violently towards the side
of the building, thrusting him half over the long wall which separates
the roof from the long drop.*)

SAMMY

What the fuck –

ANNA

How many lovers have you had in the past two years?

SAMMY

About . . . about . . .

ANNA

Yeah?

SAMMY

Twelve or so.

ANNA

For you pursuing women is like hang-gliding. They're a
challenge, something to be overcome. It's fucking outta date,
man! It's about time you learned how to love someone!
(*She shoves him so we are looking straight down, with him.*)
That's what fucking life is, baby!
(*Cut to: He lies at her feet now, on the roof.* ANNA *has spread exotic
rugs out and lit candles. There are also storm lanterns. He massages
her right foot.*)
That's it, that point's directly related to my Fallopian tubes . . .
and there, that's my small intestine . . . yes, diaphragm . . .

SAMMY

What would you do if you discovered that someone close to
you, a parent say, had done some stuff that was horrible and
unforgivable? They had ways of justifying it, of course. But still
it so disturbed you, you couldn't bear it?

ANNA

Your father? I don't know what I'd do, Sammy.

SAMMY

I don't know either, you know.

ANNA

Come here.
(*She indicates to* SAMMY *and he goes to her. They hold each other and roll away across the roof.*)

INT./EXT. COLLAGE OF COPULATION IMAGES. NIGHT

Now there is a collage of the three couples coupling. This is cut with the kids and the straggly band outside the caravan dancing in celebration of joyful love-making all over London. Some of the straggly kids play instruments or bang tins. Others are dressed in bizarre variations of straight gear – like morris dancers, pearly queens, traffic wardens, naval ratings, brain surgeons, witches, devils, etc. The cinema screen suddenly divides vertically (or would it be more appropriate horizontally?) and we see the three couples in energetic, tender and ecstatic climax, with DANNY *and* ROSIE *in the centre.*

INT./EXT. WASTE GROUND. MORNING

ROSIE *has woken up alone in the caravan. She goes out of the caravan. The straggly kids, with* DANNY *and his kid, are having breakfast outside. They eat at a long table set out in the open, the motorway above them. In the daylight* ROSIE *can see the kids have planted vegetables in the waste ground and a young black woman walks up and down with a watering can with a dildo-penis for a funnel. A number of sculptures have been built in the vegetable patch. In the background a shop has been set up in an old shack. Here customers buy vegetables, books, etc. On the long table* ROSIE *sees a printing press has been set up and the kids run off pages for books they're printing.* ROSIE *sits down next to* DANNY *and has breakfast. When she looks to the periphery of the site, beyond the barbed wire, she sees three white men standing in the open back of a lorry. One of them has a pair of binoculars. They watch the kids.*

ROSIE

(*To* DANNY)
What's going in?

DANNY

They're chucking us off this site – either today, the next day or the day after that.

INT. ANNA'S STUDIO. MORNING

ANNA *is asleep.* SAMMY *goes to* ANNA *with a tray – on it are croissants, juice, eggs and coffee. He kisses her and she opens her eyes.*

SAMMY

Let's look at the photographs you took of that place I want to buy.
(*Cut to: A little later.* ANNA *and* SAMMY *sit on the bed.* ANNA *shows him photographs of a smart and inhabited house in Fulham. Wittily, she has photographed the ridiculous yuppie inhabitants showing the place off.*)
Which'll be Rosie's room?

ANNA

I'm having an exhibition in New York. I'm going to call it 'Images of a Decaying Europe'. So I should photograph that black guy at the party. D'you know where he is?

SAMMY

On top of my wife I expect.

INT. ALICE'S LIVING ROOM. DAY

ALICE *and* RAFI *are sitting at the table having breakfast. They've almost finished.* RAFI *is eager to leave.*

ALICE

What would you like to do today?

RAFI

(*Rising, wiping his mouth*)
I think I'd better get moving, Alice. Sammy and Rosie will be expecting me.

ALICE

Why should they be expecting you? You really want to go,

don't you? Is there anything you have to urgently do? I'd just
like to know.

ALICE

Alice. I want to start writing my memoirs.

INT. SAMMY'S AND ROSIE'S FLAT. DAY

RAFI *has returned. The flat looks wrecked from the night before.*

RAFI

Sammy! Sammy!
(RAFI *goes into Rosie's study. Hearing a noise in the bedroom he
opens the door and sees* RANI *and* VIVIA *in bed. He is very shocked
and angry. He starts to abuse them in Punjabi. This is sub-titled.*)
What are you doing, you perverted half-sexed lesbians cursed
by God?

RANI

Fuck off out of it, you old bastard!

RAFI

God save my eyes from the sights I'm seeing!
(*He shuts the door and cowers behind it as* RANI *and* VIVIA *throw
stuff at him.*)

RANI

(*Raving at him*)
Come here and let me bite your balls off with my teeth and
swallow them! I'll rip off your prick with a tin opener! I'll sew
live rats into the stomach of your camel, you murdering fascist!
(*As she throws books at him*)
Who the fuck do you think you are!
(*Now she is opening the drawer and removing the weapons.*)
That pigshit bastard, I'll crush his testicles right now!
(*As she lunges with her piece of wood at him*)
Let me get at that withered sperm-factory with this and put the
world out of its misery!
(*And she bangs wildly on the door of the room. We see* RAFI *climbing
out of the window.*)

EXT. OUTSIDE SAMMY'S AND ROSIE'S HOUSE. DAY

RAFI *is climbing down the drainpipe. When he looks down he sees the* GHOST *looking up at him. Along the street* ROSIE *is getting off the back of Danny's motorbike.* RAFI *jumps the last few feet to the ground, damaging his arm as he falls. The* GHOST *walks away backwards, watching him.* RAFI *walks towards* ROSIE *and* DANNY. *He sees them warmly embrace. The police in the street look on in disgust.* RAFI *is furious, on Sammy's behalf, with* ROSIE *and* DANNY. DANNY *spots* RAFI *over* ROSIE's *shoulder. He calls out to* RAFI *as* RAFI *tries to slide past unnoticed, concealing his damaged arm.*

DANNY

Hey Rafi, why don't you come by for a talk sometime? I'd like to see you.

RAFI

I don't know where you live, Victoria.

DANNY

Here, let me draw you a map.
(DANNY *goes over to his bike for pen and paper.* RAFI *and* ROSIE *are to one side.*)

ROSIE

(*Wickedly*)
Up all night?
(RAFI *looks back at the house and sees* RANI *and* VIVIA *standing on the steps watching him.* BRIDGET *approaches* RANI *and* VIVIA *, and they talk briefly, indicating* RAFI.)

RAFI

(*To* ROSIE)
What the hell are you doing kissing this street rat and bum Danny on the road!

ROSIE

I find that rat bums have an aphrodisiac effect on me, Rafi.
(DANNY *goes over with the map, and gives it to* RAFI.)

DANNY

See you then.

RAFI

I was adored once, too.
(RAFI *walks away*. BRIDGET *comes down the steps of the house and follows him.* DANNY *and* ROSIE *embrace to say goodbye.*)

ROSIE

(*To* DANNY)
You're fond of that old man, aren't you?

DANNY

It's easy for me to like him. But it's you that makes my bones vibrate.

ROSIE

Uh–huh.
(*Pause.*)
I'd better go. Or Sammy will be anxious.

INT. THE TUBE. DAY

RAFI *is lost in the Tube. He is standing in the ticket area of somewhere like Piccadilly with all the people swirling around him.* BRIDGET *is watching him. A group of young Jewish kids are being harangued by a group of young men. They yell 'Yiddo, yiddo, yiddo!' at the kids.* RAFI *is confused and lost.* BRIDGET *is whispering to* EVA. *And* EVA *follows* RAFI *from now on, as he decides to go down a Tube tunnel.*

INT. SAMMY'S AND ROSIE'S FLAT. DAY

SAMMY *, in a good mood, has come home.* ROSIE *, alone in the flat, is sawing the legs off the bed, as it's too high. When she hears* SAMMY *she goes into the living room. He kisses her. But she is in a very bad mood.*

SAMMY

Where's Daddio?

ROSIE

He went off somewhere.

SAMMY

You didn't offend him, did you?

ROSIE

Offend him?

SAMMY

Yeah, you know, 'What's your favourite torturing method out of all the ones you know?'

ROSIE

He's been here long enough.

SAMMY

We can't just chuck the old fucker's arse out on to the street. What'll he do, become a busker?

ROSIE

Why, does he play a musical instrument? It's not as if he's poor, is it?

SAMMY

It is. We've got his money. And there are people who want to kill him. Listen, I've seen a house which would suit both of us bunny rabbits. So much room we could go for days without seeing each other. Or without seeing Pop.

ROSIE

Your father?

SAMMY

He could have the basement, or dungeon, as we could call it. (*She turns away from him, unable to share his ebullience.*) Let's try and love each other a little. Can't we try to touch each other or something?

ROSIE

How did you enjoy sleeping with Anna last night?

SAMMY

To be honest, I'd rather have stayed in and redecorated the kitchen. You?
(*Pause.*)
You're smiling inside at the thought of Danny. Did you like each other?

ROSIE

He excited me terribly.

SAMMY

And the traffic didn't get on top of you?

EXT. OUTSIDE ALICE'S HOUSE. DAY

RAFI *walks towards the house.*

INT. ALICE'S BATHROOM. DAY

ALICE *in the bathroom bandaging* RAFI's *damaged arm.*

RAFI

I can't live in that part of London. That's why I came back.
Day after day those kids burn down their own streets. It's hard
on tourists like me.

ALICE

(*Shocked, indicating arm*)
Is that how this happened – in a mad riot?
(RAFI *nods and tries to kiss her. She turns away from him.*
Cut to: They walk down the stairs, RAFI *in front.*)
I hate their ignorant anger and lack of respect for this great
land. Being British has to mean an identification with other,
similar people. If we're to survive, words like 'unity' and
'civilization' must be understood.

RAFI

I like rebels and defiance.

ALICE

You funny little fraud, you shot your rioters dead in the street!
The things we enjoy – Chopin, Constable, claret – are a
middle-class creation. The proletarian and theocratic ideas
you theoretically admire grind civilization into dust!
(*At the bottom of the stairs, in the hall,* RAFI *tries to hold her. She*
evades him.)

RAFI

Please.

ALICE

What is it, Rafi?

RAFI

Sammy and Rosie have no human feeling for me. Would it be
terribly painful to have me living here?

ALICE

You couldn't leave quickly enough this morning. There was
barely a heartbeat between your eyes opening and the Tube
doors shutting!

RAFI

I know, I know. Alice, take pity on me. I've got a lot of personal
problems.

ALICE

(*Taking his hand*)
Come. Let me show you something now.

INT. CELLAR. DAY

ALICE *takes* RAFI *through a door in the hall and down the perilous stairs
into the gloomy cellar of the house. The place is stuffed full of old furniture,
boxes, files, more Indian memorabilia – mosquito nets, hockey sticks, old
guns. As* RAFI *follows* ALICE *through all this, picking his way to the far
end, he sees that the* GHOST *is in the cellar with him, walking
immaterially through objects. To turn away from this frightening sight, he
turns to look at a framed picture. This is of* ALICE *in India as a baby,
with her ayah – the Indian servant who would have brought her up.*

ALICE

That's me as a baby, with the ayah that brought me up for the
first eight years of my life.
(ALICE *is taking down an armful of large dusty notebooks from the
shelves at the end of the cellar. Accompanied by the* GHOST, RAFI
goes to her as she opens the notebooks.)

RAFI

What is this, Alice?
(*As she flips slowly through them we can see there is an entry for*

each day through the years 1954, 1955, 1956. Each entry begins 'Dear Rafi . . .' or 'My Darling Rafi . . .' or 'Dearest Rafi . . .')

ALICE

Every day for years as I waited for you, I poured out my heart to you. I told you everything! Look, pages and pages of it! I really waited like a fool for you to come back and take me away, as you said you would. Look at this.
(She goes to an old suitcase, covered in dust. With difficulty she opens it. The GHOST watches RAFI.)
It's thirty years since I closed this case.
(Slowly she pulls out and holds up the rotting garments.)
These are the clothes I packed to take with me. The books. The shoes. Perfume . . .

RAFI

Alice . . .

ALICE

I waited for you, for years! Every day I thought of you! Until I began to heal up. What I wanted was a true marriage. But you wanted power. Now you must be content with having introduced flogging for minor offences, nuclear capability and partridge-shooting into your country.

RAFI

(To the GHOST)
How bitterness can dry up a woman!

EXT. OUTSIDE ALICE'S HOUSE. DAY

RAFI *leaves* ALICE's *house. From the door she watches him go.*

INT. SAMMY'S AND ROSIE'S BATHROOM. DAY

SAMMY *and* ROSIE *in the bath together.* SAMMY *shampoos* ROSIE's *hair.*

ROSIE

Soap?

                                    SAMMY

No, I already washed today.
(*Pause.*)
Where can the old man have got to?

                                    ROSIE

Sammy, this is all false, isn't it? I think we should try not living
together. I think we should try being apart now.

EXT. SOUTH LONDON STREET. DAY

RAFI , *with his bandaged arm and disintegrating map (that* DANNY *drew
for him), walks through the desolate tunnels and grim streets of South
London. Now it is raining.* RAFI *stops under a railway bridge where other
wretched rejects are sheltering – the poor, the senile, the insane, the
disabled. Some of them sleep in cardboard boxes, others in sleeping bags.*
RAFI *trips over someone. He turns to them. During all this, the Indian in
the filthy brown suit, with a scarf over his head, the* GHOST, *is watching
him. Further away,* EVA *watches* RAFI *with* MARGY.

                                    RAFI

(*To man*)
Will you pull off my shoe?
(*The man, who is black, tries to pull* RAFI's *shoe off.*

        Cut to: Now RAFI *walks on. The brown-suited man follows him,
carrying* RAFI's *discarded shoe.*

        Cut to: Now RAFI *is walking in another part of South London in
the pouring rain. Soaked through, bandage dangling, he is
approaching the waste ground. In the street two bulldozers are being
driven to the site. Around the perimeter of the waste ground several
big cars are parked. White men, in suits, look at the site, talk about it
and point to things. The Indian in the brown suit, the* CABBIE, *looks
on.* RAFI *walks past the nose-dived cars, ankle deep in mud. One of
the young men – the one whose mother was shot at the beginning of the
film – points out* DANNY's *caravan to him. Music blares out over the
waste ground.* RAFI *goes to* DANNY's *caravan and bangs on the door.*)

INT. DANNY'S CARAVAN. DAY

RAFI *stumbles into the caravan.* DANNY *sits writing at an old typewriter.*

A young black woman stands on a chair playing keyboards. The keyboard is slung over her shoulder like a guitar. They look up at RAFI. DANNY *goes to* RAFI *and holds him up.*

RAFI

I thought I'd take you up on your offer of tea. Is it real or tea-bags?

(*Cut to: Now* DANNY *is making tea. The woman plays the keyboards. A white rabbit runs around the caravan.* RAFI *looks around the place and at the pictures.*)

You really live here all the time? Like you it's the middle class I hate.

DANNY

This land's been bought by the property people. The government's encouraging fat white men with bad haircuts to put money into the area.

RAFI

When we first met, you and I, in the street, you were very kind to me. I'll never forget it.

DANNY

Yeah, an old woman I loved got shot up by the police. Friends of ours were pulling whites out of cars and beating them in revenge. I didn't know if I should be doing it.

(DANNY *gives* RAFI *his tea.* RAFI *looks behind him out of the window into the pouring rain. The leaves of the drenched bushes frame* RAFI*'s view of the brown-suited man who stares through the window.*)

INT. SAMMY'S AND ROSIE'S LIVING ROOM. EVENING.

ROSIE *is helping* SAMMY *learn to stand on his head. Now he is up.* ROSIE *holds him up straight.*

ROSIE

If you had to choose between sleeping with George Eliot or Virginia Woolf, who would you choose?

SAMMY

On looks alone, I'd go for Virginia. Now you. De Gaulle or
Churchill, including dinner, full intercourse and blow job.

ROSIE

(*Pause. Thinks, then*)
If we don't live together, if we live with other people, if we do
entirely different things, I won't stop loving you.

SAMMY

That's not enough. We've got to be committed to each other.

ROSIE

It's not commitment you want. It's fatal hugging that you're
into.

SAMMY

Rosie, where's the old man? D'you think he's gone back to
Alice's for a second helping of trifle?
(*Pause.*)
Danny or me?

ROSIE

That's easy.

EXT. THE WASTE GROUND. NIGHT

A meeting is taking place. The kids and RAFI *sit around a huge bonfire
discussing what they should do. Around the perimeter fence the bulldozers,
the* PROPERTY DEVELOPERS *and his cronies are discussing what to do.
Some kids play music.*

DANNY

(*To the group*)
They'll remove us tomorrow morning.

KID

(*To the group*)
What do people think we should do?

KID TWO

Not go without a fight.

KID THREE

Go peacefully. We're anarchists, not terrorists.

KID FOUR

(*To* RAFI)

You're a politician. What do you think?

(*Sitting among the kids, the man in the brown suit watches. The kids look at* RAFI *respectfully.*)

RAFI

We must go. The power of the reactionary state rolls on. But we must never, ever be defeated.

EXT./INT. THE WASTE GROUND/CARAVAN. NIGHT

It is late. Everyone is asleep. The Asian in the brown suit, the GHOST*, has walked across the silent waste ground to* DANNY*'s caravan.*

Outside he removes his suit until he is naked.

Cut to: Inside the caravan RAFI *has got up from his bed to wash his face. He runs water into the bowl. He has his back to the door of the caravan. As he washes suddenly the bowl is full of human blood and hair and bone. A noise behind him.* RAFI *turns and sees the* GHOST *covered in blood and shit, with serious burns over his body. The body is criss-crossed with wires from the electric shock treatment he received in detention. Over his head he wears a rubber mask through which it is impossible to breathe. He makes a terrible noise.* RAFI *turns and stares. The* GHOST *removes his rubber mask. We can see now that the head is half-caved in and one eye (with the bandage removed) has been gouged out.*

GHOST

I'm sure you recognize me, though I don't look my best.

(RAFI *nods. The* GHOST *sits on the bed. He pats the bed next to him.* RAFI *has got to sit next to him. The* GHOST *puts his arms around* RAFI*. Then the* GHOST *takes the pads connected to the wires which are stuck to his temples and puts the two of them over* RAFI*'s eyes.*)

You said to Rosie that I was the price to be paid for the overall good of our sad country, yes?

RAFI

Forgive me.

GHOST

How could that be possible?

RAFI

Since, I have tried to love people. And it wasn't I who did the mischief! I wasn't there, if it happened at all!

GHOST

You were not there, it is true, though you gave the order. You were in your big house, drinking illegally, slapping women's arses adulterously, sending your money out of the country and listening, so I heard, to the songs of Vera Lynn.

RAFI

The country needed a sense of direction, of identity. People like you, organizing into unions, discouraged and disrupted all progress.

GHOST

All of human life you desecrated, Rafi Rahman!
(*The* GHOST *raises his arms. Now the caravan is plunged into darkness.* RAFI *screams. Electricity buzzes.*)

INT. ALICE'S LIVING ROOM. MORNING

The following morning. ALICE *is on the phone.*

ALICE

(*To* VIVIA)
I'm a little worried about him, Vivia. Do you know where he is? Oh good. Yes I'd like to see him.
(*Writes on a pad.*)
I'll be there.

EXT. THE WASTE GROUND. MORNING

Around the perimeter fence the bulldozers are in place. The property developer's men are arriving. They discuss how to do the job. Some of the kids are spreading cloth, wool, cotton and large areas of brightly coloured material over the barbed wire. In their caravans and trucks other kids are packing up. The GHOST *in the brown suit leaves* DANNY's *caravan.*

INT. SAMMY'S AND ROSIE'S LIVING ROOM. MORNING

SAMMY *is separating the books. Rosie's are left on the shelves – Sammy's go into boxes.* ROSIE *comes into the room. She is just about to go out.*

> ROSIE
>
> Sammy, what are you doing?

> SAMMY
>
> Getting ready to leave, now the decision has been made.
> (*Continues, not bitterly.*)
> That's mine. Mine. Yours, mine.
> (*Holds up* The Long Goodbye.)
> Mine?

> ROSIE
>
> No, I bought it. When we were at college.

> SAMMY
>
> I bought it for you.

> ROSIE
>
> Whose does that make it, officially? Oh, you take it. We read it to each other in Brighton. We made love on the train.
> (*Pause.*)
> I've got to go. They're being evicted today. Any news on Rafi?

> SAMMY
>
> I wondered why I was feeling so cheerful – I haven't thought about him today. I'll find him this morning.

EXT. THE WASTE GROUND. DAY

Now the exodus has begun. The caravans are starting to move; the fence has come down. The PROPERTY DEVELOPER *and his men are moving over the site with dogs. Police accompany them. The heavies smash down the shop to clear the way. The heavies hustle the straggly young men. Caravans get stuck in the mud. Some young men are trying to dig them out.* DANNY *is at the wheel of one of these trailers. The bulldozers start to move across the waste ground, clearing the debris, flattening the earth. The* PROPERTY DEVELOPER *stands in the back of an open-roofed car yelling instructions through a megaphone. The young man whose mother was shot* (MICHAEL) *is defiant, shouting at the heavies and the police who accompany them.*

Cut to: Inside DANNY*'s caravan.* RAFI *lies moaning on the bed. Frightened by the caravan's movement, he staggers to the door.*

Cut to: Opening the door of the slowly moving caravan, we see RAFI*'s view of the waste ground. We see the convey moving slowly off, young men being pushed around, trying to organize themselves.*

Cut to: On the periphery, being held back by the police, is ROSIE, *and with her* VIVIA, RANI, EVA. *A woman in a long sable coat is watching the action – the* PROPERTY DEVELOPER*'s wife.* RANI, *standing beside her for a moment, sprays a cross in green paint on her back.*

VIVIA

(*To* ROSIE)
Your father-in-law has finally joined the proletariat.

ROSIE

What? Is he here?

RANI

Somewhere.
(ALICE *has arrived now. We see her getting out of her car and walking through the police to* ROSIE, RANI, VIVIA. *She watches the police brutally arresting young women. She is shocked by this. She takes* VIVIA*'s arm. The other women try to move forward, along with a lot of the other spectators. They are obstructed by the heavies and police. The* PROPERTY DEVELOPER *in his jeep rides past yelling through his megaphone.*)

PROPERTY DEVELOPER

Here we go, here we go, here we go! Fuck off, you lesbian communists!
(*Then he recognizes* ALICE *and she him. He stops.*)
Alice, what brings you here?

ALICE

(*Indicating everything*)
Is this you, Norman?

PROPERTY DEVELOPER

Yes, I'm proud to say – making London a cleaner and safer place.

ALICE

I'm after someone. Can I get through a minute?
(*He waves* ALICE *through.*)

PROPERTY DEVELOPER

How's Jeffrey?
(*As* ALICE *goes through on to the site,* ROSIE, VIVIA, EVA, RANI, *etc., accompany her. The* GHOST, *walking away in the opposite direction, slips in the mud and, unnoticed by anyone but the kid whose mother was shot, goes under the wheels and is broken. By now* ANNA *has arrived on site. We see her moving around quickly, photographing where she can without getting hurt.* ALICE *has reached* RAFI, *who is staggering around in the mud.*
    Cut to: Wider shot of the convoy moving away. ALICE *is taking care of* RAFI. *He is in a terrible state.* ROSIE *joins them.*)

ROSIE

(*To* ALICE)
Come on, let's get him out of here. Take him to my place.
(RANI *watches this and* ROSIE *sees her.*
    Cut to: The convoy is leaving the waste ground and heading for the road. The kids remain defiant, cheerful and rebellious, like the PLO leaving Beirut. Some of them sit on the top of the moving caravans, playing music as they go.
    Cut to: ALICE *walks away with* RAFI, *supporting him as they go.* RAFI *is raving.*)

RAFI

I'm not leaving! Take me back! We must not allow those fascists bastards to drive us away! We must fight, fight!
(*To* ALICE)
You've never fought for anything in your damn life!
(*She gets* RAFI *in the car. He collapses in the back. She is very upset by what has happened to him.*)

EXT. MOTORWAY. DAY

SAMMY, *who is driving to* ALICE's, *heads along the motorway. He stops the car, gets out. On the waste ground, looking up, we can see* SAMMY *standing on the rim of the motorway, watching it all. He calls and shouts down to* ROSIE. *He shouts with all his might.*

SAMMY

Rosie! Rosie! Rosie! Rosie!
(*But of course she doesn't hear him.* ANNA *notices* SAMMY, *though.*
She looks up and waves. DANNY *shouts to* ROSIE *from the truck.*)

DANNY

Looks like I'm on my way out!
(*A final shot, later: The convey having left, the bulldozers doing their*
work, the waste ground having been cleared, we see ROSIE, VIVIA
and RANI *walking across the waste ground.* VIVIA *carries the black*
anarchist flag which fell from the top of one of the caravans.)

INT. SAMMY'S AND ROSIE'S FLAT. DAY

It is later that day. The women – taking RAFI *with them, have gone to*
Rosie's flat to discuss the morning's events. RAFI *is in the study. The*
women, RANI, VIVIA, ALICE, ANNA, ROSIE *and* BRIDGET, *eat and*
talk.

RANI

The way Danny's lot were treated shows just how illiberal and
heartless this country has become –

ALICE

But they were illegally –

ANNA

Surely they'd been there for so long, though –
(*We get the flavour of their intense and good-natured conversation.*
As it continues, we move across to see RAFI *watching them from his*
room a moment, before shutting the door of the study. Now we are in
the room with him. The conversation from the living room can
continue over, muffled.)

ALICE

It doesn't affect the law. The law is to protect the weak from the
strong, the arranged from the arbitrary –

RANI

But they are the powerless just trying to find a place in this
rotten society for themselves!
(RAFI *moves slowly. He is tired and distressed, but there is great*

*dignity in his actions. He takes the sheets from the bed and starts,
almost experimentally, to tie them together securely. The voices
outside get louder.)*

ALICE

(Out of shot)
Their place can only be found on society's terms, not on their
own whim –
(Cut to SAMMY *has come into the flat. He stands there a while,
looking at everyone.)*

ROSIE

(To ALICE*)*
It's hardly whim, they have no given place in this society!
*(*SAMMY *goes to* ANNA *and touches her lightly. She doesn't ignore
him, but it's as if she doesn't notice him. He looks at* ROSIE.

   Cut to: Back in the study* RAFI *has proceeded quite far with the
joining together of the sheets. He climbs the ladder and ties the sheet
to the top rung. Finally we see him put the other end of the sheet
around his neck. During this, he is breathing deeply. He seems very
alert now and aware of everything.

   Cut to:* SAMMY *leans over* ROSIE.*)*

SAMMY

Where's my dad?

ROSIE

He's in his room. You OK?
(Now we hear RAFI *kill himself as he jumps from the ladder.)*

SAMMY

(To ROSIE*)*
Sure.
*(*SAMMY *goes to* RAFI*'s room. He sees his father hanging. He looks at
him.* SAMMY *leaves the study and goes back into the living room. He
watches the women talking for a moment.)*
(To ROSIE*)*
Rosie, I think there's something you should come and look at.
(She looks up and goes to SAMMY. *They go into the study. We see*
SAMMY *and* ROSIE *in the study looking at* RAFI.*)*

INT. SAMMY'S AND ROSIE'S LIVING ROOM. DAY

SAMMY *and* ROSIE *sit on the floor together, rocking each other, waiting*
for the ambulance. We can see the others leaving, solemnly, one by one,
ANNA *turning back to look at* SAMMY *as she goes. But he doesn't see her.*
It is just the two of them together.

London Kills Me

CAST AND CREW

MAIN CAST

CLINT	Justin Chadwick
MUFFDIVER	Steven Mackintosh
SYLVIE	Emer McCourt
DR BUBBA	Roshan Seth
HEADLEY	Fiona Shaw
LILY	Eleanor David
STONE	Alun Armstrong
TOM-TOM	Stevan Rimkus
BURNS	Tony Haygarth
FAULKNER	Nick Dunning
BIKE	Naveen Andrews

MAIN CREW

Director of Photography	Ed Lachman
Production Designer	Stuart Walker
Stills Photographer	Jacques Prayer
Music Consultant	Charlie Gillett
Music Composers	Mark Springer and Sarah Sarhandi
Editor	Jon Gregory
Associate Producer	David Gothard
Executive Producer	Tim Bevan
Producer	Judy Hunt
Director	Hanif Kureishi

EXT. STREET. DAY

As the credits roll we see CLINT *on the street:* CLINT *is white, fair-haired, pretty, thin, vain, with much charm and nerve. He suffers from eczema all over his body – skin broken and cracked – so he's perpetually scratching himself and twitching.*

He's carrying a large bottle of mineral water which he uncaps. He produces a toothbrush and toothpaste from the top pocket of his jacket and using the bottled water he cleans his teeth.

Then he produces a dirty old piece of soap from his pocket and once more using the water, he washes his face and hands.

Finally he wets his hair.

Cut to:

EXT. STREET. DAY

CLINT *walking purposefully through the city.*

Cut to:

EXT. STREET. DAY

Now CLINT's *checking his look in the reflecting glass of the diner. He thinks he looks fine: he's had a wash, and his clothes, at this point, are pretty good.*

Cut to:

EXT. GOLBORNE ROAD. DAY

CLINT *walking purposefully through the city. We see* HEADLEY, HEMINGWAY *and* TOM-TOM *on street.*

Cut to:

EXT. VERNON YARD. DAY

CLINT *in a secluded doorway. He's smoking a spliff as he takes out a roll of money and hides it in different bits of his clothing, including his shoes and socks. He does this quickly, as if practised at it.*

   Cut to:

EXT. STREET. DAY

CLINT *on the phone in the street, a tower of ten pences on the box, a wretched piece of paper in hand, with phone numbers on it. A young girl comes by and puts her prostitute's calling card in the glass booth. Very businesslike.* CLINT *tries to talk to her as she walks away, as well as talking into the phone.*

   Cut to:

EXT. STREETS. DAY

CLINT *walking purposefully through the city.*

EXT. STREET. EVENING

We see CLINT *on the the bridge, walking. He stops to tie his shoe-laces. Picks up something from the ground, pockets it. He's always alert in this way.*

   SYLVIE *has seen him and she watches him doing this, amused by him. She goes to him. They haven't seen each other for a while. They greet each other warmly.* MUFFDIVER *is hanging out in doorway, watching them.* MUFFDIVER *is a skinny little kid of nineteen, a wiry dirty boy without* CLINT*'s charisma. But he's tougher than* CLINT, *more determined and more organized. He's a drug-dealer and starting to move into the big time.*

SYLVIE

How you doing, Clint?

CLINT

Good, good. Not too bad. Looking for a job.

SYLVIE

Now?

CLINT

No. Come with me.

SYLVIE

Where, little Clint?

CLINT

Little rave.

EXT. MOROCCAN CAFÉ. DAY

They walk past the Moroccan café where the Moroccans sip mint tea.
They walk past the Rasta Information Centre. The street is busy and
lively, colourful and mixed. Music comes from various cafés and shops.
There is music on the street constantly. They talk and laugh, arm in arm,
though CLINT *never relaxes and glances around continually, both out of*
nervousness and interest.
  Across the street MUFFDIVER *is standing in a doorway.*

MUFFDIVER

(*To himself*)
Tsa-Tsa, she's nice.
(*He knows* CLINT *well.* CLINT *works for him. They're very old*
friends. MUFFDIVER *goes across to them.*)
Wha' 'appening?

CLINT

Going to a rave, later.

MUFFDIVER

(*Looking at* SYLVIE)
Yeah? Something 'appening.

CLINT

Sylvie 'appening. Sylvie. Muffdiver.

SYLVIE

Pleased to meet you, Muffdiver. Always nice to make new
friends.
(MUFFDIVER *looks at* SYLVIE. *She is less interested in him than he*
in her. He stares at her, fascinated. Meanwhile CLINT *calls out to*
BURNS, *who is sipping tea at a table inside the Moroccan place.*
CLINT *goes inside.*)

INT. MOROCCAN CAFÉ. DAY

> CLINT
> Burns! Burns! Yo, man, rave.

EXT. MOROCCAN CAFÉ. DAY

And BURNS, *a fat Scotsman in his fifties, comes paddling into the frame, eating. As the four of them walk,* MUFFDIVER *nudges* SYLVIE *and she does a double-take as he pulls a string of handkerchiefs out of his mouth.*

> MUFFDIVER
> Squad.
> (*Two plainclothes policemen pass in front of them. Automatically they cool down, their faces becoming masks.*
>   *When the men have gone,* CLINT *gives an Indian whoop.* SYLVIE *looks at him and laughs.*)

INT. HOUSE PARTY. NIGHT

A party. The place jumping. A mixed, black and white, party. Music. Dope. Dancing. Everything you'd expect.

    CLINT *and* MUFFDIVER *are accompanied by* BURNS. *We see them swing into the room and greet people. They're obviously well known there.*

    A couple of kids go to BURNS *and ask him questions. He's dealing. He turns away with them, putting his hand in his pocket.*

    MUFFDIVER *experimentally puts his arm around* SYLVIE *and whispers in her ear. Then he kisses her cheek. She is surprised by his attention.*

    CLINT *is surprised by* MUFFDIVER'S *move, but as usual he's concerned with other things, always curious.*

    Cut to:

INT. ANOTHER PART OF HOUSE. NIGHT

Later. MUFFDIVER *leaning back against a wall, stoned, with a joint.*

    CLINT *and* SYLVIE *talking in another part of the room.* BURNS *dancing with a girl, enjoying himself.*

    A young black MAN *goes to* MUFFDIVER. *They greet each other, their faces close.*

MUFFDIVER

Buyin'?

MAN

Na.

MUFFDIVER

Sellin'?

MAN

I hear you lookin' for Mr G. You ready for Mr G I reckon. But he want to know you properly organized and everything.

MUFFDIVER

Yeah, I appreciate.

MAN

OK, I'll fix it.
(*Indicates* CLINT)
Who that geezer?

MUFFDIVER

That's Clint. Why, he in trouble again?
(*The* MAN *winks and moves away.* MUFFDIVER *is alarmed as the* MAN *moves towards* CLINT. CLINT *gets up. The* MAN *takes* CLINT *away from* SYLVIE. *The* MAN *indicates to* MUFFDIVER *to keep out of it.* MUFFDIVER *sits with* SYLVIE.)

INT. BARE ROOM. NIGHT

The MAN *throws* CLINT *into a bare dark room, maybe with just a mattress on the floor. Pots of paint etc. There are two other guys in the room now, one* BLACK, *one* WHITE, *all young and threatening.*
    CLINT *backs away, terrified, whimpering.*

MAN

You owe me some money, Mr Clint, man, from that time you are recalling now, right?
(CLINT *is furious with himself for getting into this shit. His hands are shaking as he empties his pockets. Then, after a nod from the* MAN, *he removes a fiver from the collar of his shirt. The* MAN *takes the money but is unimpressed by it.*)
That all you carryin', boy? You strip.

WHITE MAN

Yeah.

CLINT

I got nothin'.

(CLINT *removes his clothes to his underpants. The* MAN *nods and the pants come off too. The men laugh at* CLINT'*s puny eczema-ridden body. They search his clothes. Suddenly one of them holds up money.*)

WHITE MAN

In the shoe!

BLACK MAN

In the shoe? Chew the shoe, chew the shoe, boy! Do him!
(*They all close in on* CLINT. *Suddenly one of the men hits him across the legs with a pool cue. He cries out.*)

INT. HOUSE PARTY. NIGHT

Quick cut to the loud music of the house. Here MUFFDIVER *is talking to* SYLVIE. BURNS *is eating a plate of food.*

MUFFDIVER

I've seen you around the pub and in the street, Sylvie, but I've never talked to you, though I've wanted to. For a long time.
(*Pause. He's getting nowhere with her.*)
Shall I tell you something? Burns is quite fat. He had his stomach sewn up, to stop him eating. But the bit that was left has expanded. Or maybe the stitches burst, I can't remember what he told us. A person's stomach is only the size of your fist, you know. But it's elastic.
(*Pause.

He pulls a lighted cigarette out of her ear. She doesn't respond. He pulls a lighted match from the other. She smiles.*)

SYLVIE

Where's that boy?

MUFFDIVER

You're right about him. He needs us, his friends. That's why
I'm getting us a place. Need somewhere yourself?
(*She is interested in him.*)
Why don't you come with me? Come on. We'll go somewhere.
How about it?

EXT. PARTY HOUSE. NIGHT

MUFFDIVER *and* SYLVIE *walk down the steps of the house, or stand at
the top of the steps.*

MUFFDIVER

What sort of music do you like? I like House and Hendrix. The
three Hs are for me, eh? That was a dread party. Clint's idea.
What a fool.
Cut to:

EXT. STEPS UNDER HOUSE. NIGHT

We see CLINT, *naked and covered in mud, under the steps, shivering but
then laughing as he hears his friend* MUFFDIVER*'s pretentious rap to the
aloof* SYLVIE.

EXT. PARTY HOUSE. NIGHT

MUFFDIVER *is about to put his arm around* SYLVIE *when* CLINT *rises
up.* SYLVIE *goes to him.*

SYLVIE

Clint, Clint, for God's sake, get up! Are you hurt? We didn't
know where you'd gone.

CLINT

I like fresh air, innit. Sylvie, I tell you, I'm finished with
this shit life. This eating shit fuckin' life. I'm really getting a
job.

MUFFDIVER

When?

CLINT

Tomorrow. Meet me at ten fifteen outside the diner and I'll
show you how to conduct an interview with an employer.

SYLVIE

Don't be hasty, Clint. Things are not that bad.

MUFFDIVER

And you'll have to find some clothes first, man.

CLINT

It was smoky in there, so I flogged my clothes to a man with no
trousers.

SYLVIE

Have a heart, Muffdiver.

MUFFDIVER

He brings these things on himself. Do they happen to me?

CLINT

You've got to know. It's my birthday. Now, at this moment in
the whole history of the world I'm twenty years old.

SYLVIE

Say happy birthday, Muffdiver.
(*She nudges* MUFFDIVER *to congratulate* CLINT. *He murmurs a
few words.*)

MUFFDIVER

Happy birthday, Clint.
(MUFFDIVER *makes a gesture towards* SYLVIE, *and she responds.*
CLINT *sees they're together now. He feels excluded. He moves away,
hurt.*)

CLINT

I'm just glad I spent it with friends.
(*He walks away naked.*)

MUFFDIVER

(*To* SYLVIE)
They won't let him into the Subterrania like that. They've got a
very strict door policy.

EXT. STREET. NIGHT

A shopping street at three in the morning. CLINT *walks naked along the street.* BIKE, *a young Indian kid (on his bicycle) circles around him, eating a Chinese takeaway.*

CLINT

I'm gonna live an ordinary life from now on. I know it's possible.
(*Two transvestites,* FAULKNER *and another, pass* CLINT *and glance coolly at him.*)

FAULKNER

Hi Clint. Good start.

EXT. TRASH BAGS ON STREET. NIGHT

Another part of Notting Hill. CLINT *is going through a pile of plastic rubbish bags bursting with puked Chinese dinners. But he's found a pair of trousers, and – hey presto – a filthy pair of workman's boots. These are big boots.*

CLINT *turns and sees an extraordinary apparition. A large black tramp, in rags, wild hair, covered in filth, carrying an immense number of bags (some of which are tied to his body), moves closer and closer to* CLINT, *his eyes fixed on him.*

EXT. JEWELLER'S DOORWAYS. DAWN

Three or four young people are sleeping, wrapped in cardboard, blankets and papers, one of them cowering behind umbrellas. CLINT *has spent the night here. He wakes up. He flattens his hair with spit. Then he sneaks a pair of socks from the person behind the umbrella.*

BUSY BEE *is awake, shaking out a jumper.* CLINT *watches him.*
BUSY BEE *notices* CLINT *and watches him warily.*

CLINT

I need to lend that jumper.

BUSY BEE

What's wrong with *The Times*?
(*And he throws* The Times *at him.*)

CLINT

You don't understand, Busy Bee. I got a job interview this
morning. Big interview ting.

BUSY BEE

What drugs you gonna give me, Mr Clint Eastwood?
(CLINT *grabs the jumper and runs away with it.* BUSY BEE *chases
him,* CLINT *laughing and running, pulling on the jumper.*)

INT. DINER. DAY

*We're in a busy hamburger diner at lunchtime. This is an upmarket place
frequented mainly by well-off media types. The tables are full, the activity
frantic. A young well-dressed young woman snaps her fingers and calls
sharply to a waiter.*

A young black waitress, MELANIE, *hurries over to her. The woman
speaks to* MELANIE.

At another table two SMART WOMEN *are working – looking through a
pile of papers and files, and discussing them. One of them drops a piece of
paper.*

CLINT, *who we now see is observing all this, just standing there, nips
over and picks up the papers. He holds on to the document, gaining the*
WOMAN's *attention. His clothes are too big and dirty and he sticks out in
the restaurant.*

*There is, behind the bar, throughout this film, an incredibly flash
barman, mixing complicated cocktails in a particularly theatrical way.
The* SMART WOMAN *smiles at* CLINT. *He whispers at her.*

CLINT

Need any washing done?

SMART WOMAN

What?

CLINT

Car cleaned? Washing by hand? Gardening by hand?
(*She glances at her friend and they both laugh.*)
Need any black hash? Proper ting.
(*They're interested, after a nodded consultation, but now*
HEMINGWAY, *the American manager in a suit and open-necked*

shirt, comes out, looks for CLINT, *and seeing him, takes his arm and examines his face with natural affection and interest.*

HEMINGWAY *is very cool, and sees everything about a person immediately.*)

HEMINGWAY

You Clint, yeah?
(CLINT *struggles to cope, to appear straight and normal.*)

CLINT

Yeah. Mr Clint. How you doing? Do you think you can do like what your friend promised me?

HEMINGWAY

What promise did my friend make to you, exactly?

CLINT

Get me a job here. She say the manager a wally but you know the manager intimately close, she say.

HEMINGWAY

I am the manager, Mr Hemingway.

CLINT

All this is you? Cool photos. Sturdy chairs. Top people sitting.
(*He winks at the two* SMART WOMEN.)

HEMINGWAY

OK, OK. Underneath everything you might be a good boy. Work experience?
(*Pause.*)
What work have you done?
(CLINT *thinks for a while, looking at the waitress flying spectacularly about, the barman mixing drinks.*)

CLINT

But I could pick up one of them plates.
(*And he goes to the* SMART WOMEN's *table and starts removing their plates, piling them up on his arm.*)

HEMINGWAY

All right, OK, you gotta start somewhere. It's decent work when you learn how to do it.

(*He takes* CLINT *aside.*)
Just don't mess me around, OK? Come back Tuesday
morning. I feel someone's gonna walk out on me that day.
Clean yourself up. And do one thing. Just one, right?
(*We pan down* CLINT's *legs to his boots. We see, with* HEMINGWAY,
his disgusting boots.)
You understand, don't you, that I can't have footgear like that
in my place. There is disease there. Film people come in here.
So, no new shoes – no job. No job – back on the street. Back on
the street – (*and he shrugs*) – shit!
(CLINT *nods, glances at the window to make sure* MUFFDIVER *is
outside watching all this, which he is. When he sees* CLINT *looking at
him he turns away, not acknowledging him.* CLINT *puts out his
hand.*)

CLINT

Put it there, Mr Hemingway. I wish all my problems were of
that cool order. See you Tuesday.
(HEMINGWAY *watches him go. As he goes,* CLINT *smiles at*
MELANIE, *who smiles back at him. He stops for a moment to talk to
her, but sees* HEMINGWAY *looking at him. He goes.*)

EXT. STREET. DAY

CLINT *strides cheerfully out of the restaurant.* MUFFDIVER *is waiting
outside for him and runs to catch up with* CLINT *as he walks confidently
away from the diner.*

CLINT

Start Tuesday. Everything's A-I fixed up. There's just one
thing I need –

MUFFDIVER

Clint, Clint –

CLINT

A pair of shoes. Good shoes. Great shoes.

MUFFDIVER

The job's out then. It's a dead-end, it's –

CLINT

All these people got shoes. Look. Hush Puppies, DMs, sandals, brogues, loafers, high-tops. Give me a single reason why I shouldn't get some.

MUFFDIVER

Because you a fool.

EXT. PUB. DAY

The two friends are on the street and they know a lot of people. The black kids outside the pub greet them. CLINT *calls out to a girl in the street.*

CLINT

Hey Yvonne, wha' 'appenin'? Wanna buy any E? Any bush? What about a pair of shorts?
(*And he pulls a pair of shorts out of somewhere. She shakes her head, laughing.*)

EXT. SHOE SHOP. DAY

Then CLINT *is standing outside a shoe shop. He's trying on a strong black boot which he's taken down from a display. He does a little dance wearing the one new boot. It fits and he's celebrating. The shop assistant, a young white-faced girl in black, her long hair standing straight up, watches him suspiciously.* CLINT *delicately puts the shoe back.* MUFFDIVER *is in the background.*

EXT. STREET. DAY

Later. CLINT *and* MUFFDIVER *walking quickly, heading towards a squat that's been recommended to them.*

MUFFDIVER

Fuck me? Fuck me, why, for fuck's sake?

CLINT

Because what's my life doing?

MUFFDIVER

Clint –

CLINT

It's coming together. I can make it without you.

MUFFDIVER

Yeah, sure, where's the shoes?

CLINT

You can't put me down, because the shoe is due.

MUFFDIVER

Yeah, like my arse is due. You got no money for shoes.

CLINT

I'll work for you until Tuesday.

MUFFDIVER

No. You don't even work for me now.

CLINT

What?

MUFFDIVER

You're not professional.

CLINT

And there's my new home. Our office suite. It's ready for
business occupation, right? We're swinging over there now,
yeah? It's a palace you said –

MUFFDIVER

Yeah, I said.

CLINT

I had to sleep out last night, Muffdiver.

MUFFDIVER

There's Headley.

EXT. STREET. DAY

They look across the street where HEADLEY *is walking along, a TV
interviewer with her, a cameraman and sound guy in front of her. She
talks eloquently about the area, indicating people and shops. As the crew
moves backwards, out of a doorway comes the black tramp in rags,
lumbering into shot.*

They stop shooting. HEADLEY *sees* CLINT *and* MUFFDIVER *and indicates for them to come over.*

                    CLINT
I don't wanna see her.

                    MUFFDIVER
She's business, man.

                    CLINT
She's always wanting.

                    MUFFDIVER
She's drug business, man.
(MUFFDIVER *leads* CLINT *into the gallery.*)

INT. GALLERY. DAY

                    MUFFDIVER
Let's look at some artwork for the new place.
(CLINT *and* MUFFDIVER *have joined a gallery opening. Young smart people holding glasses. Wealthy attractive people.*
    MUFFDIVER *looks at all this with much interest and envy.*
    CLINT *and* MUFFDIVER *mingle.* CLINT *takes a drink from a passing tray and hands one to* MUFFDIVER.
    MUFFDIVER, *cool and distant, doesn't take much notice of* CLINT, *who's always going on at him.*)

                    CLINT:
This squat, we're not going to be let down. Is it definite? I can't be a waiter and sleep in the gutter.

                    MUFFDIVER
What about Sylvie? Is she definite?

                    CLINT
What?
(*He's amazed.*)
With you? With Sylvie? You?

MUFFDIVER

Don't keep saying her name like that. How d'you know Sylvie
anyway?

CLINT

Sylvie. I've known her so long I can remember when she didn't
drink.

MUFFDIVER

How come I haven't seen her before, then?
(*A woman is beside* MUFFDIVER, *looking for a light.* CLINT *steals a
gold lighter from the table and lights the cigarette. He puts the lighter
in* MUFFDIVER's *pocket.*)

CLINT

Sylvie was in the drug rehab.

MUFFDIVER

But she's back on.
(*Pause. He can't tear his eyes away from the surroundings.*)
These people. Tsa-Tsa. They got clothes, cars, houses –

CLINT

Shoes.

MUFFDIVER

Maisonettes. Everything.
(MUFFDIVER *walks decisively out of the place, as if he's decided
what he must do with his life from now on.* CLINT, *as always the
deputy, walks out behind him, stealing a bottle of champagne and
putting it under his jacket as he goes.*)

EXT. BACK OF SQUAT. DAY

CLINT *and* MUFFDIVER *stand at the back of a five-storey London house,
looking up at the rear of the building.*

MUFFDIVER

Tom-Tom said it's a whole luxury place. The owner's done a
runner – he's some big criminal. We've probably got three
months of total mod-cons.

> CLINT

Great, total con-mods.

> MUFFDIVER

Okay, in through the window.
(CLINT *removes his jacket. As he does so, he talks to the world in general.*)

> CLINT

The shoe is due. The new shoe is overdue.
(*To* MUFFDIVER.)
Which floor?

> MUFFDIVER

Top.
(CLINT *vacillates, moves backwards.* MUFFDIVER *grabs him and shoves him towards the building.*)
I'll keep a sharp look-out!
Cut to:

EXT. BACK TO SQUAT. DAY

Now CLINT *is clambering up the drainpipe, about half-way up the side of the tall building. Very dangerous.* CLINT *hears a popping noise and looks down to see* MUFFDIVER *swigging from a bottle of champagne.*

   MUFFDIVER *gives him the thumbs-up and indicates for him to continue upwards.*

   Cut to:

EXT. BACK OF SQUAT. DAY

CLINT *has climbed up to the floor below the top one, and is clinging perilously to the drainpipe. From his point of view we get a high view over London. Then he turns back to the face of the building and looks into a large room.*

INT. SUFI CENTRE. DAY

This is the Sufi Centre. About twenty people holding hands in a circle and moving slowly clockwise. In the middle of the circle are four people whirling and chanting as they move.

The Sufi whirlers are all white, apart from two black girls. Mostly it's young hippyish women in casual clothes.

Outside the circle is DR BUBBA, *an Indian, instructing them what to do and clouting a drum which he holds under his arm. An old man, whirling, wearing a bow-tie, opens his eyes and sees* CLINT *suspended outside the window. He does a double-take. Then he accepts that he is having a vision and he puts his hands together and acknowledges* CLINT *as an angel, since* CLINT *has, from his point of view, developed wings.*

EXT. BACK OF SQUAT. DAY

CLING *scrambles upwards.*
Cut to:

EXT. BACK OF SQUAT. DAY

CLINT *is right at the top of the house, but the drainpipe is starting to come away from the wall.* CLINT *tries frantically to grab at things but there's nothing near by. He holds on to a grating for a few seconds but it pulls out of the wall and crashes to the ground, just missing* MUFFDIVER *who yells angrily up at* CLINT.

CLINT *looks down. He feels certain he's going to die. He is terrified. He knows he can't climb down the breaking drainpipe.*

                         CLINT
Help me MUFFDIVER, help me, man!
(*He manages to look down at* MUFFDIVER *standing there.*
MUFFDIVER *genuinely distressed and confused.*)

                       MUFFDIVER
What can I do?

                         CLINT
Call the police!
(CLINT *watches* MUFFDIVER *who takes a few paces away, but returns and indicates complete helplessness.*)
Cut to:

EXT. BACK OF SQUAT. DAY

CLINT *has grabbed another pipe above the window frame. He pulls*

*himself up and swings around the side of the building, where there's a
balcony. He clambers on to the balcony. The glass doors to the flat are
locked. He smashes one of the windows with a brick, cutting himself. But
he lands on the leopard-skin carpet, covered in blood.*

INT. LIVING ROOM OF SQUAT. DAY

CLINT, *cut and bleeding, walks around the squat, wiping the blood off
himself with a white towel.*

*The squat has clearly been burgled a few times: the TV and stereo ripped
out, and records and clothes and rubbish strewn about the place.*

CLINT *walks from room to room, taking in the thick carpets, glass tables
(cracked or smashed) and broken pin-ball machine. The living room is a
big space. There is a bar but all the bottles are empty or smashed.*

CLINT, *as he walks about, is more and more pleased with what he sees,
grunting and whistling his approval*

INT. SQUAT. BEDROOM. DAY

CLINT *in the master bedroom, lying on the bed.*

*He discovers switches beside the bed which operate the curtains; these
move furiously back and forth. He enjoys this for a while. Then he fiddles
with the lights in the room, which go off and on, dimming and
brightening. He's really like a child now, unable to believe his good
fortune.*

*Finally he hits another button and a huge TV cabinet opens. A shelf
comes out, on which there's a plate of rotting food.*

Cut to:

INT. CLINT'S BEDROOM. DAY

Now CLINT *is trying to open the main wardrobe in the room, but it is
locked. He kicks it open: it gives.*

*He touches the console beside the bed to stop the lights going on and off.
The room is semi-dark, the light red. He opens the wardrobe cautiously.
As it opens the wardrobe lights up, to reveal an illuminated row of vulgar
shoes and boots belonging to a spiv: leopard-skin and crocodile shoes,
flashy boots with spurs, cowboy boots, etc.*

When he's taken all this in, CLINT *removes his own boots and selects*

*a pair of shoes to wear, like someone choosing a chocolate from a
full box. He tries them but it's a struggle; they're too small, they'll
never fit. He tries walking in them but he falls over, laughing. None
of them fit.*

INT./EXT. BACK OF SQUAT. DAY

CLINT *shouts out of the window to* MUFFDIVER *waiting impatiently
below.*

                              CLINT
   Yo!

                            MUFFDIVER
   What's it like?

                              CLINT
   Round up the posse!
   (MUFFDIVER *is ecstatic. Under his breath, to himself, as a
   celebration, he mutters.*)

EXT. FRONT OF SQUAT. BUILDING. DAY

                            MUFFDIVER
   Round up the fucking posse! Tsa-Tsa!

EXT. STREET. DAY

MUFFDIVER *hurries through the streets, pleased. As he goes, he sees* BIKE.
Indicates for BIKE *to go over to him.* BIKE *cycles along beside him.*

                            MUFFDIVER
   Found us a place to live.
   (BIKE *hits the horn on his bike in acknowledgement.*)

EXT. DINER/STREET. DAY

Outside the diner. SYLVIE *and a middle-aged man, not extravagantly
dressed or posh, have just left the place.* SYLVIE *looks quite smart. She
smiles and talks animatedly.* MUFFDIVER *stops, then follows them. The
man waves at a cab. They both get in.* MUFFDIVER *suddenly decides to
start chasing the cab. It stops at traffic lights.* MUFFDIVER *is looking in the
window: the guy has his hand up* SYLVIE'S *skirt. The cab moves away.*

SYLVIE *pulls down the window.* MUFFDIVER *runs beside the cab.*

MUFFDIVER

(*Through window*)
We've got a place. 14 Whitehall Gardens. Top flat. OK.
(*He smiles at the guy.*

   Stay with SYLVIE *in the cab a few seconds. The guy looks at her.*
She puts her head back and laughs.)

EXT. DOORWAY/SCAFFOLDING. DAY

BURNS *standing in a doorway, his possessions around him. He's always*
cheerful, despite everything. MUFFDIVER *goes to him.* BURNS *gives him*
money. MUFFDIVER *is surprised by the amount.*

MUFFDIVER

How you doing Burns – clubs busy?

BURNS

Long weekend, big demand in the clubs up West. I could easily
shift a couple of hundred through the bouncers – I know them
all, I got most of them their jobs. Have you got it?

MUFFDIVER

More? Fuck it. I'm really short of supplies right now.

BURNS

By the way, I've had the word. Mr G's ready to see you.

MUFFDIVER

Yeah, I heard. We need him, now.

BURNS

Where shall I tell him to come?

MUFFDIVER

I've found the premises. I've got us a luxury business base.

BURNS

For all of us?

MUFFDIVER

Yeah, you'll have your own room. Burns, your posse needs you.
(*Pause.*)
How's your stomach?

BURNS

Making noises.

INT. LIVING ROOM OF SQUAT. DAY

Later that day. MUFFDIVER *and* CLINT *have taken possession of the squat and moved their gear in.* CLINT *is wrapped in the leopard-skin carpets and wearing a cowboy hat.*
    MUFFDIVER *is pacing, really wound up.*

CLINT

I did good, right, in getting this place? Muff?

MUFFDIVER

Yeah. Didn't I say I'd take care of you? Who needs shoes with
these carpets? I have to stop myself –

CLINT

What?

MUFFDIVER

Feeling too happy. In case it don't last. We can really do
something here.

CLINT

You mean parties?

MUFFDIVER

I mean as a business base. And I could kiss her here. This is
just the venue . . . for a first kiss.

CLINT

Sylvie won't even turn up. And even if she comes she won't
stay.

MUFFDIVER

She'll come.
(*Pause.*)
She's desperate.

(*Now we see the posse walk in through the door one by one, carrying their ragged possessions.* BIKE *comes in apprehensively, with nothing but his bicycle.* BURNS *is a Scotsman, unemployed, fiftyish.* TOM-TOM, *a white Rasta, late thirties, a junkie.*)

BURNS

(*To* CLINT)
Home!

CLINT

Yeah!
Cut to:

INT. LIVING ROOM OF SQUAT. DAY

They're unpacking their things and admiring the squat. They choose rooms for themselves and lay out their sleeping bags. BURNS *is changing the locks on the door and he chats away to* TOM-TOM *who's laying out his stuff in a corner of the room.*

Then SYLVIE *walks in through the door. She is carrying a trumpet and some other belongings over her shoulder.*

MUFFDIVER

You need a room here Sylvie. Only the best for you.

BURNS

Yeah, only the best.
(SYLVIE *looks around.*)

MUFFDIVER

We're gonna fix it up and everything, aren't we Burns?
Furniture. Hot water.

TOM-TOM

Cold water, even.

SYLVIE

Where's little Clint? Has he got his clothes on?

MUFFDIVER

How about a spliff? Bike, roll Sylvie a spliff.
(BIKE *scuttles off across the squat.*)

TOM-TOM

Give us a toot.

(*She plays a long sad note on the trumpet.* BURNS *looks at the others approvingly.* MUFFDIVER *watches her, utterly entranced. He's never been in love like this before.*

He thinks for a moment then he rushes into Clint's room.)

INT. CLINT'S ROOM. DAY

CLINT, *absorbed in his own world, isn't aware that* SYLVIE's *arrived. He's sitting on the bed with two pairs of boots from the wardrobe. He's trying, with a knife, to cut around the toe so they fit.*

MUFFDIVER *shoves him off the bed and then prods the mattress energetically, testing it. He also whacks the buttons on the console beside the bed. The 'effects' go crazy.*

MUFFDIVER

This is good. Total theatre, man.

CLINT

Look at these shoes. I'm on my way. Walking.

(MUFFDIVER *makes a face.*)

They're for work not for best.

MUFFDIVER

What work? You dealing for someone else?

CLINT

In the diner. They're pretty. Except they don't fit.

(MUFFDIVER *looks at the room in a businesslike manner. But still finds it difficult to broach the subject on his mind.*)

MUFFDIVER

So what exactly is happening here?

CLINT

Oh fucking no. This is exclusively my room.

MUFFDIVER

Yeah, granted. But there's one drawback.

CLINT

There's no drawback.

MUFFDIVER

Listen to me.

CLINT

I climbed the drainpipe!

MUFFDIVER

It's a double room. That interests me.

CLINT

Tsa-Tsa. But does it interest the other person?

MUFFDIVER

Yeah. It does. It interests them.

CLINT

My arse it interests. What other person is it?
(*We see, but they do not,* SYLVIE *in the room.*)
There's no other person. I'm the only other person you got.

MUFFDIVER

I love her. I'm addicted to her.
(*They turn and* SYLVIE *is standing in the doorway.* MUFFDIVER *is embarrassed, but continues, shyly, gently.*)
How would you like this room?
(*He pummels the bed histrionically while activating the lights. The TV shoots out of the wall, with the old dinner still intact on the panel.*)

SYLVIE

My God. Shoe heaven.

CLINT

Yeah, they're only for work, not for best.

SYLVIE

Will that man really give you a job?

CLINT

Yeah –
(MUFFDIVER *activates the curtains to distract her.*)

SYLVIE

(*To* CLINT)
Clint's settled in here – aren't you, little mouse?

CLINT

(*Sarcastic*)
But wouldn't this suit you? Nice duvet, nice mattress, nice
Muffdiver on top of you –
(SYLVIE *laughs.* MUFFDIVER *is furious, glares at* CLINT *and throws
a shoe at him.* SYLVIE *indicates for* MUFFDIVER *to go to her. When
he does, she puts her arms around him and kisses him. She indicates
to* CLINT *to go to her. She does the same to him. Then she gently
pushes the two of them together, encouraging them to hold each
other.*)

INT. LIVING ROOM OF SQUAT. DAY

Later that day. BURNS *and* CLINT *together.* CLINT *is getting the
practical* BURNS *to cut open the toes of an especially vulgar
pair of red cowboy boots covered in metal studs – using a big
knife.*
  SYLVIE *over the other side of the room practises the trumpet.*
  BIKE *is fixing his bicycle.*
  TOM-TOM *is asleep on the floor, on his back, music-box beside him.*
  The door to another room is open and MUFFDIVER *is hurrying about
with his possessions, settling in.*

BURNS

(*Working and eating*)
You sure this is what you want, Clint boy?

CLINT

Burns, the point is moot. I'm going to wear the boot.
(*Pause.*)
Ol' Muffdiver is starting to get pretty heavy with people. He
wasn't always like that, was he? He was sweet.

BURNS

You knew each other at school, right?

INT. MUFFDIVER'S ROOM. DAY

This room, which he's moving into, is small and virtually empty, except for several tailor's dummies on stands. Slightly eerie. MUFFDIVER *has put out two sleeping bags, side by side. Now he's adjusting the pillows, etc. He's unpacked his things neatly.*

INT. LIVING ROOM OF SQUAT. DAY

CLINT

(*To* BURNS)
There was this day, Burns, man. Me an' Muffdiver stole some LSD from someone at school. And there was another boy who wanted acid badly. So Muff got this stuff and went to him and sold it for a lot of money. I remember, we were in the school cloakroom and he had this money in his hand and his whole face brightened up like I'd never seen it before. He thought he could do anything. I reckon he wanted his whole life to be like that moment.

BURNS

Listen, Clint, these boots . . . Well try 'em on.
(CLINT *puts on the boots, with his bare toes sticking out through the end.*)

CLINT

Great. Thanks Burns, I really appreciate it.

BURNS

Why don't you just buy a cheap pair? Are you sure they're right for restaurant work?

CLINT

Clint is skint.

BURNS

What happens if it rains?
(CLINT *pulls the boots off. There are two plastic bags beside* BURNS, *in which he keeps sandwiches and food.* CLINT *empties the bags neatly, shakes out the crumbs and puts the bags over his feet. He puts on the boots again, and stands there clicking his heels together.*)

CLINT

Olé! Ready for the street.

BURNS

What you gonna sell on the street? Has he given you something?

CLINT

No. I gotta ask him now. Then I'm out sellin' for the last time.
Then I'll buy a new pair. The new shoes are due, the shoes –
(*They watch as* MUFFDIVER *calls* SYLVIE.)

MUFFDIVER

Sylvie, Sylvie.

INT. MUFFDIVER'S BEDROOM. DAY

SYLVIE *and* MUFFDIVER. *He is apprehensive . . . but determined. His
clothes on one dummy, hers on another.*

SYLVIE

All your little things . . . laid out neat and tidy.
(*Pause.*)
And my things too.
(MUFFDIVER *opens his hand to show her a bag of smack.*)

SYLVIE

Do you take smack?

MUFFDIVER

(*Slightly amused*)
But Clint does, off and on.
(*Pretentious.*)
I prefer drugs of illusion.
(*Pause.*)
Kiss.
(*He goes to kiss her. She retreats.*)
Don't. Just try me out.

INT. LIVING ROOM. DAY

Later, in the living room, the whole posse there. CLINT *and* MUFFDIVER
having a serious and loud argument.

MUFFDIVER

No, man, that's not possible –

CLINT

Please, Muffdiver, give me thirty.

MUFFDIVER

Fucking thirty!
(*To the others*)
Hey, Tom-Tom, Bike, what's he saying to me? He's saying give
him thirty!

CLINT

(*Appealing to the others*)
Yeah, that's all. Sylvie.

BURNS

What's the lad want?

TOM-TOM

Thirty Es and As to sell tonight. No chance.

MUFFDIVER

(*To* CLINT)
Come on, man, you a jerk off now. I can't take you seriously as
a salesman.

CLINT

Thirty ecstasy, thirty acid and some ME-35. Sale or return. I'm
shit-hot reliable. An A-1 salesman, like everyone here. You know
what it's for. The footwear it there, in the shop waiting for me.

MUFFDIVER

Yeah, Mr Poet, last time I leaned forward with you, you took
half the stuff yourself and gave away the rest.
(MUFFDIVER *starts to look down at* CLINT*'s feet, and pulls up his
trouser bottoms to reveal the red cowboy boots with the toes in plastic
bags sticking out at the end. He invites everyone to look.*)
Hey, hey . . .
(*The others move in closer.* SYLVIE *puts her hand in her mouth to stop
herself laughing.* BURNS *is annoyed by their mirth. But* CLINT
doesn't lose his dignity.)

CLINT

Yeah, a good price for me, a good price for you, that's how I get
the new shoe.

SYLVIE

(*Appealing*)
Muffdiver –

CLINT

You haven't had the childhood I been through. Messages from
there are still reaching me. Sexually abused. My father
shooting me up with H when I was thirteen –

MUFFDIVER

Exactly my point.

CLINT

What?

MUFFDIVER

You not used to paying for it.

CLINT

Then he got murdered –

BURNS

You gonna get murdered, son. People looking for you with iron
bars.

CLINT

Children's homes, probation officers, trials, beatings, shit, shit.

MUFFDIVER

Yeah, yeah.

CLINT

All I want is some shoes to get my life started!
(BIKE, TOM-TOM *and* MUFFDIVER *laugh.*)

INT. STAIRS/HALLWAY/BOOT ROOM/SUFI CENTRE. DAY

CLINT *and* MUFFDIVER *walk slowly downstairs,* MUFFDIVER *with his
arm around him.* CLINT *is looking very down.*

MUFFDIVER

I lose my temper, man. You know me. I'm nervous about
Sylvie. I want her so much. When I look at her I can't
understand why she isn't mine.
(*Pause.*)
Here's the stuff you wanted to sell.
(*And he gives him the Es and As.*)

CLINT

I knew you'd come through.
(*Now they stop at the open door of the Sufi Centre. Curious, they
wander in.*)
Look, look.
(*A group of people are sitting cross-legged on the floor. A
guided meditation is taking place.* DR BUBBA *leads them
through it.*)

DR BUBBA

(*To group*)
Now you're relaxed, let's concentrate on breathing. Count
your breaths in and out. One, two, three. Slowly, slowly, from
the stomach. You are not, I say not, I repeat not, blowing up a
balloon. This is to slow us down. This enables us to see our
lives clearly for a few minutes.
(*When* CLINT *turns to look at* MUFFDIVER *he sees him leaving.*)

MUFFDIVER

Business.
(CLINT *closes his eyes, takes a breath, smiles to himself relaxedly and
puts the drugs in his pocket. When he does take a squint he sees a row
of shoes. This is deeply pleasing to him.*

*He chooses an excellent pair of shoes and, removing the cowboy
boots, tries them on. They fit. Bliss.*

*He is creeping out of the door in his new shoes, blowing kisses at
them, when* DR BUBBA *is behind him.*)

DR BUBBA

You are in love with those shoes?
(CLINT *continues walking away.*)
Do they fit?

(CLINT *finally stops and turns to face* DR BUBBA.)
I am your neighbour, Dr Bubba. This morning, why didn't you
come in through the front door?
(*Pause.*)
Let's see. Are they not a little floppy, my boy? You need a size
less, I imagine. Lift up. Lift up, if you please.
(DR BUBBA *removes* CLINT's *new trainers from his feet.*)
Now, let's look here.
(*At the row of shoes*)
Mr Runcipher – asleep over there –
(*We see Mr Runcipher swaying and sleeping instead of meditating.*)
– has a smaller foot and kinder nature. You poor boy.
(*But* CLINT *hurriedly puts the cowboy boots back on, minus plastic
bags.*)

CLINT

No, no, it's OK, thanks a lot, don't worry –
(*A shot of* DR BUBBA's *sandal next to* CLINT's *foot.*)

DR BUBBA

But look, my foot and yours are entirely equal. Clearly you
favour the exposed toe. Latest fashion? May I give you my
sandal?

CLINT

Do you have strange powers, Dr Bubba?

DR BUBBA

If I had strange powers, what would you want me to do for
you?

EXT. STREET. DAY

CLINT *in the street, swallowing pills. He stands and watches people as
they walk by, looking for potential customers, nodding and hissing at
potential buyers. He's determined and single-minded.*

We see BIKE *down the street from him, looking out, checking the area,
occasionally signalling to* CLINT.

CLINT

Hash? E? A? I got some great E! What do you say? E? A?
Cut to:

EXT. STREET. DAY

CLINT *in a doorway, taking money from a middle-class white girl and giving her the stuff.*
   BIKE *is in the background.*

INT. LIFT. DAY

CLINT *in the lift of a filthy West London tower block. Two dirty fifteen-year-olds, one white, one black, are in the lift with him. The* WHITE KID *has a cut-up face: chains of stitches.*

> WHITE KID
Show us the gear, Mr Eastwood.

> CLINT
(*Distracted*)
Show us the money.
(*The* BLACK KID *pulls out a knife.* CLINT, *now quite stoned, looks at them and laughs. They look down at his feet and start to laugh.*)

EXT. STREET NR HI-TECH BAR. DAY

A couple of TOURISTS, *a German man and woman, with rucksacks, are wandering distractedly in the street. The street* DEALERS, *one by one, spot them and practically sprint towards them.*

> DEALER ONE
Germans . . .

> DEALER TWO
Tourists . . .

> DEALER THREE
Free money man.
(CLINT *shoves them aside.*)

> CLINT
They're my beauties.
Cut to:

EXT. STREET NR HI-TECH BAR. DAY

CLINT *with the* TOURISTS. *They're fascinated by his spiel . . . and his hands all over them, cajoling, wheedling, charming.*

> CLINT
>
> (*Picking up a rucksack*)
> And if you're looking for a cheap hotel . . . and you say you are. How much are you paying?
> (*Amazed*)
> You're being destroyed. Your little Aryan faces are being ripped off. Let me help you. We're all young people.

> TOURIST WOMAN
> Are you a hotelier?

> CLINT
> Yes, yes I am. Eastwood House, a hostel for young people in need. This place will cool you.

> TOURIST MAN
> But there is heating, Mr Eastwood?

> CLINT
> Underfloor heating, yeah. Overfloor heating. Everything you could want.

EXT. STREET NEAR DINER. DAY

CLINT *with a* BUYER, *a young suited man on the street, near the diner. They talk urgently and quickly. This is* CLINT *in his selling routine. He is professional and convincing, good at this, having done it many times before. He spots the* BUYER *on the street, eye contact: then he goes to him, leading him into a doorway or sidestreet. He really knows how to hustle without frightening the guy.*

> CLINT
> Yeah, what d'you want? Hash? No. E? Tabs? E, yeah? I've got some good E, burgers not capsules. The purest form. This stuff will chill you, man. Just tip it on your tongue. Taste the fizz. Yeah?

BUYER

How much?

CLINT

Twenty. These are going quickly. How many? Ten? I can do a
reduced price for ten. Yeah, going for that?

BUYER

Three.

CLINT

Yeah, little rave? You'll buzz on these. They're the best on the
street. Just gimme the money, that's sixty, and you hang right
there.

BUYER

Where you going?

CLINT

Five minutes. Two and a half. I can't carry the stuff round with
me at great personal risk. Would you?
(*The* BUYER *is reluctant.* CLINT *hardens.*)

CLINT

You've seen me about. I'm on this corner every night. If you're
not satisfied I'll refund your money.
(*The* BUYER *gives him the money.* CLINT *backs away, and then splits
quickly.*)

EXT. STREET OUTSIDE DINER. DAY

Minutes later. CLINT *has walked round to the diner. He watches the
waiters keenly. He's also looking for* HEMINGWAY.
    *Finally he spots him, talking to the barman who's making a line of
gloriously coloured cocktails.* CLINT *raised his arm in extravagant
greeting.* HEMINGWAY *waves at him and nods gravely.* CLINT *points
down at his feet, indicating that the present shoes are shit but that the
future is promising.*
    He looks at MELANIE *and she smiles at him.*
    Outside diner a man walks up by CLINT*'s side. It's the* BUYER. *His
eyes travel to the* BUYER*'s angry face.* CLINT *is very agitated.*

BUYER

(*Sneering*)
Where's my cool E – to chill me, chill me?
(CLINT *gives it to him.*)

EXT./INT. HI-TECH BAR. DAY

CLINT *enters bar counting his money in the revolving doorway of a seedy hi-tech bar in the area. A notice saying*: NO DRUGS IN THIS ESTABLISHMENT. *Open dealing going on. A guy under the notice, carving up a lump of hash on the table.*
    An old black man stands and sings drunkenly, accompanied by someone in the corner on keyboard.
    Big dealers in dark glasses sit around with their women.
    A cluster of rent boys, some in make-up, twittering around. A couple of women prostitutes, junkies with them. A handful of transvestites, all arguing and chattering.
    CLINT *speaks to several people as he walks through to the bar.*

CLINT
Wanting? Wanting? Wanting?

RENT BOY
Not from you, dear.
Cut to:

INT. HI-TECH BAR. DAY

CLINT *is clutching drinks, crisps and cigarettes which he puts down.*
TOM-TOM, SYLVIE *and* FAULKNER *are sitting at the table.*

TOM-TOM
(*Pleased with the drinks*)
Hey, this is good.

CLINT
Yeah, why not?

SYLVIE
(*Kissing him*)
Generous.

CLINT

What's that on your cheek?
(*He looks at her.*)
It's OK, I thought you were developing a second nose. Hi
Faulkner.
(FAULKNER *insists on kissing him.*)
(*To them all*)
I tell you, I had a good day at the office, I mean it. I can be a
sweet dealer when I put my mind to it.

SYLVIE

We did good too. Shopping for the squat.

TOM-TOM

And not an item paid for.
(TOM-TOM *has a new suitcase beside him which he opens. The four
of them pull out telephones, teapots, ornaments, cutlery, lamps, etc.
As they look through it* SYLVIE *sees* CLINT *scratching his face and
pulls his hand down.*)

FAULKNER

Oh yuk, yuk.

CLINT

I'm on fire. I wanna tear my arms off and smash them on the
table.

SYLVIE

How come?

CLINT

I'm kicking.

SYLVIE

Can't they take you into the rehab?

CLINT

They already threw me out.

SYLVIE

For what?

CLINT

Drug-taking.
(*They laugh.* SYLVIE *pulls a sporty cap with ear-flaps and an adjustable peak out of the suitcase and gives it to* CLINT.)

SYLVIE

Here.

FAULKNER

Oh yeah.

CLINT

Is this really for me then?
(*She and* FAULKNER *help him put it on – a big procedure, accompanied by posing and clapping and laughter.*
From across the bar CLINT *is watched by a middle-aged black guy.*)

SYLVIE

Thought it would suit you.

FAULKNER

Not quite. Put yourself in my hands.
(FAULKNER *readjusts the cap.*)
Better.

SYLVIE

Isn't he a sweetie?

TOM-TOM

Not bad for a derelict, for a disaster.
(*Among friends,* CLINT *sits back like a rent boy and puts his feet on the table, forgetting the state of his boots, which people notice. Goes into a stoned reverie.*)

FAULKNER

Clint's so good-looking, apart from the feet and the skin disease. Oh find me a man, someone. Had one today?

CLINT

We're looking after her now.

FAULKNER

Christ. The thing is, Sylvie, people don't realize what hard work it is sucking cock for a living. What a skill and trade it is,

like bricklaying. The public think, oh five minutes jaw work
and there you are, tax-free millions. But it's dirty, risky and
exhausting, your little head bobbing up and down for hours on
end. Followed by a mouthful of snot.

CLINT

I don't wanna hear about it. I'm getting a proper job.

FAULKNER

(*Laughs*)
It's only prositution by other means.

CLINT

(*Quietly, to* SYLVIE)
Can I see you?

SYLVIE

You're seeing me now.

CLINT

We should do something cultural together.
(*Pause.*)
You always liked me.

SYLVIE

I do, I do.

CLINT

You won't stay with Muffdiver. He doesn't know that yet.
You've made him fall in love with you. It's not a feeling he's
accustomed to. Then you'll let him down.
(*She looks at him, surprised by his cruelty.*)

SYLVIE

Stop it.

CLINT

What d'you want, Sylvie?

SYLVIE

What you got?
(*Pause.*)
You've got to stick with him. He's the only one who knows
what's going on.

(*The black guy taps* CLINT *on the shoulder.* CLINT *turns. The guy indicates another black guy, who gets up and takes* CLINT *out into the street.* CLINT *turns to look at* SYLVIE *as he goes.* SYLVIE *and* TOM-TOM *start to pack up their things.*)
Mr G. Tonight?

TOM-TOM

(*To* SYLVIE)
Yeah, we better get on with it. You didn't tell Clint?
(*She shakes her head.*)
You tell that boy something and it goes no further than Europe.

EXT. STREET/ELECTRIC CINEMA. DUSK

A BLACK GIRL, *early twenties, a nanny, takes* CLINT *by the arm and leads him through the streets, throwing away his new cap in disgust. Past the Electric Cinema, a few people outside. The* GIRL *walks briskly, and* CLINT *tries to keep up with her.*

CLINT

Headley want to see me? She in a good mood? What's on at the pictures?

GIRL

La Dolce Vita.

CLINT

What's that?
(*The* GIRL *gives him a contemptuous look.*)

INT. HEADLEY'S FLAT. EVENING

Weird music. The atmosphere a mixture of hi-tech late 1980s and hippy eclectic. Indian and African things. Much Third Worldism. We are in the living room. Three LITERARY TYPES *talking, a man and two young women, laughing, drinking, all expensively dressed. Various snacks on the table. Beer, wine, champagne.*
    CLINT *breaks away from the* GIRL *and takes some salmon from the table.*

LITERARY MAN
And are you a writer too?

CLINT
Yeah. I'm putting down my story. It's pretty sickening, you know.
(*To* GIRL)
Tell Headley I'll wait here for her.
(*To* LITERARY MAN)
Wanna deal with something real for a change?

GIRL
You come on.
(*And she pulls* CLINT *away.*)

INT. HEADLEY'S STUDY. EVENING

HEADLEY *is a tall, strong, imposing professor and writer. She is not the type to listen much to others. Her mood can swing from the hard to the sentimental pretty quickly.*

Anyhow, for the time being she ignores CLINT, *who tiptoes around, nervous of her and not wanting to be there at all.*

HEADLEY *is, at the moment, with a woman and baby.* HEADLEY *is pulling clothes out of a cupboard for both child and mother.* HEADLEY *talks continuously.*

HEADLEY
Why do I have to help them? Doesn't the fucking state do anything? I'm not a fucking doctor am I?
(*She stares straight at* CLINT, *who recoils and turns away moodily.*)
I'm just strong and rich, that's all. So these people come to me every day because they know I'm too guilty and weak to refuse them.
(*She talks to the baby in good Spanish, then gives the woman a gorgeous string of beads, pressing them on the unresisting woman.*)
They're Indian, from Mexico. Sell them if you like.
(*The woman goes, backwards.* HEADLEY *looks at her with contempt, then sits with her head in her hands.*)

CLINT

(*After a pause*)
Headley, I'm here.

HEADLEY

I know, dear, I can hear you scratching.
(*Put out,* CLINT *goes to the birdcage and prods the bird.*)

CLINT

How are you, parrot-face? Want some bush to get outta your
face?
(*He fishes some bush out of his bag and gives it to the bird.*)

HEADLEY

It's a toucan. Cyrano. I require that bush, Clint. I intend to get
very high.

CLINT

(*Approaching her*)
Headley, man, this stuff is fucking steep.

HEADLEY

(*Noticing his boots*)
Don't stamp dog-shit into my Persian rug.

CLINT

You haven't got a better pair of shoes by any chance? You
know, lying around. They're dear. Doesn't matter if they're
only brogues.

HEADLEY

Buy some. You street dealers earn more than I do. Or does that
other boy, the rough one, Bill Sykes, control you?
(*She looks at him. He's not answering these kind of questions. He
goes round the rug and puts the bush on the table. She makes a note
on a piece of paper.*)

CLINT

What you writing? About F. Scott Fitzgerald's books?

HEADLEY

Something about the representation of black women in film.
Women noir?

CLINT

Yeah? Oh Headley, you really know how to enjoy yourself.
(HEADLEY *slaps her knee as if summoning a dog or a baby.*
CLINT *starts to get even more nervous.*)
No, Headley, I better get going, you know. I've gotta get some
shoes lined up for my job.

HEADLEY

You want to eat, don't you? Here.
(*And she pulls him towards her.*)
Cut to:

INT. HEADLEY'S STUDY. EVENING

CLINT *is sitting on* HEADLEY's *knee. She touches his face, hair, hands,
partly out of affection, partly out of disinterested love, and partly it is
medical examination. Then she cuddles him, saying:*

HEADLEY

'Thus is his cheek the map of days outworn
When Beauty lived and died as flowers do now.'
(CLINT *stares into the distance.*)
Cut to:

INT. HEADLEY'S LIVING ROOM. NIGHT

A little later. The living room of Headley's flat. It is darker now. The three
LITERARY TYPES *are present, eating, drinking and laughing, prior to
going out for the evening.*
     CLINT *is sitting across the room with a plate of food on his knee, eating
eagerly.*
     One of the LITERARY TYPES *has removed her high heels and waves
them at* CLINT *as he eats. He glances up at her and then continues to eat,
ignoring this shit.*

LITERARY WOMAN

Let him wear my shoes, they'll suit him.
(HEADLEY *walks up and down, mainly addressing* CLINT.)

LITERARY MAN

Don't go on, Headley.

HEADLEY

There are crimes that people commit against others. Of course.
But there are, to me, more intriguing crimes, the ones that
people commit against themselves. These puzzle me,
especially as I get older and wish to live to a hundred and fifty.
What do I love? This?

(*She indicates the room.*)

My garden.

(*The* LITERARY MAN *has filled the* LITERARY WOMAN*'s shoe with
champagne and now drinks from it.*

   HEADLEY *hits a button on the CD. We hear Allegri's* Miserere
Mei.)

Jugged hare. The Beatles. But what could you say, Clint?
What do you love? Drugs.

(*And she laughs scornfully.* CLINT *is, by now, bent over, dinner on
his lap, half off the chair. He looks up at her. She drags thoughtfully
on her joint.*)

No one need make you bleed. You'll do it to yourself.

(CLINT *is angry with her. But he can't speak. He puts his food down,
and falls over on to his knees, crawls a bit, and finally walks and
runs out.*)

EXT. STREET NR DINER. NIGHT

The music continues. CLINT *has left* HEADLEY*'s place. Now he relaxes
and perks up as he walks past the diner. Two waitresses are outside,
including* MELANIE. *He's about to strike up conversation with her when
he spots* HEMINGWAY.

   Cut to:

EXT. DINER. NIGHT

MELANIE *watches* CLINT *go. He steps into a puddle, soaking the exposed
toe.*

   Cut to:

EXT. STREET NEAR OFF-LICENCE. NIGHT

Further up the street CLINT *sees* BURNS *coming out of an off-licence
carrying bottles of beer.*

He walks on. Further up he sees BIKE *on his bicycle, riding without hands, carrying booze and food. He cycles past* CLINT, *not noticing him. Maybe this is a hallucination and* CLINT *accepts it equably.*

INT. SQUAT. NIGHT

CLINT *enters the flat and sees there's no one in. He wanders around until he sees the* TOURISTS *sitting leaning against their rucksacks, with a picnic spread out in front of them.*

                    CLINT
So you got in all right?

                TOURIST WOMAN
Which is our room?

                    CLINT
Err . . . this way.
(CLINT *leads them upstairs into Burns's room, which is, naturally, full of his stuff. There are photographs of his children, his handyman's gear, clothes, etc.*)
The rent, s'il vous plait.

                TOURIST WOMAN
Now, Mr Eastwood?

                    CLINT
Yeah, on the button and no travellers' cheques accepted.

                 TOURIST MAN
But this is someone else's room.

                    CLINT
This?
(*He shoves some of Burns's gear aside.*)
Burns is moving out tonight. Make yourself comfortable. I'm just going to have a sleep, then I'm going out to buy some shoes, for work, not for best.
(*The* TOURIST MAN *counts out the money.*)

INT. SQUAT. MUFFDIVER'S ROOM. NIGHT

CLINT *goes into Muffdiver's room – sees Muffdiver's and Sylvie's stuff side by side, which surprises and hurts him. He goes through Muffdiver's things, finding nothing of interest but a knife.*

He gropes through Sylvie's things and finds three pairs of old ballet shoes that would have fitted a child, a kid and a teenager. He puts them back.

Also amongst her things he finds a number of literary paperbacks: Jean Rhys, Willa Cather, Jane Bowles, Jayne Anne Phillips. Plus several full notebooks of her own writing. He flicks through the pages, which are densely written.

At the door, on his way out, he has a brainwave. He goes to the dummies and puts his hand up inside one of them. He takes most of Muffdiver's stash of money, leaving a few quid behind, out of generosity. He is very pleased with this.

EXT. ROOF OF SQUAT. NIGHT

CLINT *puts most of the money under a brick on the roof, taking a little for himself.*

INT. CLINT'S BEDROOM. NIGHT

A couple of hours later. CLINT *has crashed out on his bed, eyes open, staring at the ceiling. The curtains move slowly back and forth, billowing in the wind. He hears noises from outside: chanting from the Sufi Centre below mixed with noises from the living room in a hallucinogenic blend. He gets up.*

INT. LIVING ROOM OF SQUAT. NIGHT

CLINT *opens the door on to an odd scene. A hallucination, the only time in this film. And only for a few seconds.*

He sees SYLVIE *wearing a ballerina's tutu and dancing.* BURNS *is dressed as Father Christmas.* BIKE, *in a yellow jersey and cycling shorts, is suspended from the ceiling on his bicycle with a tray of cocaine across the handlebars.*

TOM-TOM *is playing the guitar dressed as Keith Richards.*

There is music. The entire scene seems to be taking place in a snowstorm.

CLINT *blinks several times and the scene returns to normal. Even then it is a pretty odd scene.*

BIKE, BURNS *and* TOM-TOM *are frantically fixing the place up.*

BURNS *is installing the twee table lamps which* SYLVIE *and* TOM-TOM
stole that afternoon. (*Obviously, in the room, until now, there is only an
overhead light or some other arrangement.*)

SYLVIE *is preparing drinks for later.*

TOM-TOM *is arranging crisps.*

BIKE *is washing up.*

SYLVIE

Were you there all the time?

(TOM-TOM *hands him a dishcloth and a pile of plates.*)

TOM-TOM

Get wiping, man.

CLINT

Wipe your own arse.

SYLVIE

Mr G's coming to see Muffdiver.

CLINT

What for?

TOM-TOM

(*Indicating plates*)

I thought you were interested in restaurant work.

(CLINT *gives him a dirty look.* TOM-TOM *regards him
resentfully.*)

SYLVIE

(*Going to the trouble to explain*)

Mr G's the top man, you know that. Sign on with him and you
don't have any drug-flow problems.

(CLINT *wipes the plates, making sure* TOM-TOM *sees him.*)

SYLVIE

(*To* CLINT)

Muff's gonna do a big buy. Keep us all going for weeks.

CLINT

Which we gotta sell on the street.

SYLVIE

Yeah, it's work for all of us.

(*Making sure* TOM-TOM *is watching,* CLINT *throws one of the plates in the air and catches it on the end of his finger and twirls it around dramatically and impressively, nodding at* TOM-TOM. *Now* MUFFDIVER *hurries into the room in businesslike mood. He takes everything in quickly. Everyone working away satisfactorily, except* CLINT, *with a plate whirling on his finger.*)

MUFFDIVER

Great. Good, everyone.

(*Snaps finger at* CLINT.)

You.

(*To her*)

Sylvie. Boardroom.

(*He jabs at* BIKE. BIKE *looks at him eagerly, ready to respond.* MUFFDIVER *nods.* BIKE *obviously knows what to do.*)

INT. LANDING. NIGHT

BIKE *gets a pot of tea for three set out on a tray from dumb waiter and goes into Clint's room.*

INT. CLINT'S ROOM. NIGHT

MUFFDIVER, SYLVIE *and* CLINT *in the room.* CLINT *moves in and out of consciousness, resentful, confused.* MUFFDIVER *excited. He chops out a line of coke for himself.*

MUFFDIVER

This is an executive meeting – of the top executives of Muffdiver, Sylvie and Clint Eastwood Limited, PLC.

SYLVIE

What's PLC?

MUFFDIVER

Posse Limited Company.

(BIKE, *like a servant, is handing out the tea.* CLINT *tries to talk.*)

MUFFDIVER

You wanna speak? Right. Bike.
(BIKE *takes out a notebook and pencil. Meanwhile* MUFFDIVER *snorts up the coke, looks up and listens.*)

CLINT

You always in charge of everything.

MUFFDIVER

Yeah, I got the initiative. But it's the three of us – three business partners – doing this shit together.

CLINT

Doing what, though? What? What? What?

MUFFDIVER

Tonight, it's tonight, we're going big. This posse can deal E, A, M-25, M-26 – to the whole district. We got the contacts, the premises, the staff. The market's expanding, you know it is. Supply and demand, those cats out there can't get high enough. Course, there can't be any weak links. Weak links have to be taken care of.
(*He stares at* CLINT.)

SYLVIE

Sounds good.

MUFFDIVER

Yeah? Say yeah.

CLINT

You can't boss Clint around. It don't suit me. Gotta go my own way.

SYLVIE

(*Gently to* CLINT)
Let's give it a chance. Let's get somewhere, all of us. Think of all the shoes you'll be able to buy. In two years you can buy your own shoe shop.

MUFFDIVER

Right. Mr G'll be here in a minute. Let's make a good impression. Meeting's adjourned.

INT. LIVING ROOM. NIGHT

MUFFDIVER *is inspecting the posse in a line-up.*

>   MUFFDIVER
> Bike, don't slow things down. Burns, how's the special cool
> lighting going?

>   BURNS
> It's on.
> (*He touches a crumb off* BURNS'*s face. He inspects* CLINT'*s
> shoes, etc.*)

>   MUFFDIVER
> Right. Tom-Tom, you used to be a master chef . . . If they want
> drinks . . . Got any ice?
> (*Panicking.*)
> Mr G's only used to the best.
> (*The lights have already flickered during the line-up. Then the lights
> go completely.*)
> Burns, fix the fucking lights, man!

EXT. FRONT OF SQUAT BUILDING. NIGHT

Now we see MR G *and his posse getting out of their car, walking up to the
house.*

INT. LIVING ROOM OF SQUAT. NIGHT

The lights BURNS *has fixed up, chintzy little things, are flicking on and
off.*
>   *Cheering.*
>   BURNS *tries to fix the lights.*
>   *The front door bell rings in the living room.*
>   *The two German* TOURISTS *walk in.*

>   TOURIST WOMAN
> Mr Eastwood –

>   TOURIST MAN
> Mr Eastwood, the lights in our room are extinguishing
> onwards and offwards.

TOM-TOM

What room?

TOURIST MAN

Mr Eastwood has rented us a room upstairs. He said we could chill out. It's cool.
(BURNS *looks at* CLINT.)

BURNS

Yeah?
(MUFFDIVER *is confused. He goes to the German* TOURIST MAN *and holds out his hand.*)

MUFFDIVER

Mr G?

TOURIST MAN

Mr Wolf. Please to meet you.

INT. HALL OF HOUSE. NIGHT

MR G *and his posse have come up the hallway and are now by the Sufi Centre.* MR G *and the others look suspiciously into the Sufi Centre.*

INT. LIVING ROOM OF SQUAT. NIGHT

(*Same time.*)

MUFFDIVER

Who are these people?

TOURIST MAN

Mr Eastwood, the landlord here –

BURNS

Mr Eastwood the landlord?
(*To them*)
You sleeping in my room?

TOURIST WOMAN

It was rented to us. How do you say it? All in?
(TOM-TOM *and* SYLVIE *restrain* BURNS *as he struggles to get* CLINT.)

TOM-TOM
All in what?

INT. SUFI CENTRE. NIGHT

Meanwhile, downstairs, DR BUBBA *rises and goes forward to greet* MR G, *who has a smart young black* ASSISTANT *with him and two young women, one black, one white.*

DR BUBBA
Please, you are all welcome. Remove your shoes.
(MUFFDIVER *rushes downstairs into the Sufi Centre, behind* MR G, *and sees the indignity he is about to suffer.*

  Meanwhile the German TOURISTS *are coming down the stairs, turning to the group.*)

MALE TOURIST
I tell you nothing for something, don't stay in this place.
(MUFFDIVER *is virtually bent over double, so grovelling is he.*

  MR G *turns and sees him.*

  MUFFDIVER *gestures him and his posse out of the place, tripping over meditators as he goes.*)

MUFFDIVER
Mr G, you can't choose your neighbours, can you? Come upstairs for some refreshments. Sorry. Sorry.

INT. LIVING ROOM OF SQUAT. NIGHT

MUFFDIVER *leads* MR G *and his posse into the room.*

  MUFFDIVER *brings them in and they stand there waiting for* MR G *to sit down. The girls talk to each other.*

  Then the black woman goes to BIKE's *bicycle and takes it.*

TOM-TOM
Mr G, Mrs G, hallo.

MUFFDIVER
Welcome, Welcome.
(TOM-TOM *nods at* BIKE. *The woman climbs on to the bike and*

honks the horn. MR G *grins for the first time. We can see that* BIKE *is becoming very anxious and is about to react.*
     MUFFDIVER *glares at him.*
     BURNS *is still furious with* CLINT *about the* TOURISTS *and surreptitiously tries to whack him.*
     MUFFDIVER *glares at* BURNS.)

                         MUFFDIVER
Burns!
(MR G *finally sits down. His posse sit down, the black girl on Bike's bike.*
     SYLVIE *offers them all peanuts.*)
Cut to:

INT. SQUAT LIVING ROOM. NIGHT

MUFFDIVER – *and this is one of his specialities – is doing conjuring tricks for* MR G. *He wears a cape and top-hat. Behind,* SYLVIE, *who has dressed up rather pathetically, plays the trumpet.*
     MUFFDIVER *pulls balls out of his mouth, strings of handkerchiefs out of the white girl's ear, etc.*

                         MUFFDIVER
Is it real or is it false? No one wants too much reality, we all know that.
(MR G *has been looking around at the place with much curiosity.*)

                          MR G
When have I been here before?

                        ASSISTANT
It's Jimmy's place.

                          CLINT
He's lending it to us.

                        ASSISTANT
Really?
(*To end the act* MR G *nods at* MUFFDIVER. *It's over.*
     MUFFDIVER *bows.*
     MUFFDIVER *indicates to* TOM-TOM. TOM-TOM *takes charge.*)

TOM-TOM

This way, please, if you don't mind. Just for a few minutes, to
ensure privacy. Let's go through, I mean up.

INT. SQUAT LANDING. NIGHT

Everyone filing out of the squat. CLINT *moaning and cursing as they go,*
BIKE *protectively carrying his bicycle.*

BURNS

(*German accent*)
A word, Mr Eastwood the landlord.

INT. LIVING ROOM OF SQUAT. NIGHT

MR G *and his* ASSISTANT *and* MUFFDIVER *sit in serious conference,*
drinking. The ASSISTANT *has his briefcase open, listening to*
MUFFDIVER *as he puts his proposal.*

EXT. ROOF. NIGHT

The others, including MR G*'s girls, are on the roof of the squat.* BIKE *sits*
looking through the bars of his bicycle at everyone, especially CLINT,
whom he's happy to see with SYLVIE.

CLINT *takes* SYLVIE*'s hand and leads her to the edge of the roof.*
His hand is over the brick (where he concealed the money) as he
talks.

CLINT

I made some money today. I wanted to give you some.

SYLVIE

Oh no. What about your shoes?

CLINT

I'll take care of that tomorrow. And I start work the next day.
I'm pretty confident about things, Sylvie.

SYLVIE

(*Takes the money*)
Thanks, Clint. Thanks.

CLINT

Top of the world. I need to get out of London. Let's go . . .
Let's go to the countryside tomorrow, yeah? I know a good
place where there's not too many farmers. What d'you say?
(*She nods at him.*)

INT. SQUAT LIVING ROOM. NIGHT

MUFFDIVER *and* MR G *and his* ASSISTANT *in heavy conference.*

ASSISTANT

Everything seems agreed then. Give us the upfront investment
now, as arranged. The delivery of everything you've ordered
will be in two days.

MUFFDIVER

(*Excited*)

And, Mr G, both of you, I tell you, I've got the best on-the-
street salesmen in the area. My people are hand-trained.
Dealing's no longer for amateurs. I want to get a smooth
home-delivery service started. Like in Chicago – 'Hash-to-go',
'Call-a-snort', 'Dial-a-spliff'. Bikes, mopeds, a courier service.

ASSISTANT

Hand-trained, you say.

MUFFDIVER

Yeah.
(*Loses confidence.*)
Yeah.

MR G

Hand-trained by whom?

MUFFDIVER

By me, Mr G.
(MR G *and his* ASSISTANT *look at each other.* MUFFDIVER *gets up.*)

INT. MUFFDIVER'S BEDROOM. NIGHT

We see MUFFDIVER'*s confident, smug face as he walks towards the
tailor's dummy in the bedroom.*

EXT. ROOF. NIGHT

The others on the roof. We see CLINT*'s face, eyes closed, breathing deeply, looking up at the sky.* BURNS *eating a huge sandwich.* TOM-TOM *sitting there, talking to the girls.*

INT. MUFFDIVER'S ROOM. NIGHT

We see MUFFDIVER*'s hand reaching into the back of the dummy. We see him pulling some money out. Counts it; realizes it's not all there; gets agitated; counts it again; searches again. Searches the room for money. Finally gives up. Is furious.*

INT. STAIRS OF SQUAT. NIGHT

MUFFDIVER *tells* MR G *that the money has gone and he can't pay him.* MUFFDIVER *is speechless. The sad and comic sight of him telling them the money's gone and them rising in irritation to leave.*
    The others come back into the room, the women going out with MR G. MR G*'s* ASSISTANT *just turns and points at* MUFFDIVER.

INT. STAIRS OF SQUAT. NIGHT

Rest of troupe stand watching MR G. *leaving. We reverse on to* MUFFDIVER*'s face as everyone is filing past him.*

INT. LIVING ROOM OF SQUAT. NIGHT

MR G *and his posse have gone.* MUFFDIVER *is running around the room, screaming, attempting to smash everything, as they try to stop him.* BURNS *keeps grabbing at him. The others are hunting around, under chairs, carpets, etc., for the purloined money.* CLINT *searches especially hard.*

MUFFDIVER
Where's my fucking money, you fucking bastards, where is it, who's got it? I'll kill you for humiliating me! Mr G thinks I'm a total jerk-off and idiot fool prick total arsehole, Jesus! Search, search, you useless bastards! Who's got it?
(He grabs BURNS *by the throat, pulling a knife on him.)*

MUFFDIVER

You desperate old man, it must be you!

CLINT

Muffdiver, man –
(*He turns on* CLINT.)

MUFFDIVER

So it was you!

TOM-TOM

Bike's brother was in here too at one point.

SYLVIE

And the tourists.

BURNS

(*German accent, laughing*)
Yes it was them. Mr Eastwood the landlord.
(MUFFDIVER *sinks down in despair. The posse look at each other, some laughing.* SYLVIE *goes to him, reaching down and touching him.* CLINT *watches her. She looks up at him.*)

CLINT

Tomorrow, yeah? You an' me.

MUFFDIVER'S BEDROOM. NIGHT

MUFFDIVER *stands naked at the window of his room, trying to fix old sheets or dirty curtains to the window frame. He's banging away with hammer and nails and keeps hitting his thumb. The wind and rain blow through the window.*

When he's done this he sits in bed. He counts the money he still has and counts the tabs and capsules and 'burgers' he has in his possession.

We then see that SYLVIE *is there in the room with him. With great dignity she has put her things out on a packing case. She cleans her face with cotton wool. She moisturizes her face with care and combs her hair.*

MUFFDIVER *looks at his drugs and money and then at her. At first he doesn't catch her eye. They then look at each other. Apprehension on his face.*

She goes to him.

*From outside, through this scene, we hear the others playing
rhythmically on cans and trumpet and other homemade instruments.
It's a loud, hypnotic sound, getting faster and faster.*

INT. LIVING ROOM OF SQUAT. NIGHT

*The men – CLINT, BURNS, TOM-TOM – on the floor in the living room.
BIKE sitting beside his bicycle.*

The door to Muffdiver's room is ajar. Human noises are heard. CLINT
*glances nervously at the door. He has Sylvie's trumpet at his lips, giving it
a toot now and again.*

BURNS *watches* CLINT *and sees how disappointed and yet hopeful he is.*

TOM-TOM

(*To* BURNS)
What's your real trade then?

BURNS

Electrician, me. This line of work isn't something I thought I'd
get into when I was young, bodyguarding someone called
Muffdiver, walking round with LSD strapped to me scrotum.
Eh Bike?
(BIKE *opens his mouth to speak but some inner grief prevents him.
They all look at him in anticipation but nothing comes.*

CLINT *toots on the trumpet,* BURNS *taps an empty Coke tin with
a pencil,* TOM-TOM *drums on his knees. They grin at each other.*)

INT. SQUAT. MORNING

Next morning. CLINT *has got up early. He's finished making
sandwiches. He pops a couple of tomatoes into a bag.* TOM-TOM *is asleep
on the floor.* BIKE *also asleep, next to his bicycle.*

To his surprise CLINT *also sees* FAULKNER *asleep on the floor, covered
in other people's clothes, a pair of high heels beside him, a dress flung over
a chair.*

FAULKNER

Going somewhere?

CLINT

Tsa-Tsa – bit of fresh country air up our nostrils.

FAULKNER

All of you?

CLINT

No way.

Cut to:

INT. SQUAT LIVING ROOM. DAY

The others are stirring now. CLINT *squats down and waits at the far side of the room.* BIKE *and* TOM-TOM *are moving about.*

Finally, MUFFDIVER *emerges from his room, in leopard-skin print bathrobe, looks around, greets his posse, kisses* FAULKNER's *hand and goes to* CLINT.)

MUFFDIVER

Sleep all right?
(CLINT *nods.*)
Tsa-Tsa, you look good anyway. Combed your hair too.
(*He grabs* CLINT's *sandwich bag, looks inside and pulls out a mouldy-looking tomato.*)
What's this?
(*He notices* CLINT *is holding a rolled-up towel.*)
Going to the seaside?
(CLINT *shrugs.*)
Was it you? Tell me.

CLINT

No, man.

MUFFDIVER

Don't go anywhere today, I wanna talk about my night with Sylvie. It was the best night I ever had – ever. Don't be like that. Clint, I still like talking to you.
(*Not getting any response,* MUFFDIVER *goes off.*)

INT. MUFFDIVER'S BEDROOM. DAY

CLINT *slowly opens the door to Muffdiver's bedroom.* SYLVIE *is lying in bed, facing away from him. He holds his sandwich bag.*

SYLVIE

There are some days when you just know you're never gonna get up.

(CLINT *squatting behind her, strokes her shoulders, neck and face.*)

CLINT

We still on?

SYLVIE

What? Oh, it's you.

CLINT

For the outing. You said.

SYLVIE

What?

(*They look at each other. Now* MUFFDIVER *is behind them.*)

MUFFDIVER

What's he doing?

(*To* CLINT)

What you want in here?

CLINT

I'm calling a board meeting.

MUFFDIVER

You're up to something. The shoe is through.

(MUFFDIVER *starts to throw him out. They fight.*)

CLINT

Fuck you!

SYLVIE

Stop it, you silly boys!

(*To* MUFFDIVER)

We were just going out for the day, to the countryside. That's all!

MUFFDIVER

Tsa-Tsa, so why don't we all catch a bit of the seaside then? Get out of the filth.

> SYLVIE

But we are the filth, dear. Clint's got a place he fancies.

> CLINT

No I haven't.

> MUFFDIVER

Yeah? Where is it?

> CLINT

I can't go. I gotta buy some shoes today. I start work tomorrow morning.

> MUFFDIVER

Right then. We're on. It's a good idea to get out, with Mr G angry with us and all.
(MUFFDIVER *goes to the door, shouts out*)
Tom-Tom, fancy a trip?
(SYLVIE *goes to* CLINT *as* MUFFDIVER *organizes the posse.*)

> SYLVIE

You look dirty.

> CLINT

Thanks.

> SYLVIE

I should wash you.

> CLINT

You wouldn't.

> SYLVIE

I should give you a bath. Come on, Clint.

> CLINT

Now?

> SYLVIE

Before we go.

INT. BATHROOM. DAY

The bathroom is a large, dirty room which was once intended to be luxurious and decadent. A big kidney-shaped bath, with a shelf for sitting on. SYLVIE *has run the water and is testing it with her elbow. She turns and laughs with* CLINT. *He stands there awkwardly. She grabs his belt and pulls down his trousers. They struggle. He becomes serious.*

CLINT

What are you doing to me, Sylvie?

Cut to:

INT. BATHROOM. DAY

CLINT *is in the bath washing his hair with shampoo, as she opens a beer.*

CLINT

Whatever you do, don't look at me.
(*But she looks at him, smiling.*)
Why are you looking like that?

SYLVIE

Don't be afraid of me.

CLINT

(*Holds his arms out*)
Look at me.

SYLVIE

You're a beautiful boy.

CLINT

But you wouldn't want to hold my hand, would you?
(*She washes his hair.*)
I'd like to talk to you.

SYLVIE

What would you say, baby?

CLINT

I'd want to know where you've been. I'd love to know where you come from. Describe your mum and dad.

SYLVIE

People who . . . it's incredible . . . the police should stop certain people having children.

CLINT

I hate people who blame their parents for everything.

SYLVIE

So do I.
(MUFFDIVER *comes into the bathroom and sits down. They look at him nervously but he is abstracted.*)

SYLVIE

(*Embarrassed*)
A bath meeting.
Cut to:

INT. BATHROOM. DAY

We see MUFFDIVER *taking his clothes off. The three of them in the bath.* SYLVIE *between* CLINT *and* MUFFDIVER. MUFFDIVER *subdued, dreaming.*

CLINT

(*To* SYLVIE, *of* MUFFDIVER)
I like him when he's like this.

SYLVIE

Stoned, or thinking about his money.
(SYLVIE *and* CLINT *laugh at this.* CLINT *imitates Muffdiver's rage of the previous evening, taking off his voice.*)

CLINT

'Where's my fucking money, you fucking bastards . . . '
(*Pause.*)
We're the same blood.
(*To him*)
I could touch you, I could. And you could kill me.
(*To her*)
He could just wipe me out. Maybe he should. I make him feel soft. He hates anyone who does that to him. Even you. I wonder why he wants to be so hard.

(*She looks at him in surprise.*
   He quickly gets out of the bath. SYLVIE *sits there and shivers.*
   CLINT *holds out an old overcoat for her to get into.*)
Mum, don't get cold.

EXT. OUTSIDE FRONT OF SQUAT. DAY

*The posse bundle out of squat, in holiday mood. They've all attempted to
dress up for the occasion. They pass* DR BUBBA *standing on his balcony, in
an elegant white robe, amusedly watching them and casually eating a
piece of toast.*

                              TOM-TOM
(*Mocking*)
Om! Om! Om!
(*To* BURNS)
I've been through all that. Been through it, man!
(CLINT *is behind them, the last down the stairs, less cheerful than the
rest, seeing as* MUFFDIVER*'s ruined his day by bringing the whole
posse with him.* CLINT *is horrified by* TOM-TOM*'s mockery of*
DR BUBBA. CLINT *puts his hands together respectfully and bows
at* DR BUBBA.)

EXT. RAILWAY STATION. DAY

*The posse at Victoria Station running down the platform for a train.
They carry pizzas and beers and* TOM-TOM *has a big beat-box with
him.* BURNS *and* CLINT *carry a crate of beer.*
   *They eventually crash into the compartment of the train, out of
breath, laughing.*
   *The guard blows his whistle. The train starts off from the
station.*

EXT. COUNTRY STATION. DAY

*The posse coming out of a little country station. They are regarded
strangely by passers-by who stop and stare as they stand blinking in the
fresh air.* CLINT *spots a bus coming and starts off towards it.*
   MUFFDIVER *put on his dark glasses.*

NT./EXT. BUS. DAY

The posse climb up to the top deck of a country bus, BIKE *having difficulty getting his bicycle up the stairs.* BURNS *helps him.* SYLVIE *rushes to the front.* TOM-TOM *and* CLINT *fight to sit with her,* CLINT *winning, being the more determined.*

He turns around to cheer and celebrate but MUFFDIVER *is sitting right behind him.*

Cut to:

NT. BUS. DAY

The bus speeds through country lanes and suddenly breaks spectacularly out into open countryside. Cheering.

> BURNS
> (*Eating*)
> This is the life.
> (CLINT *shouts at people in the street*)

> CLINT
> Get down you leather queens!

EXT. COUNTRYSIDE. DAY

The posse are now standing in open countryside, a little bewildered, looking lost. They turn to CLINT, *who's the only one with any idea of where they are.*

Two local kids, a boy and girl of about fifteen or sixteen, stand looking shyly at them, these London weirdos, in admiration. This is everything they want to be when they grow up, as cool, bizarre and clearly living in freedom.

TOM-TOM *waves to them like a rock star greeting his fans.*

> TOM-TOM
> Elmore James. Chuck Berry. The Lightnin' –
> (CLINT *starts off towards the kids.*)

> CLINT
> Hey, yo, wanna buy something? Need some Ecstasy? Acid? Ice?
> (BURNS *grabs him.* BIKE *is laughing.* MUFFDIVER *looks at him steadily, neither critically nor with affection but trying to work out*

what's going through his mind. Does CLINT *really want this job?*
And why has he brought them to this place?

BIKE *cycles off down the lane.*

CLINT *steps over a stile into a field.* TOM-TOM *and* BURNS *follow*
him. SYLVIE *takes* MUFFDIVER'S *arm and tries to guide him over*
the stile. He won't go over it.)

SYLVIE

What's the matter?

MUFFDIVER

My boots.
(*And he indicates his superb boots which he refuses to get dirty.*)

EXT. COUNTRYSIDE. DAY

The posse walking through a wood. They're in a cheerful mood – and
drinking. Music from TOM-TOM'S *beat-box.* BURNS *hides behind a tree*
and jumps out on BIKE, *making donkey noises.* MUFFDIVER *bends over*
to try and clean his boots, which are already muddy. The two local kids
follow them through the wood, intrigued.

CLINT

(*To* BIKE)
Fancy some country grass?
(BIKE *takes a spliff.* CLINT *takes one himself.* CLINT *offers one to*
TOM-TOM. TOM-TOM *waves him away.*)
This country grass will fly you into the eternal moment.

TOM-TOM

Talk about something else. Foliage. Tree bark. Ten years I've
been a junkie and I can tell you, druggies are boring, small-
minded and stupid. The people are enough to put you off
taking the stuff. Don't you know anything else?

CLINT

I want to, Tom-Tom.
(MUFFDIVER *takes* SYLVIE'S *arm.*)

EXT. POND IN WOOD. DAY

They walk beside a large pond deep in the woods, watched by the two local kids from across the other side. TOM-TOM *wading in the water by himself, talking to himself.*

> TOM-TOM
>
> Otis Redding.
> (*Pause.*)
> Marvin Gaye.
> (*Pause.*)
> Smokey. Smokey Robinson.
> (*Still in dark glasses,* MUFFDIVER *suddenly tries to shove* BURNS, *who's watching* TOM-TOM, *into the water. He gives him a hard shove but* BURNS *is immovable, as he munches another pizza.*)

> BURNS
>
> (*Without turning*)
> I bet you were a real fucking bully at school.
> (TOM-TOM *wades out further.*)

> TOM-TOM
>
> Sam Cooke. Bob Marley. Aretha.

EXT. COUNTRYSIDE. DAY

Later. They all walk along a high ridge with a view down to a cottage. In the garden LILY *is hanging out some washing. She has a little boy with her, aged seven or eight.* BURNS *is on the bike,* BIKE *himself beside* BURNS. TOM-TOM *and* MUFFDIVER *together,* MUFFDIVER *nodding as* TOM-TOM *goes on with his list.* SYLVIE *and* CLINT *together, watched by* MUFFDIVER.

> CLINT
>
> (*To* SYLVIE)
> Six months I'd been at the rehab. As a reward, not a punishment, as a reward, they send us on this outward bound shit. We're trudging up a mountain, ten deviants, with four social workers and all.

TOM-TOM

(*Off camera*)
J. J. Cale.

CLINT

I've done something wrong and no one's allowed to talk to me
Suddenly I see this carpet of mushrooms, magic mushrooms.
They're everywhere, just growing out the earth. I'm behind a
tree gobbling them down. Soon the mountain's breathing and
the trees are dancing and the sky is swirling with energy and
atoms. And I can see the people are sly and cunning and
ignorant. I can see that the people who won't let anyone talk to
me are in love with power and cruelty. They don't love me.
And I know what I want to do. Get back to London and be
with the only people for me, having adventures.

TOM-TOM

Phil Spector.

MUFFDIVER

(*Looking at* CLINT)
Where's he going . . . with my money?
(*And* CLINT *is running downs the hill towards the cottage, making
Red Indian whooping calls.*)

SYLVIE

I think he's spotted a new pair of shoes.

EXT. OUTSIDE COTTAGE. DAY

From LILY's *point of view we see the posse, with* CLINT *running down
the hill, coming towards her.* BIKE *cycles down the hill.* SYLVIE *dances
down the hill.*

LILY *is a damaged, nervous woman, smoking constantly, early forties,
been through a lot. The cottage has only recently been bought and is in the
process of being done up.*

*The posse, seen from the house, are a higgedly-piggedly bunch,
threatening and risible at the same time.*

LILY *examines them closely. She becomes tense and then joyful.*

EXT. FIELD. DAY

LILY *walks and runs towards them.*

> LILY
>
> Is it you? Yeah, it would be, it is you!
> (*She goes to kiss* CLINT *but* CLINT *holds back, not going to her. We look at* SYLVIE *looking at them, puzzled.*)

> CLINT
>
> These are my friends. And this is Sylvie.

> LILY
>
> Hallo Muff.

Cut to:

EXT. FRONT OF COTTAGE. DAY

Minutes later, they're all walking towards the cottage, LILY *with her arm around* CLINT.

> LILY
>
> (*To* BIKE)
> We've only had the house a few months.
> (*Indicating* CLINT)
> I expect he wants to have a look
> (*Pause.*)
> My boy's come back.
> (*She turns to look at* MUFFDIVER *who is arguing with* SYLVIE *as they walk.* BURNS *very interested in the house, striding towards it.*)

INT. LILY'S HOUSE/KITCHEN. DAY

LILY *is putting the kettle on. She is with* CLINT. *The others have gone through into the parlour.*

> LILY
>
> Don't take this the wrong way – but you haven't come to ask for anything have you?

> CLINT
>
> Mum, I've got money.

LILY

Why, what have you and Muff been doing? I can guess.

CLINT

No. Here.
(*He gives her the head he stole from Headley's room.*)

LILY

Thanks. It's dead.

CLINT

It's Japanese. I always bring you something.
(*Pause.*)
I want a photograph of Dad. Have you still got that one of the three of us?

LILY

I'll have to look for it.

CLINT

Why, haven't you kept much from our old house?

LILY

Some.

INT. PARLOUR. DAY

While LILY *and* CLINT *are in the kitchen, the others have gone through into the parlour,* BIKE *carrying his bicycle of course,* TOM-TOM *soaked,* BURNS *trying to organize them and* SYLVIE *upset and trying to get heroin out of an irritable* MUFFDIVER. *She pleads with him.* LILY *and* CLINT *come through with tea.*

LILY

(*To* BIKE)
Wouldn't you like to leave that machine outside?

BURNS

He takes it everywhere with him, love.

LILY

Well, tell him to wipe his tyres.

BURNS
(*To* BIKE)
Wipe your tyres.

LILY
Hallo Muff.

MUFFDIVER
Hallo Lily.

BURNS
There's a cracking fire through there – mind if Tom-Tom gets his clothes off in front of it?

LILY
No, no. My husband'll be back in a minute.

BURNS
How much did you pay for the place, love?

LILY
Dunno.

INT. LILY'S HOUSE. DAY

LILY *is showing them the house. It's been a run-down place which she and* STONE *are doing up.* BURNS *touches walls, examines woodwork, electrics, etc.* LILY *perks up at* BURNS*'s interest but keeps looking nervously at* CLINT.
    Cut to:

INT. LILY'S HOUSE/VARIOUS ROOMS. DAY

Another room, more finished.
    A huge framed poster of Elvis. The only other ornamentation in this room is Elvis paraphernalia – good stuff, well presented, not too tacky.
    A photograph of STONE *dressed as Presley which* BIKE *examines and poses as, trying to make* CLINT *laugh – which he doesn't.*
    LILY *explaining to* TOM-TOM *what they're doing with the cottage.* BURNS, CLINT *and* SYLVIE *looking on.*

CLINT
Stone'll be back soon. Not my dad – Mum's new husband. Stoneface.

LILY

Don't you start. He's not new. Eight years we've been together.
(*To* MUFFDIVER)
I wish I'd known you were coming, Muff.

MUFFDIVER

I wish I'd known, Lily. I thought I was going to the seaside.
Clint, why didn't you say you wanted to see your mum?

CLINT

Stone – on Saturdays he dresses up as Elvis.

BURNS

I used to do that.

CLINT

Stone hates my guts.

LILY

Have you come home for a slap? Look at the mud on your feet.

BURNS

When did you get this place?

LILY

We got it a year ago. It was derelict. We've saved it.

BURNS

I bet you're right proud of yourself.

LILY

We've given it all our love and attention.

CLINT

I'm going to have a shower.

BURNS

They haven't got any books.

TOM-TOM

Music says everything I want to know. This place has music.
Listen.

BURNS

I wish I had a house.

INT. KITCHEN. DAY

Later. LILY *goes into the kitchen and finds* SYLVIE *going through the medicine cupboard, restless and agitated.*

LILY

Headache, love?
(SYLVIE *shakes her head.*)
Need something else?
(LILY *gives her a Valium from her handbag.* LILY *knocks over an open jar of honey that spreads like an opening flower across the table.*)
He'll murder me.

SYLVIE

Come on.
(*They clear it up together.*)

SYLVIE

Lily, he's a sweetheart.

LILY

Is he? Yes he is, my little Clint.

SYLVIE

Why –

LILY

His dad was addicted to everything, you name it, and violent. What he did to me. Someone chopped him up. Good job. What a life – I thought it was over. Then I moved into John Stone's. You should know, I'll tell you, he loves me. He has me three times a day. Sometimes more. You can't say fairer than that. There's no heaven and no God, is there?

SYLVIE

I have to ask. When you went to John Stone's why didn't you take Clint with you?

LILY

You saying I'd just leave my boy? Stone took him in too. He was kind to him. And what did Clint do? He puked in bed. He shouted names at Stone's friends in the Territorial Army.

He injected himself and nearly died. The day came. Sylvie, I had to choose.

                          SYLVIE
Between your son and your lover.

EXT. OUTSIDE LILY'S HOUSE. DAY

John STONE, *middle aged, owns a second-hand shop selling porn, guns and knives. His dog sits beside him in his car, a pink Cadillac. He's turned into the yard of his cottage to see* BIKE *doing wheelies. Further away, sitting on a wall, are the two local kids, watching with juvenile interest as* BIKE *performs for them.* BIKE *stops when* STONE *turns up.* STONE, *cool, grim, gets out of the car with his dog and walks past* BIKE *ignoring him.*

INT. KITCHEN. DAY

Through the window LILY *sees* STONE *coming towards the house. She is nervous.*

                          LILY
Here he comes now. Please go and calm them all down for me.
    (SYLVIE *leaves the kitchen.*)
Cut to:

INT. KITCHEN. DAY

John STONE *comes into the kitchen. He steps unwittingly into a pool of honey which has been overlooked. She looks at him worriedly and then goes to kiss him.*

                          STONE
Lily. It's all right.

                          LILY
Let's have a drink.
    (*She pours two large Scotches.*)

INT. UPSTAIRS CORRIDOR OF COTTAGE. DAY

MUFFDIVER *walks along the top corridor of Stone's house, past a bedroom in which he glimpses* SYLVIE *standing with her back to the door, combing her hair. He goes in and gives her a bag of smack. Another room is the bathroom and* MUFFDIVER *sees his friend* CLINT *leaning against the sink and staring at himself in the mirror. They look at each other in the mirror.*

The last room is Stone's study, a large room. MUFFDIVER *opens the door slowly. The room is full of weapons mounted on the wall: rifles, handguns, antique guns, old swords and daggers.*

The room is also a shrine to Elvis, with Elvis gear everywhere. The room's major item is an Elvis costume, beautifully made, obviously Stone's, mounted on a dummy.

MUFFDIVER *is fascinated by all this stuff and moves further into the room, taking down a dagger and a gun.*

He tries on Stone's Elvis jacket and looks at himself in the full-length mirror, posing with the gun and dagger.

MUFFDIVER

Somebody.

INT. KITCHEN. DAY

STONE *and* LILY *in the kitchen.*

STONE

What's that blackie doing in the yard, love?
(*Pause.*)
Has your boy come back? For good – or what? What do you want to do with him? Is he the same? Is he?
(*She gets up. She gestures in distress.*)

INT. STONE'S LIVING ROOM. DAY

STONE *goes into the living room where* TOM-TOM *is fiddling with the piano.* STONE *goes to him.*

STONE

How you keeping?

TOM-TOM

Not well. You?
(TOM-TOM *plays 'Are You Lonesome Tonight?' and* LILY *starts to hum the melody.* STONE *moves snakily, as Presley, impressed by*

TOM-TOM's *playing. As* LILY *hums and* TOM-TOM *plays*
STONE *does the speaking section of the song, with* BIKE *looking*
through the window behind him. BIKE *laughs and urges* TOM-
TOM *on. He catches* STONE's *eye.* STONE *gives him a look. Now, as*
this continues, water starts dripping through the ceiling on to
STONE's *head. He notices. Looks up. And dashes out of the*
room.)

INT. ROOM IN THE COTTAGE. DAY

STONE *dashes through into another room where* BURNS'S *fat carcass is*
laid out on the sofa, watching TV, a beer and a plate of sandwiches in
front of him. As STONE *dashes through the room to the opposite door,*
BURNS *gets up with a sandwich clenched between his teeth, knocking the*
beer over.
Cut to:

INT. STAIRCASE/ROOM. DAY

STONE *is going upstairs quickly.*
  STONE *is on the top floor of the house. Now he shoves the door of the*
bedroom and sees SYLVIE *with her jeans around her knees injecting*
herself in the crotch.
  In the corridor once more he sees, at the far end, MUFFDIVER *standing*
guiltily outside the door of STONE's *study wearing his Elvis jacket.*
STONE *jerks his thumbs at him, indicating that he should take it off and*
get out. MUFFDIVER *moves.*
  Now STONE *bursts into the bathroom and pulls back the shower*
curtain. CLINT *is in the shower.*

STONE

Get outta there, boy, the water's coming through.
(CLINT *jumps out.* STONE *turns off the water, getting wet himself,*
and several tiles fall off the wall.)

CLINT

Those tiles must have been stuck up by a moron.

STONE

Jesus. Jesus.

(STONE *starts throwing the tiles on the floor.* CLINT *is not frightened yet and continues to dry himself, not concealing himself and his eczema-scarred body.* STONE *is shocked rather than hostile.*)
Someone shove you in an acid bath?

CLINT

I got a job, Stone.
(STONE *goes slowly towards* CLINT. CLINT *retreats.* STONE *reaches out to touch him.*)

STONE

What kind of strange little boy are you?

CLINT

Don't you touch me.

STONE

Still using shit, Clint? Don't even reply, you're an addict and therefore a complete liar.
(*Now* SYLVIE *is at the door behind them, not seen by* STONE.)
Your mother loves you but what you done but break her heart?

CLINT

Have I?

STONE

Apologize to her.
(SYLVIE, *laughing at* STONE, *comes into the room towards him, not in the least scared.*)

SYLVIE

Oh mister. Mister.
(*She goes to* CLINT *and helps him up, holding him.*)

STONE

You're smart, girlie. What you doing with these bad boys?
You're above them.

SYLVIE

Me? I'm not above no one.

INT. LIVING ROOM OF COTTAGE. DAY

All the posse present now, in the living room.

    LILY *and* BIKE *come into the room carrying tea and biscuits. The atmosphere is no longer relaxed, as it was when they first came into the cottage. They look at each other expectantly, as if to say: 'Should we leave?'*

    MUFFDIVER *and* SYLVIE *lie on the sofa together, whispering and playing with each other.*

    CLINT *stands there drying his hair after the shower, hurt and disturbed, looking to* MUFFDIVER *for support.* MUFFDIVER *ignores him.*

    BURNS *sits forward in an armchair, worried, as always, about all the others.*

    TOM-TOM *is at the piano, tinkling a melancholy tune.*

    LILY *pours the tea and* BIKE *hands it around to the others.*

LILY

(*To* BIKE)
There's a good boy.
(*Now* STONE *comes into the room and stands there, looking at the posse individually, puzzled, as if trying to work out how the posse came to be this way, this loathsome.*

    BIKE *hands tea to* BURNS. BURNS *puts his tea down immediately. He's made a decision after seeing* STONE*'s face.*)

BURNS

Let's get off then.

STONE

I've said nothing.

BURNS

I can smell . . .
(*and he sniffs*)
contempt.

STONE

(*Parodying* BURNS*'s sniffing*)
I'm getting it too. From you. You think everything respectable
I've built up with my hands somehow belongs to bums like you
That I don't deserve it. That I've stolen it. I haven't. You people –

BURNS

Here we go.

STONE

You listen for once to someone who isn't stoned, who can
speak the English language, fat man. You only desire to be . . .
what you are now. This. The lazy dregs of society.
(*Glancing at* MUFFDIVER)
And superior. But none of you know fuck-all. That boy for
instance.
(*He indicates* CLINT)
I know him. Absolutely useless. He knows nothing about
nothing. He can't do fuck-all.

BURNS

(*Shaking his head furiously*)
No! There is intelligence –

STONE

You're slaves of sensation, just slaves –

BURNS

Your way of life, that's slavery, habit, repetition –

STONE

Without will or strength or determination. You'll always take
the easy way.

SYLVIE

If only you know, Mr Stone, how hard it is when you're out of
tune with the straight world and what strength and
determination you need when you've got nothing. On the
street . . .

STONE

To tell the truth, girlie, I pity you. I pity people who don't know
the purpose that real work gives you.

BURNS

I can wire a house. I can install a shower.

CLINT

(*To* LILY, *of* STONE)
More than he can.

STONE

(*Looking scornfully at* SYLVIE)
I saw you upstairs. Addiction is the most pathetic and
wretched thing.
(TOM-TOM *has hung his head during this.* MUFFDIVER *tries to
catch his eye. Tension is rising all round.* MUFFDIVER *shows*
TOM-TOM *the knife.* TOM-TOM *laughs wryly.*)
Because you think you can be happy by sticking a needle in
you. You're yellow cowards, afraid of life.

SYLVIE

(*To* LILY)
Lily, when I look at your man, Stone, I think: that person will
never understand anything about other people's hearts.
(*Indicates* CLINT)
Whereas he loves . . .

LILY

(*Shouts*)
No, that's a lie. Stone loves! He loves me!
(*To* STONE)
Yes?

STONE

(*To* SYLVIE)
If you want to die, go and do it in a corner and don't commit
no crimes on ordinary people.
(STONE *spits on the floor.* MUFFDIVER, *who's been preparing
himself throughout this, hurls himself at* STONE *with his knife.
But* STONE*'s a fighter.* MUFFDIVER *and* STONE *struggle,*
LILY *screaming, everyone yelling. The knife eventually falls from*
MUFFDIVER*'s hand.* TOM-TOM *picks it up.*
    And BURNS *holds* STONE. SYLVIE *and* CLINT *hold*
MUFFDIVER.
    BIKE *turns away.*)

                          BIKE

(*To* TOM-TOM)
I don't think they'll ask us back.

INT. KITCHEN. DAY

BURNS, BIKE, TOM-TOM, SYLVIE *and* MUFFDIVER *going out through
the kitchen door.* CLINT, *last, about to follow them, when he spots a pair
of shoes parked in the corner of the kitchen, sitting on newspaper, freshly
cleaned. He quickly removes his boots and puts on the good shoes,
carefully putting the old pair in their place.*

                         CLINT

The shoe is overdue.
(*Now he goes through into the hall.*)
Mum.
(*At the top of the stairs he sees the little boy, now in pyjamas and old
dressing gown, coming slowly downstairs. At the top of the stairs is*
LILY, *preoccupied.*)

                          LILY

I'm just coming.

EXT. FIELD. AFTERNOON

The posse moves off across the field, SYLVIE *being given a piggy-back by*
BURNS.
    Now LILY *runs after them, carrying the shoes that* CLINT *left behind.
She stops and shouts, running until she catches up with* CLINT.
    Seeing this, MUFFDIVER *has the others continue, into the distance.*

                          LILY

(*Breathless*)
Stay, stay. Stone says . . . it's OK.

                         CLINT

Tomorrow I start work, Mum.

                          LILY

Whose shoes are those? You left yours.
(*She looks down.*)

Oh no, give them back.
(*He shakes his head.*)
He'll take it out on me. You can't do it! Clint! Thief!
(*She throws the old pair at him.*)

TOM-TOM

Elvis Aaron Presley.
(*And* STONE *is standing there dressed as Elvis, with a Rottweiler.*)

EXT. COUNTRY STREET. LATE AFTERNOON

*An old hippy is coming out of a house with guitar cases, putting them in
the back of a big van – watched from across the road by the posse.*
　　MUFFDIVER *looks at* CLINT. CLINT *goes over to the hippy.*
　　Cut to:

EXT. COUNTRY STREET. LATE AFTERNOON

*The van pulls away with them all sitting in the back. We watch this event
from the point of view of the two local kids, deeply in awe of the entire
event.*
　　*Then the van is gone. Music from the beat-box hangs in the air for a
while, then silence; desolation. The local kids turn away.*

EXT. OUTSIDE THE DINER. NIGHT

Doors of the van burst open. BIKE *cycles out of the van. The others tumble
out after him. The hippy's van draws away. The posse on the pavement,
dispersing in different directions.*
　　CLINT *standing outside the diner, watching, ready to wave. He spots*
MELANIE. *But at the table she is serving at, he sees Mr G's black*
ASSISTANT *and Mr G's two women friends eating and laughing.*
　　Now FAULKNER *crosses the road with one rent boyfriend.*

FAULKNER

So you're back, Marco Polo. Jesus. Phew. You're dead meat,
man. All of you.

CLINT

Mr G? He not bothered about us. He amused.

FAULKNER

Not Mr G. Mr Gangster whose place you're squatting. He's
heard about it. He's very angry about you sitting on his toilet.
He's coming over.

(CLINT *hurries away after the posse.*)

EXT. OUTSIDE THE SHOE SHOP. NIGHT

CLINT *hurries past the shoe shop.* BUSY BEE *in the doorway starts to
unpack his paltry belongings and make himself comfortable for the night.*

BUSY BEE

Where's my jumper?

INT. HALLWAY/SUFI CENTRE. NIGHT

CLINT *stands outside the Sufi Centre, watching the chanting and
revolving. He catches* DR BUBBA'*s eye and is about to go to him. But*
SYLVIE, *carrying groceries, is behind him.*

SYLVIE

What a fabulous man, Dr Bubba.

CLINT

But what are they doing, these people? What do they want?

SYLVIE

I talked to one of them. They chant and meditate to get serene.
To clear their heads. They want to stop wanting all the time
and start really living.

CLINT

Yeah?
(*They remove their shoes and practically dash to join the group.
They join the circle and revolve,* CLINT *looking pretty awkward.
The others smile and encourage him. He watches* SYLVIE.
    *After a good whirl, as the circle gets smaller and smaller, they stop,
and separate, in a circle.*)

DR BUBBA

What do you all feel, if you don't mind? Let us compare
calmnesses.

(*There are several replies from the group: 'Yes, calm . . . happy . . .*
OK . . . tired . . . not religious. Not spiritual.'
    Then it's CLINT's *turn. They look at him.*)

CLINT

Sexy . . . Just . . . sexy.
(*People freeze, not knowing how to take this. They look at*
DR BUBBA. DR BUBBA *starts to bend forward and straighten,*
bend and straighten.)

SYLVIE

(*To someone in group*)
He all right?

PERSON IN GROUP

Dr Bubba is doing his laughing meditation.
Cut to:

INT. SUFI CENTRE. NIGHT

SYLVIE *putting on her shoes.* CLINT *looking for his shoes.*

CLINT

Hey, some bloodclaat's swiped my shoes! Hey, yo, Dr Bubba,
man!
(*But* DR BUBBA *is talking to someone else.*)
Where are they! Give them back!

SYLVIE

The shoe has flew!
(CLINT *starts to smash the place up, throwing things around.*)

CLINT

Where are they! Where are they!
(DR BUBBA *comes across and removes his own shoes, Indian*
chappals. Very flimsy sandals. He gives them to CLINT *who is very*
distressed. CLINT *takes them resentfully.*)

INT. LIVING ROOM OF SQUAT. NIGHT

CLINT *standing in the living room barefoot, waving the sandals about.*
BURNS *playing cards with* BIKE.

> CLINT

Look, look! Some religious fucker has stolen my fucking shoes!
(BURNS *replies in German.*)

INT. SQUAT BATHROOM. NIGHT

SYLVIE *is alone in the bathroom. She tries to shut the broken door. She
has cotton wool and a bottle of disinfectant. And a razor blade. She rolls
up her sleeve and slowly, carefully, as if she's done this before – the dark
scars are visible – cuts herself. She cuts herself five times until the blood
comes. She watches herself in the mirror. She bathes each cut.*

INT./EXT. OUTSIDE BATHROOM DOOR. NIGHT

SYLVIE *comes out of the bathroom.* CLINT *is outside, waiting for her.
She is not certain if he's seen her.*

> CLINT

Sylvie, what are you doing?

> SYLVIE

Don't follow me round.

> CLINT

Where are you going now, then?

> SYLVIE

Muffdiver's taking me out.

> CLINT

Let's go out for a drink first. It's only a few hours before I start
work. How about a quick drink?
(*She looks at him and finally relents. He is pleased.*)

INT. HI-TECH BAR. NIGHT

CLINT *and* SYLVIE *go into the hi-tech bar with* BIKE, *minus his bike for a
change. The place is pretty full.*
  TOM-TOM *is at the bar. A* DWARF *springs around, collecting glasses.*
  As usual, as CLINT *comes in numerous people talk to him, saying
'Buyin', sellin', got any M-25?', etc.*

CLINT

I'm retired. In a new business. Got a day job.
(CLINT *and* SYLVIE *push through the crowd. Then* CLINT *steps in a puddle of beer, wetting his feet and cursing.*)

DWARF

(*Laughing*)
You wanna get some new shoes, innit?
Cut to:

INT. HI-TECH BAR. NIGHT

CLINT *has got them drinks.* SYLVIE *is sitting down, beside* FAULKNER.

SYLVIE

You love him –

CLINT

I mean it, you an' me, we've got to finish with him. We mustn't get dependent.

SYLVIE

But we need him. Look at us, people like us, wasted trash –

CLINT

Yes, he'll take us down.

SYLVIE

We can't do nothing for ourselves. He's a sparky little kid with a dream.

CLINT

Of money, only. Powerful people, they're the worst, they always want to take you over.

FAULKNER

Oh stop it you two.
(CLINT *stares at* SYLVIE. *Kisses her cheek. She sighs. He gets on his knees and under the table, between her legs.*)

FAULKNER

Is he?
(SYLVIE *nods*)
When he's finished, ask him to do me.

(*The camera on* SYLVIE'*s face.* FAULKNER *dabs her forehead with his handkerchief.*)
Cut to:

INT. HI-TECH BAR. NIGHT

Under the table. We see CLINT *on his knees with his head under* SYLVIE'*s skirt. As he withdraws for a breather, he notices* FAULKNER'*s excellent shoes which, unlike the rest of him today, are entirely conventional.*

   Now SYLVIE *kicks* CLINT *to continue, which he does, while at the same time he's clumsily putting one sandalled foot beside* FAULKNER'*s.*

FAULKNER

Lick my toe-caps baby.
(*To* SYLVIE)
Clearly no shoe is safe in this boy's company.

CLINT

Can I borrow them, Faulkner, just for the day?

FAULKNER

No you can't.
(*But there's a struggle under the table as* CLINT *frantically tries to wrench* FAULKNER'*s shoes off, and* FAULKNER *tries to get rid of him.* SYLVIE *laughing.*)
Help me, help me!
(*We see* BURNS *and* TOM-TOM *looking at this from across the bar and laughing approvingly.*
   BURNS *turns as five or six policemen come into the bar through two entrances.*
   As CLINT *comes out from under the table a pint of beer tips off the table and down his back. He gets up quickly, very pissed off, and sees what's happening.*)

CLINT

Oh no, oh Christ, what's happening? They can't arrest me, not now. I'm only a waiter.

SYLVIE

Get rid of your stuff!

(*He stands there petrified, looking around.*)
Clint!
(*Meanwhile everyone in the place reacts fast. They know what to do.
We see this in comic detail: people dropping their drugs on the floor;
others swallow theirs; a white man, standing beside* TOM-TOM,
drops his stuff into TOM-TOM's *pocket, even as* TOM-TOM *drops his
own stuff on the floor.*

*We see feet kicking stuff under tables. One man pops his shit out of
the window. Someone else throws a lump of dope in the air and
catches it in his mouth.*

FAULKNER *punches* CLINT *in the balls.*

SYLVIE *grabs* CLINT *and holds him, going through his pockets,
finding his stuff and throwing it on the floor, kicking it under a table
into a corner.*)

EXT. OUTSIDE THE HI-TECH BAR IN THE STREET. NIGHT

*This isn't a major bust. Two police cars, a couple of arrests. People drifting
away.*

CLINT *and* SYLVIE *stand to one side, having seen it all before.*
TOM-TOM *is being hauled off by the police.*

CLINT

(*To* TOM-TOM)
Sid Vicious.
(CLINT *cracks up laughing.* SYLVIE *nudges him and they see*
MUFFDIVER *across the street, dressed up, looking very smart.*)

MUFFDIVER

(*To* SYLVIE)
Hi baby. Tsa-Tsa.

SYLVIE

Yeah, look at you, it's nice.
(MUFFDIVER *takes* CLINT *to one side.*)

MUFFDIVER

I'm taking Sylvie out for a bit of grub and then to a little rave.
So give me the money you owe me for the hundred and give me
the ones you haven't sold.

(CLINT *goes through his pockets.*)
(*Sarcastic*)
Thanks for the day out, man.
(*He looks at* CLINT *and is sorry for his sarcasm.*)
No.
(CLINT *gives him money.*)

CLINT

I had to get rid of the rest of the stuff in there.
(*Pause.*)
I won't be working for you no more, Muff, man. I start work
tomorrow.
(MUFFDIVER *looks down at* CLINT'*s sandals. Does a double-take.*
Looks at him sympathetically.)

MUFFDIVER

I'll never let something as bad as that happen to you.

CLINT

Have a good evening.
(*He walks away, crying.* MUFFDIVER *yells after him*)

MUFFDIVER

I won't let them do it to you, I promise, Clint, I won't!

EXT. SQUAT BUILDING. NIGHT

CLINT *walking back to the squat. Outside the house several cars are*
parked on the pavement. A HEAVY *is throwing out the dummies from*
Muffdiver's room.
    CLINT *sees the black tramp dressed in rags walking towards him.*
    CLINT *runs towards the house.*

INT. HALLWAY/SUFI CENTRE. NIGHT

CLINT *walks upstairs past the door of the Sufi Centre.* DR BUBBA, *who's*
been waiting to catch him, comes out.

DR BUBBA

Remain down here for some time. Some men are looking for you
boys, courtesy of the previous occupant. They don't love you.

(*As* CLINT *looks up the stairs, the posse's gear is being thrown out of the door.* BIKE *suddenly flies down the stairs and is thrown out. He struggles with the* HEAVY *but is ejected, his bicycle thrown down after him.*

    The HEAVY *turns and glares at* CLINT)

HEAVY

This squat is closed. You Muffdiver?

CLINT

(*Aggressive*)
Why?

HEAVY

Someone's looking for him.

DR BUBBA

(*About* CLINT)
This young man is my personal assistant.
(*The* HEAVY *looks at him and goes. From the top of the stairs we hear* BURNS *complaining, arguing and fighting with the* HEAVIES.

    CLINT *quickly dives back into* DR BUBBA's *place, which is deserted at this time.*

    DR BUBBA *watches him walking nervously around the place. He watches him go to the window, open it and look up at the drainpipe up which he originally entered the house. He starts to climb out of the window.* DR BUBBA *restrains him.*)
Stay here.

CLINT

I had some money for shoes stashed up there. I've gotta get it.

DR BUBBA

They won't let you up, boy. And you must warn your other friends. Don't come back here. Go. Go.

EXT. FRONT OF SQUAT BUILDING. NIGHT

CLINT *is walking quickly away from the squat – backwards. He watches the* HEAVIES *throwing the posse's belongings out into the street.*

   BURNS *is picking up some of the things and putting them into a supermarket trolley. The* HEAVY *shoves* BURNS *hard and pushes the trolley over.*

CLINT *talks to himself as he turns and runs.*

EXT. DINER. NIGHT

CLINT *walks to the diner and looks in through the window. He sees* MUFFDIVER *and* SYLVIE *sitting at a table eating and talking amicably, drinking wine.*

CLINT *watches them. He can't decide whether to go in or not. He's about to step inside when he sees* HEMINGWAY *putting his coat on and preparing to leave.* MELANIE *is also putting her coat on.*

CLINT *conceals himself as the two of them come out,* MELANIE *putting her arm through* HEMINGWAY's *once they're outside. They go.* CLINT *watches them.*

He turns and BUSY BEE, *whose jumper he nicked, is standing beside him.*

> BUSY BEE
>
> Where's my jumper?
> (*Instinctively,* CLINT *turns and runs.*)

INT. HEADLEY'S FLAT. NIGHT

CLINT *is in the hall of Headley's flat, trying to get past her.*

> CLINT
>
> Let me in, Headley.
> (*He's in a terrible state, exhausted and wretched.*)

> HEADLEY
>
> But yesterday you ran out, all independent.

> CLINT
>
> Just for a little while.

> HEADLEY
>
> To hide from the law. What a gas. Gimme some more of that bush then.

> CLINT
>
> I swear I got nothing, Headley.

HEADLEY

What's the point of you then? Got your bloody shoes?
(*She looks at him, in a pitiful state. Then down at his ridiculous sandals and wet feet.*)
What happened to you?

CLINT

It's a long story, Headley.

INT. HEADLEY'S STUDY. NIGHT

HEADLEY *lies face down on her sofa.* CLINT *is brusquely instructed to rub her back.* CLINT *sits over her arse.*

HEADLEY

Ummm . . . yes. There, right, down a bit, harder, move those fingers. Knead my cheeks, darling.

CLINT

I'm not going no further.

HEADLEY

Hey. Don't you need the money?
(*We should play this off* CLINT's *face: the humiliation, the calculation, the wild thinking and then, with the* MAN's VOICE, CLINT's *fear of being beaten up. Suddenly there's an American* MAN's VOICE *outside and hard knocking on the door.*)

MAN'S VOICE

Headley.
(CLINT *is terrified and looks around for a window to escape through.*)

HEADLEY

How are you, dear?
(*To* CLINT)
Don't stop now.

MAN'S VOICE

Am I allowed to come in?

HEADLEY

Goodness, no, I'm not quite ready for you.

MAN'S VOICE

All right if I take a shower then?
(*Pause. The* MAN *goes.* CLINT *gets up.*)

HEADLEY

Stay, stay.

CLINT

I'm not getting into nothing weird. I've been sexually abused
before. And I'm starting work tomorrow. I've only got tonight
to find a pair of shoes – or get some money to buy some
tomorrow morning. Give us some dosh, Headley.

HEADLEY

But you haven't earned it.

CLINT

I beg you, Headley, give us thirty quid, thirty fucking quid,
that's all. Give me the money, Headley!

INT. HEADLEY'S FLAT. NIGHT

CLINT *walks quickly through Headley's flat. He sees the man's clothes
flung over a chair. But of course he doesn't know they belong to*
HEMINGWAY.

    *Beside the chair is a pair of boots, American boots, tough and colourful
and easily distinguishable. The best boots he's seen so far.*

    CLINT *quickly removes his own Indian chappals and examines these
American boots, caressing and sniffing and holding them. He's about to
put them on when the door from the shower opens.*

    CLINT *scarpers, quickly.*

    Cut to:

INT. HEADLEY'S FLAT. NIGHT

HEMINGWAY *comes out of the shower, a towel wrapped around him. He
looks down and sees a pair of knackered Indian sandals where his own
splendid boots were.*

HEMINGWAY
Headley! Headley! God dammit!

EXT. SHOE SHOP. NIGHT

CLINT *prepares to sleep in the doorway of the shoe shop. A couple of other people are already there, including* BUSY BEE *whose jumper he nicked.*
    The others have blankets and rudimentary pillows and stuff, while CLINT *has virtually nothing but an old coat, which he pulls around himself, his feet, with the magnificent boots, sticking out.* CLINT *spits in his hand and cleans the boots.*

BUSY BEE
Where's my fucking jumper?

CLINT
Tsa-Tsa.

EXT. STREET/NOTTING HILL TUBE. MORNING

The rush hour. Well-dressed, motivated and employed people dash around. CLINT, *eager to join the employed world, moves in and out of the crowd, feeling self-conscious about his wretchedness.*
    Across the street BURNS *sees him and calls out.*

BURNS
Clint!
(*He tries to get through the traffic to* CLINT *but* CLINT *fails to hear him and moves off quickly.*)

EXT. STREET NEAR TUBE AREA. MORNING

CLINT *walking in another part of Notting Hill.* BURNS *has finally caught up with him.*

BURNS
Listen. Christ.
(BURNS *just grabs him and pulls him off the street.*)
Come on. This way.

CLINT
Burns, man, I got a job waiting for me. Right now this minute.

BURNS
You're with me, little boy, yes you are.

CLINT
No! What are you doing?
(*But* BURNS *is strong.*)

BURNS
We're going to see the boss, my wee man. And wipe your feet too.

EXT./INT. HOTEL. DAY

BURNS *drags* CLINT *through the doors of a seedy hotel in the area.*

INT. HOTEL ROOM. DAY

BURNS *drags* CLINT *into a hotel room, shuts the door and leaves him standing there, a little bewildered.*
MUFFDIVER *and* SYLVIE *are in the room, quite panicky,* MUFFDIVER *stuffing things into a small bag.* SYLVIE *is getting changed into her Gothess gear.*
The two of them look different, older perhaps, more involved with each other. Still, the atmosphere is tense.
Once more CLINT *feels excluded, but confident about his future.*
SYLVIE *and* MUFFDIVER *are warmer towards him than they've ever been, which disconcerts him.*

CLINT
What are you two playing at?

MUFFDIVER
The owner of that squat is looking for us. It's a fact he's very pissed off. So we're going to chill out.

SYLVIE
You should make moves too.

MUFFDIVER
We'll meet somewhere in a few days. We'll rendezvous. In Portsmouth.

CLINT

Portsmouth?

SYLVIE

It's for your sake, baby.
(*Now* MUFFDIVER *puts a long black wig on.* SYLVIE *hands him a black-leather studded jacket.*)

MUFFDIVER

I'm disguising myself as Goth in order to leave town without trouble. Sylvie's going as a Gothess.
(*He glances in the mirror at himself. A touch of vanity.* CLINT *can't help laughing at him.*)

CLINT

Yeah, Mr Goth, and I'm starting work in ten minutes time.
(*Points.*)
Look man, the shoes has come true.

SYLVIE

Sit down. We've got you a birthday present.
(MUFFDIVER *hands him a plastic bag. To his delight* CLINT *pulls out a pair of huge DMs.*)

CLINT

(*To them both*)
Thank you. Thanks.

SYLVIE

You're escaping as a skinhead, Clint.
(*She runs her hands through his hair, kisses his cheeks and pulls out a pair of scissors. She starts to cut his hair, cutting out a big lump.*)

CLINT

No! I gotta go. See you!
(*He struggles. She tries to hold him.*)

MUFFDIVER

Be cool, Clint, brother. Put the boots on and get your hair off.
(MUFFDIVER *tries to remove* CLINT*'s boots and replace them with the DMs.*)

CLINT

(*Distressed*)

No, you be cool, man. Christ. Sylvie. Christ. Sylvie – I loved
you and everything. Both of you. What are you doing? I loved
you.

(*And* CLINT *backs away towards the door, trying to stop crying.*)

MUFFDIVER

Clint!

SYLVIE

No! Stay!

(*And* CLINT *dashes out of the door.*)

EXT. STREET. DAY

CLINT *hurries towards the diner, upset, and trying to fix his hair. He stops
and tries to look at himself in a mirror on one of the market stalls to see if
the missing hank of hair is noticeable. He sees that it is.*

   Walking through the market he steals a cap from a stall he's passing.
BIKE *stops beside him and shouts at him to stop.*

   *Then he hurries on, only stopping to check his shoes and adjust the hat.
He's ready for* HEMINGWAY.

INT. DINER. DAY

The diner is crowded. The two SMART WOMEN *are there, and they
recognize* CLINT. *Waiters fly about, including* MELANIE, *who smiles at*
CLINT. *Behind the bar the flash barman mixes fantastic cocktails.*

CLINT

(*To* MELANIE)
Is Mr Hemingway here?

MELANIE

He expecting you?

CLINT

Oh yeah, Melanie. Tsa-Tsa.
Cut to:

INT. DINER. DAY

CLINT *desperately trying to arrange himself.* HEMINGWAY *emerges.*

CLINT

Here I am, you know, Mr Hemingway, this is me as arranged.
The job hasn't gone to another?
(HEMINGWAY *smiles and shakes his head.*)

HEMINGWAY

Let's have a look at you.

CLINT

(*Turning around*)
You know I'm counting on this gig.
(HEMINGWAY*'s eyes start at the top of* CLINT*'s body and move
slowly downwards. During this process of examination* CLINT *looks
out of the window of the dinner and sees* MUFFDIVER, *in full heavy
Goth gear, standing outside.*

With him, also disguised, is SYLVIE, *with black lipstick,
eyeshadow, etc., in long black velvet clothes.*

MUFFDIVER *knocks on the window and indicates for him to come
out.*

MELANIE *looks at them and at* CLINT. CLINT *looks away. Then*
MUFFDIVER *and* SYLVIE *walk on.*

Now HEMINGWAY*'s eyes continue. At last he takes in the shoes.
And suddenly looks up to* CLINT*'s face. He looks down to the boots
again, and once more up at* CLINT.

CLINT *smiles broadly, happily, his smile spreading across the
screen.*)

CLINT

Whaddya say, Mr Hemingway – the boot is cute, right? The
boot is a hoot, yeah?

INT. TRAIN. DAY

MUFFDIVER *is standing in the corridor of a train as it rushes through the
English countryside. He is proud, disdainful, and still dressed as a Black
Sabbath man.*

SYLVIE *has her head out the window, hair blowing.*
From her point of view we see the countryside rushing away.

EXT. TRAIN IN STATION. DAY

The train has stopped in a station. MUFFDIVER *is now sitting on a seat, looking out of the window. Some of Sylvie's belongings are on the seat next to him. The train starts to move away from the platform. He looks out of the window and sees* SYLVIE *on the platform, walking away from him. She turns and waves. He gets up and gesticulates, but the train is moving away. It is too late. He turns to see her take off her vampire wig and throw it away.*

INT. DINER. DAY

CLINT, *in waiter's gear, subserviently stands by a table; two smart white men in suits are deciding what to eat.* CLINT *has his pad at the ready. As the end titles roll, we see* CLINT *in the restaurant, putting plates down, removing others, running around. Freeze frame on his face.*

My Son the Fanatic

CAST AND CREW

EXT. FINGERHUT HOUSE. DAY

A large modern house in the country, surrounded by land.

INT. LIVING ROOM. FINGERHUT HOUSE. DAY

In the living room. MRS FINGERHUT, *prim, snobbish, middle class, has been entertaining the assembled group for some time, as* FINGERHUT *is late.*

The atmosphere is strained. MRS FINGERHUT'*s daughter* MADELAINE, PARVEZ, MINOO *and their son* FARID – *all in their best clothes – sit on hard chairs.* PARVEZ *is both terrified and ecstatic to be there.*

MRS FINGERHUT *puts down a photograph album she has been showing everyone.*

> MRS FINGERHUT
>
> Madelaine was a delightful girl.
> (*Pause.*)
> She still is, of course.
> (MADELAINE *and* FARID, *both uncomfortable, glance at one another.*)

> PARVEZ
>
> (*Smiling at her*)
> And a little bit plumpish at times . . . as you said, twice.

> MINOO
>
> Rice is very good.
> (MRS FINGERHUT *looks bewildered.*)
> For reducing diet.

> PARVEZ
>
> Cricket is excellent. Farid was Captain. I warned, don't you ever go professional, career is over in f*i*ve years. MRS FI-GERHUT – Hilda – this boy of ours, I can assure you he is all-round-type; going whole hog, but not on field!

                              MINOO

Oh yes. But in garden?

                              PARVEZ

(*To* MINOO, *sharply*)
One minute.
(*To* MRS FINGERHUT)
At school he carried the prizes home. Now at college he is . . .
he is top student of year.

                             MADELAINE

Not difficult.
(MRS FINGERHUT *looks at* MADELAINE, *who scratches.* FARID
smirks. They sit there a moment: tense.)

EXT. FINGERHUT HOUSE. DAY

*Fingerhut's chauffeur-driven car turns into the drive, stopping beside
Parvez's battered taxi, which* FINGERHUT *regards with aversion as he
walks past it. The house dogs rush towards him, barking.*

INT. LIVING ROOM. FINGERHUT HOUSE. DAY

                              PARVEZ

(*Hushed voice*)
The Chief Inspector.

                          MRS FINGERHUT

(*Going to the door*)
About time.

                              PARVEZ

The law never sleeps at night.
(*Looks at* FARID, *who is cringing.*)
Perhaps a career in the police could be guaranteed for you.
Let me mention it to Chief Inspector.

                              FARID

Papa.

                              PARVEZ

Leave the matters of business opening to me. Put on cheerful
face – blast it! – this is happiest occasion of life.

MINOO

(*In Urdu, subtitled*)
I want the toilet.

PARVEZ

(*In Urdu, subtitled*)
Not again. They'll think we're Bengalis.

MINOO

They couldn't tell the difference between a Pakistani and a
Bengali. We're all –
(MINOO *is halted by the expression on* PARVEZ's *face.*
     FINGERHUT *grandly enters the room and looks around at
everyone.* PARVEZ *goes to him, kissingly.*)

Cut to: FINGERHUT *and* PARVEZ *together.* FARID *watches this,
embarrassed and repelled.*

PARVEZ

I will arrange all engagement party details personally. Our
tradition is beautiful in this respect.
(FINGERHUT *appears to make a face.*)
You enjoy our food when I bring it personally to police station.
(*Leaning closer*)
Chief Inspector, please inform me absolutely in confidence:
Farid is top police material, isn't he?

FINGERHUT

Isn't he training to be an accountant?

PARVEZ

Law and order might be more reliable. Crime is everywhere
out of control, wouldn't you confirm?
(*Looking at* FARID, *who is cringing.*)
My boy says the same.

FINGERHUT

He would know, would he?

Cut to:

PARVEZ

(*To* MINOO)
Get camera. Now is moment!

Cut to:

(*To* FINGERHUT)
Please, sir, would a pose be all right for private use exclusively?
Fingerhut appears to nod.
(*To* MINOO)
Bring champagne, too.
(MINOO *pulls a camera and a bottle of champagne out of a bag.*)

*Cut to: A photograph is being taken, by the chauffeur, of the whole
group.* MRS FINGERHUT *stands next to* PARVEZ, *who has his arm
around* FARID. MADELAINE *is beside* FARID. MINOO *and* CHIEF
INSPECTOR FINGERHUT.
*We see all the faces. There is a flash. Other photographs, in other
combinations. And finally,* PARVEZ *and* FARID *together – both drinking
champagne, clinking glasses,* PARVEZ *laughing to himself.*
Titles in.

INT. CAR. NIGHT

*We cut inside the car and pull back from one of the photographs – now a
little curled and yellowing. Then,* PARVEZ's *face, as he gesticulates, shakes
his head and waves at other drivers; we see him singing to himself.*
    *Low on the track, an Asian radio station is playing Nusrat Fateh Ali
Khan, or something similar.*
    PARVEZ *is a Pakistani in his early fifties. He wears an old suit, scuffed
shoes and inevitably looks scruffy. He is unshaven in places, his hair
stands up, his askew tie is stained, his sweater unravelling. But he is a
lively and engaging man with a lovely face.*

EXT. NORTHERN CITY. NIGHT

A high shot – a Northern city.

EXT. STREET

Parvez's taxi cab drives through the frame – away from the city.

EXT. AIRPORT. NIGHT

We see the flickering lights, planes overhead, open air, foreign travel – and businessmen with briefcases hurrying through the exits.

INT. AIRPORT. NIGHT

PARVEZ *stands by the barrier with a cardboard sign that says 'SHIT' in large letters. A smaller letter 's' has been added to the end of this legend.*

  PARVEZ *keeps getting elbowed aside by the other taxi-drivers, but he is tenacious; he pushes forward and waves the sign at a likely figure, who backs away when he sees the piece of cardboard.*

  Behind this man the GERMAN *strides through the gate.*

INT./EXT. CAR

Cut to: PARVEZ'*s talking mouth.*

  He is driving the man into town.

> PARVEZ
> You are brand-new in town, sir?

> GERMAN
> That's why I passed through the airport a few minutes ago.

> PARVEZ
> Ah-uh. Interested to see something of our glory, sir?
> (*This is an opportunity for* PARVEZ *to show off his knowledge of his adopted city, its geography and history. He talks about the mills, the great nineteenth-century entrepreneurs, the first Pakistani immigrants, and he points out their shops. (He begins cautiously, to see whether the passenger will respond, and then becomes more voluble.) It is an animated if garbled flow, and we should have shots of the relevant places.*
>
> *The* GERMAN *is amused and interested by* PARVEZ, *who, encouraged, continues, until . . .)*

INT./EXT. RESTAURANT. NIGHT

They pass the large and swanky front of an Indian restaurant where PARVEZ *slows down and stops.*

> PARVEZ
> Good, good, final decoration is done. Here we will be having my son's getting engaged party. He is marrying Madelaine,

Madelaine Fingerhut, the top policeman's daughter. He
impressed her no end. I am working extensive hours to make
the money.
(*He turns round.*)
The restaurant, sir, belongs to my friend, Fizzy. There, fattish
one. We came together to this country. He had five pounds,
which he borrowed from me. Look now. And look at me!
(*We see* FIZZY, *avuncular and affluent in a good but loud suit,
greeting guests at the door.* PARVEZ *beeps his horn and waves.*)
Your name too small on front, yaar!
(FIZZY *notices* PARVEZ *with some irritation. The place he has
recently opened is trying to be posh. He comes over.*)

FIZZY

Don't block parking space! Come – eat!

PARVEZ

I'm eating to capacity, when I get one minute of silence!

FIZZY

I must have date of engagement party.

PARVEZ

Yes, yes, coming up.

FIZZY

(*Sharply*)
Tomorrow for definite.
(PARVEZ *is surprised by this tone, and indicates the passenger in the
back.*)

PARVEZ

Okay, okay.
(FIZZY *gives* PARVEZ *his card and winks.* PARVEZ *hands it to the*
GERMAN.)
(*driving on*)
Top class place, almost. You like our food?

GERMAN

I try everything.
(PARVEZ *considers this, before turning the car in another direction.*)

INT./EXT. SEEDY STREETS. NIGHT

Cut to: The cab now passes a row of unprepossessing prostitutes in a seedy nineteenth-century street. Several of the women are perilously young and the others, in their mid-thirties, some black, and one in her mid-forties carrying a little dog, are standing in the wind and cold, stamping their feet, awaiting trade.

The GERMAN *perks up and turns around in his seat.*

> PARVEZ
>
> Local people and religious types don't like. Condom and all, you know, hanging from rose-bushes.

EXT. SMART HOTEL. NIGHT

The city's smartest hotel. PARVEZ *staggers with a bag in each hand and one under each arm to the door of the hotel, where he knows the porters. He isn't fit and his back hurts. He stops and rubs his lower spine, before proceeding painfully.*

The GERMAN *gives him a good tip.* PARVEZ *shakes his hand and gives him his card.*

> PARVEZ
>
> (*After attempting some German*)
> Thank you, sir. And please, sir, let's meet again. Call me personally by name, Parvez. That's me. Or at home.

INT. CAR. NIGHT

PARVEZ *sitting in his car. With the tip on one side, he counts the day's takings. Then he counts it again, unable to believe it is so little.*

The voice of the CONTROLLER *on the radio interrupts him.* PARVEZ *tries to compose himself.*

INT. NIGHTCLUB. NIGHT

The early hours of the morning. PARVEZ *standing in the entrance to a nightclub, chatting with the white bouncers, who are condescending.*

Through a spangled curtain we see coloured lights and hear music. (We see this club later.)

> PARVEZ

The Chief Inspector – all Fingerhuts are close personal friends of mine – is very concerned about scene of nightclubs, noises and all. But I've told him –

> BOUNCER

(After glancing inside)
Your ride.
(A white MAN *crashes through the curtain, and* BETTINA *follows him.)*

INT./EXT. STREET OUTSIDE CLUB AND IN CAR

PARVEZ *follows them to the car. The* MAN *is high-spirited but almost collapses on the back seat.*

> MAN

Turn it up!

> PARVEZ

(Turns on a Tony Bennett record)
Romantic tune for romantic evening, sir?

INT./EXT. STREET AND IN CAR

The white MAN *is groping and fondling* BETTINA *– who both placates him and keeps him away.* PARVEZ *watches them in his mirror.*

> MAN

(To PARVEZ*)*
Stop, stop! I'm going in my pants!

> PARVEZ

Do not water new upholstery, sir!
*(*PARVEZ *halts hastily, rushes round to the backseat and hauls the* MAN *out of the car.)*

Cut to: The MAN *is pissing against the wall outside a row of Asian shops.*

PARVEZ

I told a German about you. Rich-smelling. New in town.

BETTINA

(*Surprised*)
Ta very much. You'll be wanting commission next.

PARVEZ

Am I later taking you home?

BETTINA

(*Indicating punter*)
He's paid for an all-night job, but I think he's looking a bit on the bright side.

PARVEZ

I will wait, then.

BETTINA

Will you? Thanks. How have you been?

PARVEZ

Same. You know, I liked –

BETTINA

What?

PARVEZ

Out little talk –

BETTINA

Several talks –
(*The* MAN *staggers against the side of the car, and falls in again.*)

PARVEZ

Please sir, no smoking indoors, smell is deafening.
(*The* MAN *grabs* PARVEZ *by the back of the neck.*)

MAN

Go!
(PARVEZ *reaches down for the thick piece of wood he uses to defend himself.*)

PARVEZ

Don't touch me, sir, in case I go left instead of right.

(*The* MAN *drags the rear-view mirror to one side and adopts an Indian accent and waggles his head.*)

                          MAN
Look straight ahead, sir!

INT. CAR

As they drive, the MAN *fucks* BETTINA *in the back of the car. As* PARVEZ *hears the* MAN *cry out, we cut to:*

INT. BEDROOM OF TERRACED HOUSE. NIGHT

The noise of a clattering dustbin lid awakens a middle-aged Pakistani woman asleep in bed.

INT./EXT. WINDOW OF TERRACED HOUSE. NIGHT

The Pakistani woman hurries to the window and is alarmed to see the shadowy figure of a man rooting in the bins.

EXT. BACK OF TERRACED HOUSE. NIGHT

PARVEZ *is examining the contents of his own dustbins. Along with the remains of many messy Indian dinners, he pulls out LPs and CDs, as well as crumpled posters of rock and sporting heroes.*

EXT. BACK OF HOUSE. NIGHT

The back door of the house opens. A light is switched on, illuminating him. Parvez's wife MINOO – *in her nightie and dressing-gown – looks nervously around the door.*

PARVEZ *looks up, ignores her, and then holds something up to the light and examines it.*

                          MINOO
Papu, it is you? I was frightened.
(*He grunts.*)
You are like a dirty tramp.

                          PARVEZ
Why does he throw this rubbish out?

MINOO

He has always been a clean boy.
(PARVEZ *comes towards her. She can see him now. He moves quickly past her.*)

PARVEZ

(*Bitterly*)
Why can you never give a straight answer!

INT. FARID'S BEDROOM. NIGHT

Quietly PARVEZ *opens the door to his son's bedroom. He is about to venture a few tiptoed paces into the room when* MINOO, *behind him, pulls him out and shuts the door.*

INT. UPSTAIRS LANDING. NIGHT

MINOO *watches* PARVEZ *to ensure he doesn't go back in.*

PARVEZ

Don't stand there like the police!

INT. FIZZY'S RESTAURANT. EVENING

The restaurant is almost full with well-off whites, and a few besuited and bejewelled Asians. FIZZY *is unctuously elaborating over a white couple – opening napkins, pouring wine, discussing the menu.*
    PARVEZ *looks a bit out of place in his crumpled clothes, but he surveys everything keenly: the fountains, the fancy foliage, the comfy sofas and Indian effects. A* WAITER *hurries towards him.*

WAITER

He say wait in function suite. Busy in here.

INT. FUNCTION ROOM IN FIZZY'S RESTAURANT. EVENING

Kept waiting, PARVEZ *has been walking about disconsolately in a large room above the restaurant, which is full of broken chairs, boxes and unwanted kitchen equipment.*

FIZZY

(*Coming in hurriedly*)
I'm rushing, but here we can have food on tables. Another

small kitchen there. I'll make it magnificent for entire
Fingerhut tribe! And there –

PARVEZ

And the food not too . . . fierce, yaar?

FIZZY

What?

PARVEZ

Toilet is far away for older guests.
(FIZZY *isn't much amused by this.*)

FIZZY

But why is date not fixed? What problem is going on?

PARVEZ

No, no, I am awaiting full confirmation from high up.

FIZZY

Your boy is taking you up in the world – at last.
(*Beat*)
One time a fare said to me, 'So what's new in the taxi
business?' I racked my head and . . . there was nothing but
abuses and little money. That was the day I threw down my
keys, cleared out and took a loan. Do or die, yaar.

PARVEZ

Some of us have become traffic wardens but personally
you'll never find me walking alone. All I want is to pay
mortgage.

FIZZY

Maybe you will – five minutes before you die, eh?
(PARVEZ *turns and walks away.*)
That will please Minoo at last, eh?

PARVEZ

Oh God.

FIZZY

She is very strong-willed, yaar. You never got her under
control, that has been problem.

(They look at one another. As they walk away they slap one another on the back, consolingly; old friends.)

EXT. STREET OUTSIDE CAB OFFICE. NIGHT

Later that night.
     This is a seedy part of town. Two prostitutes can be seen touting for custom across the street as PARVEZ *pulls up in his cab outside the office. He looks across the street at the prostitutes, but* BETTINA *isn't amongst them.*
     Other cabs and their loquacious drivers, leaning against the bonnets of their cars, smoking and gossiping, are lined up outside the office.

INT. CAB OFFICE. NIGHT

PARVEZ *enters to find a* PROSTITUTE *waiting.* RASHID, *another driver, younger than* PARVEZ *and rather aggressive, has been joshing her.*

PROSTITUTE
Parvez, take me back home, my kids are on their own. I'm not going with any of these –

RASHID
It's useless going with Parvez – he accepts only money!

PROSTITUTE
Fuck off, Rashid, I'll pay you tomorrow!

PARVEZ
(In a hurry)
Not now.

PROSTITUTE
Don't be a bastard! Sorry, sorry, I didn't mean it!
*(*PARVEZ *moves away from her towards a door leading to an inner office which is occupied by the radio* CONTROLLER, *visible through a glass panel in the walls.*
     RASHID *puts his arm around the prostitute's shoulders and laughs.)*

RASHID
Pay me later – and if you can't –
*(*RASHID *puts his hand up her skirt and pinches her, much to the raucous amusement of the others.)*

INT. RADIO ROOM OF CAB OFFICE. NIGHT

PARVEZ *enters the room to find the* CONTROLLER *very busy talking to cabs on the road, taking bookings, etc.*

This is a larger area of busted furniture. A TV with a video showing Indian action films. A boys' school atmosphere: men playing cards, stuffing their faces with chapatis, talking, shouting out jokes.

Two men are arm-wrestling over a table, with others watching, urging them on. This wrestling contest continues throughout the film – with sometimes one man about to win, and sometimes the other. There is never a result.

The CONTROLLER *is pleased to see* PARVEZ, *but this conversation is interrupted by calls.*

CONTROLLER
Parvez, yaar, I never speak to you in flesh! How's the exam boy? He studies more than anyone in country.

PARVEZ
These sons can be a bag of trouble, yaar.

CONTROLLER
Everyone know Javad's boy got in jail. They say it Javad's fault. How's the engagement coming? Everyone say you don't get parking tickets now.

PARVEZ
Tell the truth, Farid has gone very far inside himself these days –

CONTROLLER
Up and down, yaar, rather than in and out?
(*Just as the* CONTROLLER *sees his friend is troubled,* PARVEZ *cuts the conversation short. Through the glass pane he has seen* BETTINA *enter the outer office.*)

PARVEZ
(*To the* CONTROLLER)
Thanks for the extra work.

CONTROLLER
You're looking tired, yaar.

(*Shouts after him and around at the other drivers*)
But no one slacking!
(*The* CONTROLLER *watches* PARVEZ *and* BETTINA *go.*)

EXT. CAB OFFICE. NIGHT

BETTINA *and* PARVEZ *come out of the office and get into* PARVEZ's *cab.*

> BETTINA
>
> Have you eaten today?

> PARVEZ
>
> Which day is it?

> BETTINA
>
> Come on
> (*Parvez drives off.*)

EXT. MOBILE ROADSIDE CAFE. EARLY MORNING

A lay-by on a windy hillside overlooking the city. A mobile cafe/catering van. Bacon sizzling on a hot-plate. The owner, whom PARVEZ *and* BETTINA *both know, squirts mustard into the bacon butties, looks at* PARVEZ, *and squirts more in. They laugh.*

   PARVEZ *bites into his sandwich with pleasure, sighs, and considers the night and the landscape.* BETTINA *stands beside him, enjoying her butty, licking her fingers, ogled by a couple of lorry drivers parked nearby.*

> PARVEZ
>
> For weeks I haven't slept ten minutes. He throws away his things. He won't talk. Who would have sons?

> BETTINA
>
> Will you say something about what you've noticed?

> PARVEZ
>
> I am observing daily. I don't want to be some fool interfering with his freedoms. He gets easily rude with me now – his mother's side of the family.

> BETTINA
>
> What does your wife say?
> (PARVEZ *is about to reply, but just shakes his head.*)

INT./EXT. TAXI. EARLY MORNING

BETTINA *takes a tape from her bag, puts it in the cassette-player and fiddles with it until she finds the piece of music she wants to hear (maybe a reggae track). She listens then, leaning her head back, hums and smokes.* PARVEZ *glances at her. He is about to tell her something – but her good mood and company relaxes him.*

> BETTINA
>
> I haven't seen you for a few days.

> PARVEZ
>
> I'm going further and further afield for work, but earning less. They're sacking the drivers who won't work night and day. Sometimes I think – if I hit that tree what difference?

> BETTINA
>
> You wouldn't see that.

INT./EXT. TAXI. EARLY MORNING

As the taxi reaches the top of a hill they are confronted with a view of the dales. But they are looking at one another – with some curiosity.

> BETTINA
>
> Can we walk?

> PARVEZ
>
> Walk?

> BETTINA
>
> In the fresh air. The breeze is lovely. Let me show you a place.

> PARVEZ
>
> Surely there is air everywhere about?
> (*She laughs and gets out of the car. He has no choice but to follow her.*)

EXT. THE DALES. EARLY MORNING

BETTINA *and* PARVEZ *walking away from the car.* BETTINA *enjoys herself, but* PARVEZ *is uncertain. Suddenly she runs down a hill.* PARVEZ *has no choice but to follow, unathletically.*

Cut to: She approaches a stream. On a far side is a ruin on a hill, surrounded by trees. This is the spot BETTINA *wanted to show him and, although he is breathless and finding it hard going, its beauty impresses him.*

> BETTINA

Well?

> PARVEZ

Yes, it is magnificent. There were places, back home, I used to go.
(*He laughs*)
With a girl, actually.
(BETTINA *looks at him, before skipping across the stream.* PARVEZ *follows uncertainly. Halfway across, his foot slips on the wet stones and he finds himself standing knee-deep in water.*)

> PARVEZ

Oh God, there are icicles going inside!

> BETTINA

Those trousers will have to come off.
(*He looks at her in horror and she laughs.*)

INT. PARVEZ'S HOUSE. EARLY MORNING

We see MINOO *trying to scrub Parvez's shoes in the kitchen, his trousers are hanging up to dry.*

PARVEZ'S LIVING ROOM

PARVEZ *is in the living room. He's changed into salwar kurta, and is sipping a glass of whisky and relishing the taste, in a good mood.* MINOO *comes into the room.*

> MINOO

We can't afford new shoes. You're not a coolie to carry baggage through mud.

> PARVEZ

There are many abnormal occurrences in taxi business.

MINOO

Not usually involving a wet bottom.

PARVEZ

Hamid had to transport a tortoise in a box to Newcastle.
(*Pause.*)
There was a strange building last night, which reminded me of
your grandfather's house in Multan. All tumbled down, like his
after the hurricane.

MINOO

Take me, Papu.
(*He puts his bare feet into her lap. She caresses them.*)

PARVEZ

I must speak with Farid.

MINOO

About what?

PARVEZ

(*Thinks*)
Engagement party.
(*She works on his feet.*)
Minny, how has Fizzy done so well?

MINOO

He was always greedy . . . for things.

PARVEZ

He was a greedy little boy.

MINOO

You are easily made happy and like things to be always the
same. That's why you never made a success.

PARVEZ

Not a success?

MINOO

Driving taxi for twenty-five years is not –

PARVEZ

All right.

MINOO

If I'd been given your freedom . . . think what I would have done . . .

BETTINA

What such marvellous stuff then, bloody hell?

MINOO

I would have studied. I would have gone everywhere. And talked . . . talked.

PARVEZ

Talked – who the hell to?

MINOO

Anyone. And not stood here day after day washing filthy trousers.

PARVEZ

It's easy to say.
(*She gets up and goes.*)

Cut to: PARVEZ *is contemplating a display of Farid's cricket and swimming trophies on the mantelpiece. Also, a photograph of him, with a cricket team, holding a cup.*

INT. LIVING ROOM. PARVEZ'S HOUSE. MORNING

MINOO *is hoovering the muddy footprints from the carpet around the bottom of Parvez's trousers.* PARVEZ *has fallen asleep on the sofa. Some of Farid's discarded belongings lie alongside the empty bottle on the floor.*
    The front door slams. PARVEZ *wakes up.*

INT. LIVING ROOM WINDOW OF PARVEZ'S HOUSE. MORNING

He goes to the window and sees FARID *in the street arguing with* MADELAINE, *who has just turned up.*
    Also parked outside, with its boot open, is a car belonging to a young Asian man. FARID *has handed him a guitar, amp and speaker.*

This conversation is from Parvez's POV through the window. He can't make out much of it.

MADELAINE

I only wanted to see you –

FARID

(*Coldly*)
I told you truth from day one, and everything has been discussed several times –

MADELAINE

Oh, what has happened to you –

FARID

Leave me in peace –
(*She turns to go.*)
Don't come again!
(*We see* FARID *watching her go. At one point she turns. The two of them look at one another.*)

EXT. PARVEZ'S HOUSE. DAY

PARVEZ *standing at the window.*

EXT. PARVEZ'S HOUSE. DAY

PARVEZ *runs barefoot out of his house to confront* FARID.

PARVEZ

Where is she going?
(FARID *shrugs.*)
Why are you fighting?

FARID

Why do people fight?

PARVEZ

What is problem here? Farid, can I help you?

FARID

Papa –
(*Farid's Asian* COMPANION *is getting impatient.*)

COMPANION

Farid –

(FARID *puts the rest of the stuff in the car and the* COMPANION
gives him a wad of money which he immediately pockets.)

PARVEZ

(*To* FARID)

Where is that going? You used to love making a terrible noise
with these instruments!

(FARID *bends his knees and imitates a ridiculous rock guitarist.*)

FARID

You said all the time that there are more important things than
'Stairway to Heaven'. You couldn't have been more right,
Papa.

PARVEZ

Y-Y-Yes.

(*Pause.*)

Where are you going?

(FARID *looks down at Parvez's bare feet.*)

FARID

To college. Go inside, you'll catch pneumonia.

(FARID *picks* PARVEZ *up in his arms and carries him indoors –*
PARVEZ *continues to talk all the while.*)

PARVEZ

I've been driving twelve, fourteen hours non-stop. Many times
I've gone through the red light. Everywhere I am hurting. It is
hell on wheels.

FARID

Don't do it for me.

PARVEZ

Who else to do it for?

(FARID *puts him down and then turns and continues up the street.*)

Farid . . . ?

(PARVEZ *turns back.* MINOO *has gone. His clean shoes stand in the
middle of the hall.*)

INT. FARID'S BEDROOM. DAY

PARVEZ *surveys Farid's almost bare room. Even last night's boxes have gone, and the shelves are practically bare. On the walls are the marks of removed posters and pictures.*

He sees, sticking out from under the bed, the handle of a cricket bat. He pulls it out. On it are the signatures of a triumphant Pakistani cricket team captained by Imran Khan.

Cut to: In a drawer he finds an airline ticket – which he examines.

Cut to: As he goes, PARVEZ *picks up a discarded folder full of photographs of Farid, which he has had professionally taken to get modelling work.*

Next to it is a piece of crumpled-up paper which PARVEZ *tosses in the air and hits across the room at the door, just as* MINOO *comes in, surprising him.*

> MINOO
>
> You know how you complain when your food goes cold.
> (*As he follows her to the door he picks up the crumpled piece of paper. It is a signed picture of* MADELAINE *and* FARID *– taken during the opening scene – with lipstick kisses on it and the words: 'Love you always, handsome.'*)

INT. HOUSE. DAY

He goes downstairs, examining the picture, and is about to speak to MINOO, *but sees she is on the phone, at the bottom of the stairs.*

> MINOO
>
> There is someone calling you. A . . . shit.

> PARVEZ
>
> Shh . . . Minoo!
> (*He takes the receiver. Realizes who it is.*)
> Ah, Herr, Mr Schitz, coming, coming, directly on call, immediate service.

EXT. DISUSED VICTORIAN MILL COMPLEX. DAY

PARVEZ *drives up to the mill gates with the* GERMAN – *Schitz – where a group of suited Asian and white businessmen are waiting, holding briefcases.*

SCHITZ

(*As he gets out*)
One hour.
(PARVEZ *watches* SCHITZ *being received deferentially by the businessmen.*

PARVEZ *drives off fast – the crumpled photograph of* MADELAINE *and* FARID *on the dashboard in front of him.*)

INT. BANK. DAY

A big imposing place.
PARVEZ *walks quickly through the – mostly white – queue, embarrassed but determined, and in a hurry.*

PARVEZ

Sorry, sorry. Urgent personal matter.
(*He stops and stares at the official he's seeking –* MADELAINE. *She's pretty, but thin and fragile looking.*)

PARVEZ

Is that Madelaine? Miss Fingerhut.
(*She looks up at him and nods.*)
Farid's dad – Parvez and all.

MADELAINE

(*To customer*)
Excuse me.
(*Now* PARVEZ *is there he doesn't quite know what to say.*)

PARVEZ

Food is waiting anytime. Why not come Sunday, eh?

MADELAINE

We've packed up.

PARVEZ

Engagement is off?

MADELAINE

He didn't tell you?

PARVEZ

Suddenly you don't like my boy?

MADELAINE

He wanted to start again, with new friends.

PARVEZ

What type of friends?

MADELAINE

I wanted to meet them. Didn't want to be narrow like some
folks round here. But they wouldn't –

PARVEZ

What?

MADELAINE

Meet women.

PARVEZ

Everyone wants to meet women, surely!

MADELAINE

I thought you were arranging a marriage for him? A month ago
he took me out to tell me.

PARVEZ

But all this time I have been preparing party!

MADELAINE

He wanted someone he had more in common with. He has
become inflexible.
(*She shakes her head. Behind* PARVEZ *people are complaining.*)
I have been ill.

PARVEZ

I will break open his face until he obeys!
(*Thinks.*)
Best thing – I will discuss with your father.

MADELAINE

You don't know anything, do you?
(*Parvez looks at her.* MADELAINE *is reluctant to repeat the slur.*)

Farid told my father he was the only pig he'd ever wanted to eat.

(PARVEZ *looks at her in horror.*)

EXT. WEAVING SHED. DAY

PARVEZ *drives fast up to the gates only to find the area deserted. Annoyed by missing his appointment he gets out of the cab and runs around the deserted buildings in the hope of finding* SCHITZ. *The mill is vast and his footsteps echo around the massive silent buildings.*

   PARVEZ *notices a door has been left unlocked. He enters.*

INT. WEAVING SHED. DAY

PARVEZ *peers around the dark cavern of the shed, empty except for a few odd bits of broken machinery.*

   As he is about to go outside again SCHITZ's *voice rings out. He is standing outside a cabin on a platform some twenty feet off the floor.*

                              SCHITZ
We should have a party here.

(PARVEZ *looks around, confused, for the source of the voice, and makes his way towards* SCHITZ *until he is standing at the foot of the ladder leading to the cabin.*

                              PARVEZ
Mr Schitz, here I had my first job in England. Fizzy and I. Five years double shift, seven day a week. They wouldn't put me in the team.

                              SCHITZ
(*Laughs.*)
I wouldn't put you in the management team either.

                              PARVEZ
Cricket team. We were the best players. I could spin a little.
(*He trots across the floor and illustrates how he could bowl. The* SCHITZ *laughs.*)
What business are you doing here?

SCHITZ

Out of town shopping. Everything under one roof.

PARVEZ

The land and the labour is cheap, eh?

SCHITZ

Like the women. Remind me – what is the name of the one you recommended?

PARVEZ

Bettina.

SCHITZ

Tried her yourself?

PARVEZ

Sir, I only joke with them and all.

SCHITZ

I want to see her. Where do you boys hang out?

PARVEZ

Not nice place, sir –

SCHITZ

Let's go, little man. Instruct her to be there. And tell her to wear boots.
(*Sings*)
Spanish boots of Spanish leather.

EXT. ROUGH PUB. DAY

PARVEZ *follows the striding* SCHITZ *up to the pub. Several taxis are parked outside.*

INT. ROUGH PUB

This is a rough and noisy place frequented by prostitutes, taxi-drivers, local lads, drug dealers.
   As PARVEZ *crosses the pub a fellow* DRIVER *addresses him.*

DRIVER

Getting sociable at last, Parvez, eh?

PARVEZ

Working as usual, yaar.

SCHITZ

These are all your colleagues?

PARVEZ

Sir, a lot of these drivers are very low-class types. They can hardly speak English.

SCHITZ

You're not a snob are you, Parvez?

PARVEZ

The 'gentleman' is my code.

SCHITZ

And it stops you enjoying women?

PARVEZ

There is respect, sir, but not degradation.

SCHITZ

Respect is no substitute for pleasure. What of life do you enjoy then?
(PARVEZ *looks puzzled.*)
Your family?
(PARVEZ *nods unconvincingly.*)
I left mine.

PARVEZ

That's not a very nice thing, sir.

SCHITZ

What do you know about it?

Cut to: BETTINA *walks in.*

PARVEZ

There, sir.
(SCHITZ *looks at her approvingly.*)

SCHITZ

(*To* PARVEZ)
We boys are going to start to enjoy ourselves.
(*She comes over and stands by the table.*)

PARVEZ

Bettina.
(SCHITZ *gets up and kisses her hand. The other prostitutes and drivers watch with some interest.*)

SCHITZ

Couldn't you just kiss every part of her?

BETTINA

(*To* PARVEZ *of* SCHITZ, *with considerable charm*)
Couldn't you just kick every part of *him*?
(PARVEZ *looks nervous.* SCHITZ *laughs, then turns to the barman and gives him a twenty-pound note.*)

SCHITZ

Get her a drink!
(*To* BETTINA)
Have some lunch.
(*To* PARVEZ)
Good. Very good. Let's go.
(*He heads for the door. Bewildered,* PARVEZ *follows, shrugging apologetically to* BETTINA. *She snatches the twenty-pound note from the barman and pockets it.*)

EXT. TAXI OUTSIDE PROSTITUTE'S HOUSE/STREET. NIGHT

PARVEZ *pulls up outside the house.* BETTINA *gets in.*
    As they drive away they're startled by a drug-addict PROSTITUTE *jumping out and banging on the window.*

PROSTITUTE

Bastard, bastard, giving her a lift! Bettina always gets her ride, does she? What about me!
(PARVEZ *accelerates.* BETTINA *turns and watches the woman.*)

PARVEZ

She wanted a ride but didn't have no money.

BETTINA

All her money goes into her arm. She even sold her floorboards. You didn't buy any did you? They were riddled – like her.

PARVEZ

(*Alarmed*)
Is that what drug types do?
(*She looks at him.*)

INT. PARVEZ'S PARKED CAB. NIGHT

PARVEZ *has parked the car with a view over the moors or hillside. Over the radio we hear the car* CONTROLLER *calling for* PARVEZ, *who turns down the volume.*

We see the concentrating faces of PARVEZ *and* BETTINA, *and her hand – its rings and bracelets – as she sketches a joint, various pills, a pile of coke, etc.*

BETTINA

(*Gently*)
Look out for sweats, mood changes, frequent visits to the bog. Also, the eyes. Are they big or small, bloodshot, tired . . . vacant. And his arms –
(PARVEZ *is listening carefully and nodding. He looks down at Bettina's legs; her coat has come open, her underwear is exposed. He is stirred.*

BETTINA *notices him looking at her. She passes the piece of paper to him. There is an intimate moment between them as they regard one another.*)

PARVEZ

It's better the other drivers don't know this. They are envious of Farid winning the prizes. But you have always seen what I am so concerned about.

BETTINA

You talk about Farid a lot. And you like to hear about my daughters. The other drivers like to pretend they don't have families.

PARVEZ

He used to love his clothes. At weekends he worked in those
fashion shops. I've never known a boy with such enthusiasm
for ironing. I was worried he'd gone homo. I told you, he did
some modelling. In London they wanted him. I thought –
anything he wants he can do. Now he has become – I never
before cursed the day I brought us to this country.

EXT. PARVEZ'S HOUSE. DAY

PARVEZ *arrives outside his house to see* FARID *putting a box full of his
things into the boot of a friend's car before going back into the house.*
PARVEZ *gets out of the cab and, giving the driver a perfunctory nod, goes
in.*

INT. PARVEZ'S HOUSE. DAY

As PARVEZ *enters he sees serious* FARID, *carrying a cardboard box under
his arm, coming downstairs and making for the front door.*

PARVEZ

Why are you getting rid of those things? Farid!

Cut to: PARVEZ *is consulting Bettina's piece of paper.*

Cut to: PARVEZ *follows* FARID. *When he catches up with him, he takes the
box from him and puts it down. While holding him,* PARVEZ *looks into his
eyes.* MINOO *comes out of another room.*

PARVEZ

Put light on, Minoo.
She does so. PARVEZ *gets closer. Then he takes Farid's hand and
pushes up his sleeve.* FARID *gives in, leaning back against the wall
and letting him do it, staring sardonically into his father's eyes.*
     PARVEZ *glances mechanically at Farid's arm, not really knowing
what to look for.* FARID *slowly rolls down his sleeve and does up the
buttons.*

FARID

I can always tell when you've been reading the *Daily Express*.

EXT. PARVEZ'S HOUSE

FARID *goes out of the front door to a waiting car into which he puts the box before heading back to his room.* PARVEZ *gets his breath back and continues to follow him.*

FARID'S ROOM

                         PARVEZ
Farid, please, do me the credit here, yaar, tell me something!
Why make me into the fool?
(MINOO *is packing the remaining discarded items into another box and generally helping to clear out the room.*
   As FARID *passes him,* PARVEZ *tries another tone.*)
Madelaine not coming over tonight? Why not?
(*His blood pressure is rising.*)
That's what I'm asking here.
(FARID *shakes his head as he walks past.*)

                         PARVEZ
Where are you going?

                         FARID
To see Asad.

                         MINOO
I'll get your coat.

                         PARVEZ
Playing squash?
(FARID *shakes his head.*)
Have you got rid of the racket I bought?
(*He and* FARID *look at one another. Pause.*)
I worked my arse to pay for that – overtime!

                         MINOO
(*Standing at the door*)
All the time you shout and swear! That's why no one speaks
here! Let him go, you useless –!

                         PARVEZ
Useless? Who earns the money!

MINOO

I don't know what games you play out there in the mud, but it's
practically nothing now –

PARVEZ

Who spends it!

MINOO

There's nothing to spend after all these years! Look at Fizzy.
His wife went on a cruise.

PARVEZ

Ex-wife. All you do is send my money to your lazy relatives!
What are they eating there – diamonds?

MINOO

I wish I were with them.

PARVEZ

Go then!
(*To* FARID, *desperate to retrieve the subject.*)
I met Madelaine.
(FARID *looks at* MINOO. *The mood changes.*)
Yes! What about the engagement, and this other marriage I am
arranging, eh?

FARID

I am intending to marry.
(MINOO *nods approvingly.*)

PARVEZ

Yes, Madelaine is so nice. Minoo has written to all three people
she knows in Lahore, announcing.

FARID

I have asked trusted people for a suitable girl.

PARVEZ

You go to them secretly when I have hand-picked Miss
Fingerhut!
(*Pause.*)
You used to kiss her?

MINOO

Stop!

PARVEZ

Is it wrong to find out if our son is normal, eh?

MINOO

Normal is not perverted like in your mind.

PARVEZ

Keep quiet!

FARID

(*Intervening*)
You might not have noticed – Madelaine is so different.

PARVEZ

How?

FARID

Can you put keema with strawberries?
(*Surprised by this,* PARVEZ *moves closer to his son who hesitatingly continues.*)
In the end our cultures . . . they cannot be mixed.

PARVEZ

Everything is mingling already together, this thing and the other!

FARID

Some of us are wanting something more besides muddle.

PARVEZ

What?

FARID

Belief, purity, belonging to the past.
(*Beat*)
I won't bring up my children in this country.

PARVEZ

What types are these new friends?
(MINOO *goes to* PARVEZ. *She is trying to get him out of the room.*)

MINOO

They are not like the bad English stealing and drugging.

PARVEZ

How do *you* know?

MINOO

The mothers tell me.
(PARVEZ *looks at them both in exasperation as she ushers him out of the room.*)

PARVEZ

How long have you known this?
(*She looks at him.*)
I am made into ignoramus. Why?

MINOO

He has had many things to take in. What world are you living in? You don't notice us.

PARVEZ

(*Devastated*)
I am nowhere else. After everything, don't I satisfy you?

MINOO

It is you . . . never satisfied with what we do.
(*Minoo looks at him.*
   A desperate PARVEZ *watches* FARID, *who has moved towards the door, having picked up the last box.*)

PARVEZ'S HOUSE LIVING ROOM. DAY

PARVEZ *in the front room with a drink, standing at the window watching* FARID *get into a car driven by one of the young acolytes we will see later.*

INT. CELLAR IN PARVEZ'S HOUSE. DAY

PARVEZ *sits in the cellar – this is his private domain – surrounded by wine and beer-making kits, tools, old newspapers and records.*
   He takes the piece of paper on which BETTINA *has written the names of the drugs, and drawn pictures of different kinds of pills, a joint, etc., and looks at it. Then he screws it up and places it beside the screwed-up picture of* MADELAINE.

PARVEZ *hears* FARID *enter the house and go up to his room.*

PARVEZ *is listening to Louis Armstrong, but after a short time he becomes aware of a new sound. He switches the record off and listens.*

INT. THE STAIRWELL OF PARVEZ'S HOUSE. DAY

PARVEZ *emerges from the cellar and heads upstairs, following the sound.*

INT. OUTSIDE FARID'S BEDROOM. DAY

Farid's bedroom door is slightly ajar and through the crack PARVEZ *sees his son praying.*

On the wall has appeared a gilt framed picture of the Kaaba.

INT./EXT. CAB. NIGHT

PARVEZ *driving. Parvez's face, as he attempts to take in what has befallen him.*

The illuminated 'Taxi' sign on the roof has developed a fault and flickers on and off. PARVEZ *thumps the ceiling occasionally to try and make it work properly.*

INT. /EXT. PROSTITUTES' STREET. NIGHT

He enters the 'street of prostitutes' and slows down beside the women. He speaks to a young prostitute – MARGOT.

> PARVEZ
> Hey, Margot, seen Bettina?

> MARGOT
> Not tonight.

> PARVEZ
> (*To another woman*)
> Where is she?

> WOMAN
> She's been lucky.
> (*The Controller's voice comes on the radio.*)

CONTROLLER

Your foreigner friend's asking for only you at the Atlantic.
(*In Punjabi, subtitled*)
He's giving me a hard time. Please hurry . . . get moving.
(PARVEZ *hurriedly turns the car round.*)

EXT./INT. HOTEL. LATER THAT NIGHT

PARVEZ *has parked outside* SCHITZ's *hotel.*

INT. HOTEL

Already late, he hurries in, out of breath, straightening his tie, brushing his hair. SCHITZ *is at the desk, talking to the concierge. He turns and sees* PARVEZ.

PARVEZ

Sorry, sorry, four minutes only held up.

SCHITZ

(*Cheerfully*)
Tonight, little man, we are accompanied.
(PARVEZ *doesn't quite understand* SCHITZ. *He turns away and sees a smartly dressed woman coming down the stairs.*)
She's wearing the finest cotton, cashmere, satin and silk.
Don't you just love the sound of silk on skin. Her boots are shining. Puss in Boots I'm calling her now.
(PARVEZ *looks at her again, and wonders why she's smiling at him. He recognizes* BETTINA, *wearing a wig.*

Pulling himself together, PARVEZ *hurries away to hold the door for them.*

There in the lobby SCHITZ *looks* BETTINA *over, brushes her coat, adjusts her hair, before walking out with her.* PARVEZ *then rushes to the car to hold open the doors.*

As they get in:)

BETTINA

(*Whispers to* PARVEZ)
Looks like I've got the 'shits'.
(*She imitates his accent*)
We are going to look around the place, Puss in Boots.

(SCHITZ *overhears this and is amused.*)

INT. CAR. EVENING

A hand going up a skirt to pinch a plump thigh.
    PARVEZ *driving;* SCHITZ *in the back with his arm around* BETTINA.
PARVEZ *watches them in the rear-view mirror.*

> PARVEZ
> Why come to our town, sir?

> SCHITZ
> Ten years I worked in Munich, Lyon, Bologna. I wanted to try
> a strange and awful place where everything was new to me.

> BETTINA
> How is it?

> SCHITZ
> We will see. Tonight, we will experience some Northern
> English culture?

> BETTINA
> We'll be in bed by nine, then.

> SCHITZ
> Come along, Parvez, you join us.

> PARVEZ
> Oh no, sir.

> SCHITZ
> I book you for the whole evening, little man.

> BETTINA
> That's right, you've got no choice.

INT. CLUB. EVENING

SCHITZ, BETTINA *and* PARVEZ *go down the stairs of the club. One
bouncer stares lasciviously at* BETTINA. *The other bouncer attempts to
bar Parvez's way.*

SCHITZ

He looks after me.
(*He slips the bouncer some money.*)
Come, friends.

INT. CLUB. EVENING

The open mouth of a comedian.

The smoky club is packed with raucous drinking men and women. On stage a fat vulgar comedian is telling a stream of coarse jokes – lesbians, mothers-in-law, etc.

BETTINA, SCHITZ *and* PARVEZ *are sitting together at a table. Clearly the* SCHITZ *can't follow the comedian and he leans over* BETTINA.

SCHITZ

Explain me his gist!
(BETTINA *attempts to explain.* SCHITZ *throws his head back and laughs.*

PARVEZ *isn't paying much attention to the comedian.*

While SCHITZ *talks into one of Bettina's ears, asking her to explain what is going on – and she attempts some kind of translation –* PARVEZ *talks into the other.*)

PARVEZ

. . . Bettina, you've no idea how relieved I am that the weight of drugs has gone from my head. But why has he never discussed this new direction with me?

BETTINA

(*Touching him*)
We all need something to hold on to, don't we?
(PARVEZ *considers this.*)
You must have it out with him.

Cut to: Suddenly the spotlight is on Parvez's face, and the comedian is telling Paki, Rushdie and Muslim jokes. PARVEZ *realizes everyone is turning to look at him, laughing and jeering. He is the only brown face there. He looks at the hostile faces, confused.*

As the comedian addresses him directly SCHITZ *patronizingly puts his arm around* PARVEZ. BETTINA *refuses to laugh and looks disgusted.*

At the next table a white man has picked up a bread roll and is about to lob it at PARVEZ. BETTINA *throws a glass of beer over him. Everyone freezes. The bouncers move towards them.*

The spotlight moves from Parvez's face, the comedian starts on another joke and the atmosphere changes.

BETTINA *gets up. She takes Parvez's arm and is about to walk out.*

BETTINA

(*To* SCHITZ)
Coming?

SCHITZ

(*Getting up*)
I like a plucky girl.
(*He ushers* PARVEZ *and* BETTINA *out past the bouncers who stand between them and the crowd. As they go he looks at the hostile faces around them.*)
And this is the celebrated Northern culture?

EXT. OUTSIDE PUB. NIGHT

PARVEZ, BETTINA *and* SCHITZ *hurry across the car park to the car. Rough white men stand at the back-door of the club watching them, whistling and jeering.* SCHITZ *enjoys the exhilaration.*

SCHITZ

I will inform the police of this disgust.

BETTINA

They were sitting at the next table.
(*To* PARVEZ)
You all right?

INT. CAR. NIGHT

PARVEZ *drives off as fast as he can, looking around to see if they've been pursued.*

INT. HOTEL CORRIDOR. NIGHT

A lift door opens on Parvez's face. For a moment he stands there unaware of where he is.

Then he struggles up the hotel corridor with bottles of champagne, beer and water, his arms full of crisps and cigarettes.
Pushes the door and goes in.

INT. HOTEL ROOM. NIGHT

PARVEZ *brings the stuff into the room and looks for a place to put it.*
Music is playing.
BETTINA *has one foot up on the table, with her dress pulled up, her boot on.*

SCHITZ
(*To* PARVEZ, *checking the bottles*)
Ah, good.
(*The* GERMAN *sees* PARVEZ *glancing at* BETTINA *and smiles, before resuming cutting out a few lines of coke.*)

SCHITZ
Now bring here the dark younger pussy I saw just now on the corner.

PARVEZ
Margot? What for?

SCHITZ
To sing to me.

PARVEZ
Can't Bettina sing?

SCHITZ
Her voice is too deep.

BETTINA
Your pockets better be.

SCHITZ
Here Puss, Puss, Puss.
(*She laughs.*)

PARVEZ
Behind the wheel is my racket.

SCHITZ

Haven't the people here got no ambition? The Puss want to
work, but I thought you immigrants were busy too.

PARVEZ

Sir, where has it got us, and how many of us are happy here?

SCHITZ

I feel sorry for you people, I really do.
(SCHITZ *looks at him, turns up the music and nods at* BETTINA.
She comes over and snorts her line. PARVEZ *looks very uncertain; he
isn't sure what they're doing.* SCHITZ *indicates that* PARVEZ
should try. PARVEZ *looks at* BETTINA.)

PARVEZ

What is it?

BETTINA

It's good coke.

PARVEZ

A drug?

SCHITZ

Thank God there's something good in this town.

BETTINA

(*To* SCHITZ)
Not since you arrived.
(*Shrugs; to* PARVEZ)
After a certain age there's no point in saying no to everything.
(PARVEZ *looks confused.* BETTINA *smiles and goes into the
bathroom.*

    SCHITZ *indicates for* PARVEZ *to open the champagne – three
glasses. Then he joins him across the room, out of Bettina's earshot,
and speaks to him in a low voice.*)

SCHITZ

For you there's a good drink.
(*He gives him some money.* PARVEZ *pockets it gratefully.*)
Enjoy yourself with Bettina when I've finished. I see how you
look at her. She is delicate, isn't she? How all the parts of
women sing out.

(*Pause.*)
Run along, little man, and bring the dark beauty for double
fun! The quality of pussy is not strained, it falleth from street
corners like sweet rain.
(*Beat.*)
My English is even better than yours!
(*He gives* PARVEZ *more money. Then his towel slips.* SCHITZ
*ostentatiously removes it and we see he is wearing underneath a pair
of silk French knickers. As* PARVEZ *looks at him in surprise,*
SCHITZ *winks and whistles a happy German song, if there is one.*)

Cut to: At the door PARVEZ *turns and sees* BETTINA *come out of the
bathroom, wearing her long overcoat, stockings, boots.* SCHITZ *goes to her,
wiggling his arse.*

   PARVEZ *stands for a moment looking at them, before forcing himself to
get out.*

EXT. STREET OF PROSTITUTES. NIGHT

PARVEZ *jumps out of his car near the young black prostitute,* MARGOT,
who is just about to get into another car.

                          PARVEZ
Can you sing?

                          MARGOT
That's one thing no one's asked me to do.

                          PARVEZ
Get in – Bettina waiting. Good job.
(*She first has to get rid of the first, now rather angry, driver, who
gesticulates violently at* PARVEZ, *and gets into Parvez's car.*)

                          MARGOT
I didn't know you –

                          PARVEZ
Favour only.

                          MARGOT
Long as the ponces don't find out.
(PARVEZ *looks nervously at her. She laughs.*)

EXT. STREET OUTSIDE HOTEL. NIGHT

PARVEZ *under a lamp-post attempting to mend the 'Taxi' light on the roof of his car. He reaches in through the window and throws the switch.*

The light flickers. PARVEZ *thumps the fitting: sparks fly, there's a bang, the light dies.*

He steps back and looks up at the lighted windows of the hotel, wondering what is going on in there.

Cut to: BETTINA *and* MARGOT *skip out of the hotel.* MARGOT *sticks her head in the cab window and ruffles Parvez's hair.*

> MARGOT
> Thanks for the work, Parvez.
> (*To* BETTINA)
> Coming?
> (BETTINA *shakes her head.* MARGOT *nods approvingly and walks off in the other direction.*)

Cut to: In the cab BETTINA *waves money at* PARVEZ.

> BETTINA
> We are doing very well in Europe. I am all for the Union. Next stop Maastricht!

EXT. OUTSIDE A ROW OF HOUSES. NIGHT

PARVEZ *has parked.* BETTINA *is getting out.*

> BETTINA
> Thanks for helping me out.
> (*He nods. On his face as he watches her go into the house.*)

Cut to: He is about to drive away. Suddenly he changes his mind, gets out and hurries after her. Then he is standing in front of the row of houses, unsure of which is hers.

> PARVEZ
> (*Shouts*)
> Bettina! Bettina!
> (*A moment on his face as he waits.*)

INT. BETTINA'S HOUSE. EARLY MORNING

As BETTINA *prepares food in the kitchen* PARVEZ *is in the living
room, looking around, more nervous and uncertain than he is in
the cab.*

INT. BETTINA'S LIVING ROOM. EARLY MORNING

BETTINA *is not well-off, but the small flat is neat and cosy. Photographs
of her children on the sideboard; ornaments and knick-knacks
everywhere.*

   *For the first time we see her without wig or make-up. She wears jeans
and a sweatshirt. Classical music is playing.*

   PARVEZ *stands at the door watching her, looking at her hands, face, as
she works, hums and sings a little.*

> PARVEZ
> We were only little kids when we came. And the second we
> stepped from the boat we never stopped working for our
> families here. Over twenty-five years passed away. I never saw
> my mother's face again! How I miss them, my parents, and
> they've been dead all this time! What I would give to see their
> faces now, for just one minute! But my father was very cruel,
> and I have tried to love the boy . . .
> (*Tearfully he turns away.*)

Cut to: Later. They are eating breakfast together.

> Thing is, my father used to send me for instruction with the
> Maulvi – the religious man. But the teacher had this bloody
> funny effect; whenever he started to speak or read I would fall
> dead asleep – bang!
> (PARVEZ *illustrates this narcoleptic state, with snores, impersonating
> also the Maulvi's monotonous voice.*)
> Naturally I also annoyed him by asking why my best friend, a
> Hindu, would go to Kaffir hell when he was such a good chap.
> His eyes would bulge fully out.
> (*He illustrates.*)
> So he would clip my arms and legs with a cane – like this. Tuck,
> tuck – until the blood came!

(PARVEZ *illustrates.*)

But it took no effect. Still I would drop off. He selected another solution.

BETTINA

Yes?

PARVEZ

He took a piece of string and tied it from the ceiling to my hair – here. When I dropped off I would wake up – like thus! (*His head starts up.*)

After such treatment I said goodbye permanently to the next life and said hello to – to work.

BETTINA

Who can blame the young for believing in something beside money? They are puzzled why a few people have everything and the poor must sell their bodies. It is positive, in some ways.

(*But* PARVEZ *looks gloomy.*)

There is one thing you can try. Give him a better philosophy.

PARVEZ

What type?

BETTINA

How do you feel about things? The purpose of life, and all that. How should we treat each other?

PARVEZ

Good, I think. Where possible. But I cannot explain the origin of the universe.

BETTINA

Leave that till later.

INT. BETTINA'S HOUSE, HALLWAY. MORNING

A little later. BETTINA *and* PARVEZ *at the door.*

PARVEZ

I am full. See you tomorrow.

BETTINA

Call me Sandra – when we are alone.

PARVEZ

That is the password, eh? To you.
(*She kisses him on the cheek and then on the mouth. He is surprised.*)

BETTINA

I don't know when I last kissed a man. Sorry. Do you mind?

INT./EXT. CAR/STREET. MORNING

PARVEZ *drives through the deserted streets – a strange, unreal*
atmosphere – listening to music on the radio, touching his face with
his hand, as if to feel her kiss on him.
    We see an old bearded Pakistani sitting in the back. They pass the
young prostitute, MARGOT, *on the street – running towards a car – and*
the old man spits and curses in Urdu.
    PARVEZ *picks up Bettina's comb from the dashboard and puts it to his*
face.

BEDROOM. PARVEZ'S HOUSE. MORNING

PARVEZ *is coming out of his bedroom, unshaven, with his hair standing*
up. (In bed he wears salwar kamiz.)

INT. HALL. PARVEZ'S HOUSE. MORNING

He sees, further down the hall, MINOO, *with a tray of drinks and snacks*
going into Farid's room – backwards with her head bowed and covered.
    She looks up and sees PARVEZ.

PARVEZ

Is he still home?

MINOO

Farid is busy.
(PARVEZ *flinches with annoyance, moves past her and goes to the*
door. Without knocking he goes into Farid's room.)

INT. LIVING ROOM. PARVEZ'S HOUSE. MORNING

Five bearded earnest young men in white salwar are sitting in a circle on the floor. In the centre is a tablecloth with tea and biscuits on it. Some of the men lie back; one smokes a pipe. Another is in a wheelchair.

They're reading aloud passages from the Koran and discussing their meaning and relevance. PARVEZ *watches this.*

He murmurs some words from the Koran.

He indicates to FARID. *At first* FARID *tries to ignore him.* PARVEZ *irritably repeats his gesture.*

> PARVEZ
>
> I've informed Fizzy we're going tonight to his place.

> FARID
>
> Tonight there is a meeting for some friends.

> PARVEZ
>
> Isn't it written that you will respect your father?
> (FARID *gives a little nod of reluctant assent.* PARVEZ *is pleased with this move.*)

Cut to: Outside PARVEZ *stands there a moment, ear at the door, listening to the murmuring voices.*

EXT. STREET. DAY

In his car PARVEZ *has been waiting in a nearby street for the group to leave the house. Some of them split off, but he follows the main group, with* FARID.

EXT. STREET OUTSIDE MOSQUE. DAY

They have arrived, with PARVEZ *following, at the mosque. A group of young men, in salwar kamiz, have gathered outside.*

FARID has just joined them. They shake hands, embrace and greet each other enthusiastically, before going in.

EXT./INT. MOSQUE. DAY

PARVEZ, *following his son, hurries into the entrance of the mosque. It's been so long since he's done this that he forgets to remove his shoes.*

A man takes Parvez's arm and points down at his feet. PARVEZ *takes off his shoes and stands holding them in holed socks, looking around at the numerous faces and different types of people, concealing himself behind a pillar.*

Farid's group are entering a room at the far end of the mosque, but as they go in there is an altercation with a older group of men, who try to prevent them going in. Raised voices.

PARVEZ *addresses a man in a Post Office uniform.*

> PARVEZ
>
> What's doing here?

> MAN
>
> These boys are not welcome. They are always arguing with the elders. They think everyone but them is corrupt and foolish.

> PARVEZ
>
> What do they want?

> MAN
>
> They are always fighting for radical actions on many subjects. It is irritating us all here, yaar. But they have something these young people – they're not afraid of the truth. They stand up for things. We never did that.
>
> (*The boys finally gain access to the room, and go in.*
>
> PARVEZ *stands there alone. For a moment he looks around and considers praying, but decides not to. And leaves.*)

INT. PARVEZ IN HIS CUBBY HOLE. EVENING

With a shaking hand, PARVEZ *takes one of his favourite records out of its sleeve and puts it on the deck.*

INT. CUBBY HOLE DOOR. PARVEZ'S HOUSE. EVENING

He sticks his head around the door and sees FARID *has come downstairs.*

INT. CUBBY HOLE. PARVEZ'S HOUSE. EVENING

PARVEZ *puts the record on as* FARID *comes past the door.*

PARVEZ *has dressed up, in an old suit and dismal tie, and has combed his hair. He is nervous and drinking to give himself courage.*

PARVEZ

(*Doing a little dance*)

I'll tape this for you.

(*Pause.*)

Or did you sell the player?

(*As* PARVEZ *takes a last swig of his drink, Farid leaves.*

MINOO, *who has obviously been hovering, goes to* PARVEZ *hopefully. He smiles at her, and burps.*)

MINOO

But you are drinking already!

(*He pushes past her.*)

I'll be waiting. Papu, I have such hopes for this evening.

(*She watches him go.*)

EXT./INT. FIZZY'S RESTAURANT. NIGHT

As FARID *and* PARVEZ *walk up to and enter the restaurant* PARVEZ *straightens his tie and looks critically at* FARID, *as if he were a schoolboy; he even reaches out and attempts to brush his hair.* FARID *moves away in annoyance.*

PARVEZ

It has been so long since we had a real enjoyable chatterbox!

(*Indicates front of restaurant*)

What a magnificent joint! Bloody old Fizzy has done good.

INT. FIZZY'S RESTAURANT. NIGHT

As they go in:

FIZZY

(*Approaching them with two glasses of champagne*)

What a handsome big man he has grown into! Is he good?

(FARID *waves away the champagne as* PARVEZ *drinks his.*)

PARVEZ

(*into Fizzy's ear*)

Lately he has been having some funny ideas we must straighten out!

FIZZY

And with engagement party coming up. Come – see the room.
(PARVEZ *and* FARID *are reluctant to move.*)

INT. FUNCTION ROOM. NIGHT

FIZZY, *smoking a cigar and sipping champagne, has been, once more,
pointing out the qualities of the room.*

FIZZY

And over there the beautiful couple will come in, and here we
can arrange for . . .
(PARVEZ *and* FARID *stand there, unable to look at each other or
speak. Fizzy's flow isn't stemmed by their embarrassment.*)

PARVEZ

(*Whispers*)
Have you really made up your mind about this thing.

FARID

She is absolutely not right for me. But perhaps for you . . .

PARVEZ

You are becoming very disrespectful. I can still clip your ear.
(FIZZY *turns and sees them arguing.*)

INT. KITCHEN. NIGHT

FIZZY *has taken* PARVEZ *and* FARID *into the kitchen, introduced him to
the chef and is proudly showing them the kitchen equipment.*
  *The chef stuffs a big white napkin into Parvez's collar: it remains there
until they leave the restaurant. Meanwhile the chef has* PARVEZ *try all the
dishes, holding the spoon to his mouth.*

FIZZY

Many thanks, yaar, for the German. Those Krauts certainly
stuff themselves up.
(*As the chef leads him around the kitchen* PARVEZ *swoons
enthusiastically at each mouthful, until he is practically fainting in
appreciation.*)

PARVEZ

Again tasty! Extra tasty! More tasty!

(FIZZY *goes to* FARID.)

FIZZY

On our last day there his mother made me promise to look after him. You must cherish your father.

FARID

Fizzy, uncle, haven't we lost our way here?

FIZZY

What? Some of us are doing real good.

FARID

Even so, we lack something inside.

FIZZY

Leave that crap to the old men, yaar. We are getting on.
(PARVEZ *looks over at him.*)
(*To* FARID)
Good boy, eh?

INT. THE RESTAURANT. EVENING

PARVEZ *sits down opposite his son and indicates the restaurant, smiling at people at other tables.*

PARVEZ

(*Indicating the place*)
Bloody old Fizzy. But as your mother correctly confirms independently, he is greedy and all.
(FIZZY *comes over with two large glasses of whisky which he puts down in front of each of them.* PARVEZ *is a little embarrassed, since he imagines* FIZZY *might have overheard his last words.*)

FIZZY

Tonight you drink and eat as my guest!

PARVEZ

No. Fizzy –

FIZZY

Without a quibble! Wedding present, yaar!
(FIZZY *bows and leaves them.* PARVEZ *adjusts his napkin and takes a long drink of whisky.* FARID *pushes away his own glass.*)

PARVEZ

If I'd know it was free I would have missed lunch!
(*He leans forward and says confidently*)
I tell everyone, eat here and you'll never be constipated again!
(*The* WAITER *comes over with plates.*)

WAITER

We will bring a good selection.

PARVEZ

This is my only son.
(*To* FARID)
Have a beer with dad.
(FARID *shakes his head, and the* WAITER *goes.*)

FARID

Don't you know it's wrong to drink alcohol?
(FARID *is looking at him steadily.* PARVEZ *bangs his glass down on
the table and laughs dismissively.*)
It is forbidden. Gambling too.

PARVEZ

I am a man.

FARID

You have the choice, then, to do good or evil.

PARVEZ

I may be weak and foolish, but please inform me, am I really,
according to you, wicked?

FARID

If you break the law as stated then how can wickedness not
follow? You eat the pig. In the house.

PARVEZ

A bacon butty? Tasty! You loved them too.

FARID

(*A little shiftily*)
Perhaps. I didn't force mother to eat it.

PARVEZ

(*Laughs*)
Force – her lips were twitching!
(*Pause.*)
In the days of the Prophet the pig was contaminated meat.
Farid, this purity interest. What is it about?

FARID

Who in this country could not want purity?
(*A* WAITER *brings a tray of various foods.* PARVEZ *looks at it with enthusiasm.*)

PARVEZ

Good man!
(*To* FARID)
Try that. Or this! Delicious.
(*He leans towards* FARID *and says confidently*)
Seriously, these English, you'd be a fool to run them down –

FARID

I have been thinking seriously.

PARVEZ

Good.

FARID

They say integrate, but they live in pornography and filth, and
tell us how backward we are!

PARVEZ

There's no doubt, compared to us, they can have funny habits
and all –

FARID

A society soaked in sex –

PARVEZ

(*Eating*)
Not that I've benefited! Where do you think the drugs come
from? It is Rashid's relatives sending them, yaar! Anyhow, how
else can we belong here except by mixing up all together? They
accuse us of keeping with each other.

FARID

Yes!

PARVEZ

But I invite the English. Come – share my food! And all the years I've lived here, not one single Englishman has invited me to his house – apart from Fingerhut, who is a top-class gentleman! But still I make the effort.

FARID

You see, we have our own system. It is useless to grovel to the whites!

PARVEZ

Grovel!

FARID

It sickens me to see you lacking pride.

PARVEZ

Fill up for two days.

FARID

Thing is, you are too implicated in Western civilization.

PARVEZ

Implicated!
(*He stares at his son and burps. The* WAITER *is hovering by the table. To him*)
You hear what clever words my boy is using against me? Implicated!
(WAITER *goes.*)

FARID

Whatever we do here we will always be inferior. They will never accept us as like them. But I am not inferior! Don't they patronize and insult us? How many times have they beaten you?

PARVEZ

With my cricket bat I have always defended without fear!

FARID

How can you say they're not devils?

PARVEZ

Not everyone, I am saying! Farid, this is not the village but our home country, we have to get along. Tell me something useful, boy. Is it true you don't love Madelaine?

FARID

What is that kind of love? Here all the marriages last five minutes. Respect and devotion is better. Are you in love?

PARVEZ

I'm beginning to see what it is. There is curiosity. Fascination. The feeling that the other person is . . . more important than anyone else. And it is . . .

FARID

Lately you've become very introspective.

PARVEZ

I found something . . . an airline ticket, you know, in your room.

FARID

What were you doing in there?

PARVEZ

(*With a mouthful of food*)
Eh? A little dusting.
(FARID *can't help himself – he laughs. A moment of spontaneity.*)

FARID

Why snoop around?

PARVEZ

What is the ticket for?

FARID

Papa, I want you to do something for me.

PARVEZ

Have I ever refused you one thing?

FARID

Papa, there is a wise maulvi from Lahore. He is a good man
and we have invited him to offer us a little instruction. Can't he
stay a few days?

(*Without thinking,* PARVEZ *picks up his whisky and drinks, waving
his drink approvingly at a waiter.*)

PARVEZ

In our house?

FARID

(*Excessively polite*)
If you would give permission.
(FARID *sees* PARVEZ *give a little confused and perfunctory nod. The
waiters bring more food and drink. Parvez's mouth is messy with
food, and he drops keema and dall on to his trousers.*)

PARVEZ

That is what the money was for? You're not going anywhere?

FARID

(*Shaking his head*)
He can stay?

PARVEZ

(*Nods*)
Our house is open. Why haven't you told me about this
interest?

FARID

(*Shifty*)
The irreligious find belief difficult to comprehend. Those who
love the sacred are called fundamentalists, terrorists, fanatics.

PARVEZ

And this is why you've left Madelaine? Her father, Chief
Inspector Fingerhut of the police force –

FARID

(*Sighing*)
Papa –

PARVEZ

I don't want this anti-Fingerhut face!

FARID

But you are reminding me of something disgusting! Surely you grasped how ashamed I was, seeing you toadying to Fingerhut.
(PARVEZ *stares at him, a handful of chapati at his mouth.*)

FARID

The girl is okay. But Fingerhut . . . Do you think his men care about racial attacks? And couldn't you see how much he hated his daughter being with me, and how . . . repellent he found you? I never want to see those people again.
(PARVEZ *is in shock, drinking, shaking his head to clear his brain, and looking around the restaurant, as if for assistance. He is starting to get drunk.*)

PARVEZ

(*Watching* FARID)
All right. If this is reality, that I am disgusting, that I have never been a good man, and never done anything worthwhile, I must face it. After all, you have observed me for a long time.
(*Pause.*)
But tonight I am determined to get one good thing. Tell me that at least you are keeping up with your studies.

FARID

Papa, there are suffering men in prison who require guidance.

PARVEZ

What guidance? If they're inside they must be fools!

FARID

I have never met men more sincere and thirsty for the spirit. And accountancy . . . it is just capitalism and taking advantage. You can never succeed in it unless you go to the pub and meet women.
(PARVEZ *starts to yell. Customers look around at him. Waiters and* FIZZY *stand watching concernedly.*)

PARVEZ

Fool, you're beginning to irritate my arse! What's wrong with women!

FARID

Many lack belief and therefore reason. Papa, the final Message is a complete guidance –

PARVEZ

You donkey's dirty arse, this evening you have shown only one thing –

FARID

This is the true alternative to empty living from day to day . . .
. . . in the capitalist dominated world we are suffering from! I am telling you, the Jews and Christers will be routed! You have taken the wrong side!

PARVEZ

One thing, one thing I know –

FARID

Papa, please, it is not too late! I beg you to seek Allah's forgiveness for your mistakes!

PARVEZ

Please, boy, don't go too far with this thing!

FARID

No. It is you who have swallowed the white and Jewish propaganda that there is nothing to our lives but the empty accountancy of things . . . of things . . . for nothing . . . for nothing.

PARVEZ

I am swallowing nothing but brother Fizzy's dinner, and it will give me indigestion now.
(*By mistake he sweeps a dish from the table.*)
But a wasp has gone into your gullet!
(FIZZY *rushes over to see what the commotion is.*)

FIZZY

Mayor is sitting over there! Eat!

PARVEZ

I have lost my appetite! The boy is massacring my life!
(PARVEZ *is choking and distraught.*)

EXT. FIZZY'S RESTAURANT. NIGHT

FARID *is leading* PARVEZ *out.*

FIZZY

I've never seen him like this. A drinking taxi-driver is a bloody
fool.

FARID

Who gave him the alcohol?
(FIZZY *stares at* FARID. *Just then, they run into* SCHITZ *and*
BETTINA *coming in, arm-in-arm.*)

SCHITZ

Little man, you are everywhere!
(PARVEZ *is unable to stop looking at* BETTINA, *who smiles at him.*)

BETTINA

(*Indicating* FARID)
This is him.
(*She is about to put out her hand, but stops herself.*
   SCHITZ *addresses* PARVEZ.)

SCHITZ

I am organizing party, for business acquaintances. Your friend
here can fix food –

PARVEZ

Yes, yes.

SCHITZ

But I can leave the girls to you? Diversification, eh? Only the
best Puss in Boots, like Bettina, eh? Good, good . . .
(*As* SCHITZ *and* PARVEZ *talk,* BETTINA *and* FARID *are left
together.* BETTINA *is unsure whether to say anything. At last she
decides to do so.*)

                         BETTINA

Your father talks about you 'non-stop', as he puts it.
(FARID *smiles politely.*)
Your exams are going well?
FARID *nods a bit.*
What will you do later?

                          FARID

Something good.

                         BETTINA

I hope so.

                          FARID

And you?
(*She looks at him.*)
How do you know Dad?

                         BETTINA

I see him about.

                          FARID

What do you do?

                         BETTINA

I am in . . . industry.
(FARID *looks her up and down.* PARVEZ *has seen this. He takes
Farid's arm and leads him away.*)

Cut to: PARVEZ *turns and watches* SCHITZ *put his arm gently around
Bettina's waist and leads her down to the door of the restaurant.*

EXT. STREET. PARVEZ'S CAB. OUTSIDE RESTAURANT. EVENING

PARVEZ *is attempting, drunkenly to clamber into the driver's seat. He
slips and almost falls.* FARID *tries to manoeuvre him into the back.*
   FIZZY *and a waiter stand in the doorway of the restaurant, watching
with concern.*

                          FIZZY

(*Shouting to* PARVEZ)
Rear seat, yaar!

FARID

Yes, Papa, please –

PARVEZ

Don't pull! Haven't you destroyed me already?

FARID

Better not lose your licence too.
(FIZZY *runs down and helps manoeuvre the flailing* PARVEZ *into the back.*)

INT. CAR. NIGHT

By now PARVEZ *is in the back and* FARID *is driving.*

FARID

(*Into car radio*)
Papa's clocking off.

CONTROLLER

Passed any exams today, Farid?
(FARID *snaps the radio off.*)

PARVEZ

(*To* FARID)
You think you're a smart mister, but you are taking us wrong route!

FARID

I will show you something.

PARVEZ

Go to hell!
(FARID *smiles bitterly to himself – used to this. He drives in another direction.*)

Cut to: A few minutes later. Lying back in the car, PARVEZ *is talking, ignoring where they're going.*

I know what it is . . . you see, I haven't loved life here apart from – Farid, I have loved your company, as a baby, and as a boy. I would get out of bed only to look at your face. For you it was just growing up. For me the best of life itself.
(*Meanwhile* FARID *picks up, from the dashboard, a lipstick and comb*

belonging to BETTINA, *and looks curiously at them.* PARVEZ *sees this.*
FARID *throws them down and turns the car into a housing estate.*)

INT./EXT. CAR. CONTINUOUS TIME

FARID *drives into a rough part of a nearby run-down estate. Many of the*
houses are boarded up, the cars abandoned or burned out; a lawless
atmosphere.

A bunch of white and black kids are hanging out under the street lights,
watching one of the gang doing handbrake turns in a stolen car. They're a
wretched bunch, fighting and shoving each other around. Music from
someone's ghetto-blaster. This would be a part of town that PARVEZ
wouldn't know much about.

FARID *slows down and* PARVEZ *sits up to look out.*

PARVEZ

Where have you brought us?
(FARID *gets out.*)

PARVEZ

Farid!
(PARVEZ, *afraid, leans over the seat and pulls out his piece of wood.*
  Noticing FARID, *two older* LADS *approach him. Seeing they're*
friendly, PARVEZ *gets out, holding the piece of wood, and maintains*
himself upright by holding onto the roof.)

LAD

Hey, Farid, Farid. Not on the rides like your old man?
(FARID *shakes his head.* PARVEZ *is trying, drunkenly, to present*
himself respectably, and puts out his hand – transferring the piece of
wood clumsily to his other hand.
  As the LADS *greet him,* PARVEZ *is unable to prevent himself from*
retching and coughing. He eventually straightens up and takes some
deep breaths.)
What's he on?
(FARID *looks at* PARVEZ *in disgust.*)
(*To* FARID)
Sorted?

FARID

Got everything I need.

LAD

Lucky lad.

FARID

What you doing?

LAD

Starting fires, yeah.
(*Chants*)
Burn it down, burn it down!
(*As* FARID *chats to the* LADS, PARVEZ, *feeling better but requiring fresh air, stands up and walks towards the houses, people and children around him. It is cold and desolate.*)

Cut to: FARID, *with the two* LADS *behind him, has joined* PARVEZ. *They stroll around a little until they come to a group of kids playing around a bonfire, and throwing stuff onto it.*

PARVEZ

We have come from one Third World country to another.
(*A little kid comes towards* FARID *and whispers something in his ear.* FARID *shakes his head, smiles in a kindly way, shrugs and sends the boy away.*)
Those boys are selling the drug.

FARID

I was at school with those lads, until they burned it down.

PARVEZ

They did it? What will happen to them?

FARID

Some will die, or get snuffed. Many will go to prison. The lucky ones stay here, and rot.

PARVEZ

This shows we must –

FARID

I was like them, going to hell in a hurry.

PARVEZ

When?

FARID

Before I learned there could be another way.

PARVEZ

But you were studying.
(FARID *shrugs.*)
You fooled us.

FARID

For months I was high and low at the same time, lying on the
floor in bloody terrible places. I thought I could never get back.

PARVEZ

But what of Madelaine? You went to the Chief Inspector's
house every night, to study and all.

FARID

She was the same.

PARVEZ

Never lie to me!

FARID

We did everything together.

PARVEZ

Under his nose? But not now?

FARID

I have returned from something – clean and serene.

PARVEZ

Why didn't you tell me?
(FARID *shrugs.*)
How could such a thing have happened?

FARID

Evil is all around. The brothers have given me the strength to
save myself. In the midst of corruption there can be purity.

Cut to: Retching, PARVEZ *gets back into the car and as he vomits on the
back seat:*

PARVEZ

(*To* FARID)
Oh God, not on new upholstery.
(FARID *hands him some tissues.*)
Fizzy's food. Remind me to insist on refund.

INT./EXT. STREET. EVENING

*A bit later. The car halts at traffic-lights. On the corner three prostitutes
are standing – one of them* MARGOT.
    They recognize PARVEZ *in the back of the car, and wave and call out to
him.*

MARGOT

Give us a lift!
(*For a moment he smiles, and then, catching Farid's alert eye in the
mirror, he turns away, ignoring the girls.*)

FARID

Filthy women, near the children's school.

PARVEZ

What can be done with human nature, boy?

FARID

Send them away.

PARVEZ

Soon everyone will go away. They're building a shopping
centre outside the city where people will buy everything. The
small shopkeeper has had his chips. We might as well go home
again.

INT. HALLWAY. PARVEZ'S HOUSE. NIGHT

MINOO *is waiting when they come back. She opens the door to see* FARID
and a distressed PARVEZ. *As* PARVEZ *gets past them* FARID *whispers
quickly to Minoo.*

FARID

I am going ahead with all arrangements.

MINOO

He agreed?

FARID

He is beginning to see things from another point of view.
(MINOO *looks surprised.*)

INT. BEDROOM. NIGHT

PARVEZ *is sitting on the edge of the bed.* MINOO *comes in.*

MINOO

Well? Tell me, man. Speak, speak – if you can!
(PARVEZ *gestures and waves as if everything is beyond his
comprehension. Then, slowly, he starts to move.*)

PARVEZ

I'm going out . . . to work and all, you know, what else?
(*She shakes her head. He attempts to get up. Then he gives up.*)
Later, then. Can't you help me?

MINOO

All my life I have helped you.
(*Impatiently she goes to him and starts undoing his shirt.*)

PARVEZ

Touch me then, here.
(*In illustration, he rubs his forehead. She continues with the buttons.
    He starts to stroke her; he puts his hand between her legs. She is
unresponsive.* PARVEZ *opens the front of his trousers.*)
Minee. Minee, can't you –
(*She brushes his hands away.*)

MINOO

Today I am exhausted.

PARVEZ

It must be exhausting, sitting here all day –

MINOO

Shut up, clown.
(*Suddenly he grabs her and viciously forces her onto the bed.*)

What are you doing! No, no! Leave me! Leave me! Parvez you
have become an animal!
(*She is not strong, but he is drunk. They continue to struggle, and*
PARVEZ *is very determined.*

*Finally she shoves him, and he crashes off the bed and lies there
winded. She gets to her feet, shocked, pulling her clothes down.*)

MINOO

Don't ever do that to me again! I will kill you!
(*She abuses him in Urdu.*

*He looks up at her, before rolling over and facing in the other
direction.*)

INT. LIVING ROOM. DAY

PARVEZ *wakes up on the sofa in the living room, hears a noise and heads
out into the hall to see what it is.*

INT. HALL. DAY

FARID *and a couple of his student friends cleaning the whole house, as
quickly and thoroughly as they can.*

FARID *looks up and smiles at* PARVEZ. *Another student is on his knees
scrubbing the hall tiles.*

PARVEZ

Don't miss a bit and do my shoes while you're down there.
(MINOO *struggles through the front door with several shopping bags,
accompanied by another student who is also carrying bags.*

*Through the open door we see that Parvez's car is being cleaned
by a student.*)

PARVEZ

Don't scratch my bonnet!
(*To* FARID, *who has come out*)
What is this?

FARID

Surely you remember?

EXT. PARVEZ'S HOUSE. DAY

Outside, Rashid's cab draws up and he beeps his horn. PARVEZ *looks confused.*

                    PARVEZ
And that donkey?

                    FARID
Get dressed, Papa.

INT. HALL. PARVEZ'S HOUSE. DAY

MINOO *comes to* PARVEZ *and* FARID. *For* PARVEZ *she has freshly cleaned shoes; for* FARID *the new white salwar.*
    PARVEZ *looks at them both, conspirators.*

EXT. OUTSIDE THE HOUSE, MOMENTS LATER. DAY

On the front path, FARID *and* PARVEZ, *wearing their new garments, have a sudden heated argument, watched by various others, including* MINOO *and* RASHID.

                    PARVEZ
Is it what you want, or what they've ordered you to do –

                    FARID
Papa, you gave your word –

                    PARVEZ
Put this man in a hotel! The Atlantic, I can get a special price –

                    FARID
More boasting.

                    PARVEZ
He'll stir up the pots, you don't know what these religious
people are like, imposing mad ideas –

                    FARID
Papa . . . the people are thirsty, thirsty –
(PARVEZ *walks away, towards the car.*)

                    PARVEZ
I'm beginning to feel bloody thirsty.

INT./EXT. PARKING AREA. AIRPORT. DAY

RASHID – *the spiteful colleague from the taxi firm – is leaning against his cab, picking his teeth.* PARVEZ *stands next to him.*

> RASHID
>
> How long is he putting up in your house?
> (PARVEZ *glances irritably at him.*)
> Haven't been informed, eh? You are in a good mood.

> PARVEZ
>
> Why not, monkey face?

> RASHID
>
> You've changed. I wonder why.

> PARVEZ
>
> It would be worse to be the same.
> (RASHID *looks up and hastily sprays air-freshener into his car.* PARVEZ *puts his paper away and looks up.*
> *The long-bearded* MAULVI *from Pakistan has arrived. He walks out of the airport surrounded by five or six young men, carrying his luggage – including* FARID, *who has sponsored him.*
> *The* MAULVI *is tall and thin, wearing elegant long robes. He is a little effete, and rather self-important. And he is younger than* PARVEZ *had imagined.*
> RASHID *and* PARVEZ *open the car doors.*)

INT./EXT. CAR. STREET

The MAULVI *is sitting in the back of Parvez's cab with another student beside him.* FARID *sits beside* PARVEZ *but talks, very respectfully, to the Maulvi.*

> FARID
>
> That extremely tall chimney on the left perfectly symbolizes the overblown egos of nineteenth-century British industrialists. It was built that high so the smoke from it would blow over the house of one of his rivals.
>
> Actually, Ayatollah Khomeini wore a robe made here. The place where it was manufactured used to be on the right. Unfortunately it was demolished some years ago.

INT./EXT. CAR. PROSTITUTES' STREET

PARVEZ *is amused. He turns the wheel of the car. The* MAULVI *is looking out of the window.* FARID *notices that they are driving up the street of prostitutes.*

>   FARID
>
> (*Whispers to* PARVEZ)
> Wrong way!

>   PARVEZ
>
> Let him see true life, yaar!
> (*To the* MAULVI)
> On the right we have –
> (*But on the left are the line of prostitutes which the Mullah looks at.* PARVEZ *sees* BETTINA *and smiles. She waves at him.* FARID *sees her too, remembering her, of course, from the restaurant.*
>   *An Asian family with several children pass the prostitutes.*)

>   FARID
>
> (*Embarrassedly to the* MAULVI)
> In the West everywhere there is immorality.

>   MAULVI
>
> You take no action?

>   PARVEZ
>
> The wild spice and variety of life is goes on everywhere – like in Lahore, and Karachi. Eh?
> (*And he slaps his son playfully on the knee. Then he turns and gets a good look at the* MAULVI.)

INT. PARVEZ'S HOUSE. DAY

The MAULVI *is looking around Parvez's front room. Everyone holds their breath, awaiting his approval. At last he nods.* MINOO *in the doorway.*
   The place is not only preternaturally tidy, but the furniture has been moved around.
   With the MAULVI, PARVEZ *looks around quizzically, wondering what has happened.*

                            MAULVI
I will feel as if I am at home.

                            FARID
We couldn't ask for more.
(*They sigh with relief.*
     PARVEZ *stands to one side, looking on with envy and cynical amusement.*)

INT. KITCHEN. PARVEZ'S HOUSE. DAY

FARID *comes out of the kitchen with a tray of food.*

INT. DINING ROOM. PARVEZ'S HOUSE. DAY

The MAULVI *sits at the table, studying a religious book.* FARID *puts the food in front of him and sits down opposite.*
     PARVEZ *comes into the room, sees the* MAULVI *and looks around uncomfortably, before sitting down. He is about to take a mouthful when he notices the* MAULVI *is not eating.*

                            PARVEZ
Eat, eat.
(MAULVI *reaches across for food. He isn't about to make conversation.* PARVEZ, *about to tuck in, looks up to see where* MINOO *is. He notices, then, that no place has been set for her.*)

                            PARVEZ
Where's your mother?

                            FARID
(*Uneasily, glancing at the* MAULVI)
Busy in the kitchen, I think.

                            PARVEZ
(*To* MAULVI)
We always eat together as a family, otherwise we would see one another even less.

INT. KITCHEN. PARVEZ'S HOUSE. DAY

PARVEZ *goes into the kitchen to find her eating alone.*

> PARVEZ
> Come.
> (*She shakes her head. He picks up her plate and takes it to the door.*)
> Come!

INT. LIVING ROOM. PARVEZ'S HOUSE. DAY

He goes into the living room with the plate, puts it down on the table.

> PARVEZ
> I will not eat without you!
> (*The* MAULVI *remains silent.* MINOO *has not shifted from the kitchen.* PARVEZ *looks at* FARID.)

INT. KITCHEN. PARVEZ'S HOUSE. DAY

In the kitchen, in front of MINOO, PARVEZ *ostentatiously scrapes the food from his plate into the bin.*

INT. CELLAR. DAY

A romantic record is playing; PARVEZ *is wearing just a shirt, new tie and socks. He has damp hair. Having placed a mirror against a shelf, he is snipping at the hair in his nostrils, ears and eyebrows with a inconveniently large and blunt pair of scissors. He stands back and regards himself.*
   He hears a noise behind him and turns around nervously.
   MINOO *comes in with a plate of food and cutlery.*

> PARVEZ
> You've thrown away my bottle! What am I working for if I can't even wet my mouth!

> MINOO
> When you drink you play that music.

> PARVEZ
> What's wrong with Louis Armstrong? You don't know.

MINOO

(*Pause.*)
It's too trumpety. Here.
(*She offers him the food.*)

PARVEZ

You eat too.

MINOO

I am full.
(*She watches him, as he puts on his trousers.*)

PARVEZ

(*Self-conscious*)
German likes me to dress well.
(*Pause.*)
I must start getting like Farid and his longbeard best friend –
laying down the law for other people. I don't know how you
can talk to that man without wanting to give his whiskers a
hard tug. I might do it myself – then we'll see what's
underneath!
(*He illustrates.*)

MINOO

(*Stopping a giggle*)
Papu!

PARVEZ

I will tug – so!

Cut to: MINOO *has gone.* PARVEZ *puts 'Mack the Knife' (or similar) on
the record-player and opens the door. As he lets the first notes blare out
into the house, he laughs to himself. He leans out of the door before the
enquiring head of the* MAULVI *appears at the living room door, followed
by Farid's head.*

PARVEZ *enjoys the mischief for a moment, before banging a pair of
headphones over his head and doing a little dance to the music. He is quite
excited.*

Cut to:

INT. HOUSE. EVENING

PARVEZ *tiptoes past the door of the front room where the Mullah, surrounded by acolytes, is talking.*

EXT. STREET. NIGHT

PARVEZ *helps an elegant* BETTINA *out of the car, outside Fizzy's restaurant.*
   A smart white couple, seeing, of course, that it is a taxi, wave at PARVEZ, *who dismisses them irritably.*

> PARVEZ
> Not for hire or sale! How beautiful you look tonight, my love.

INT. RESTAURANT. EVENING

Tonight it is crowded. PARVEZ *points out* FIZZY, *who glances over but doesn't immediately respond.*

> BETTINA
> Did you make a booking?

> PARVEZ
> Silly, Fizzy used to carry my cricket bag. His father –

> BETTINA
> Why did you want to come here?

> PARVEZ
> Best place. This is the bloody life, yaar! I am so glad to get out of that house. And Farid says the cultures cannot mix. Jesus, they can't keep apart.
> (FIZZY *comes over, puzzled by Parvez's sartorial care and by his beaming happiness.*)
> (*To* BETTINA)
> This is my first-friend – Fizzy.

> FIZZY
> And who is this friend?

> PARVEZ
> Bett – Sandra.

FIZZY

Madam.
(*He takes her hand; to* PARVEZ)
We are fully booked, yaar.

PARVEZ

Fizzy, yaar –

FIZZY

Okay, okay. Upstairs everything is good.
(*As the waiter leads them away*)
Where have I seen that tart?

WAITER

She came with the German who ate the whole kitchen and
then said it was too salty.
(FIZZY *watches and nods.*)

Cut to:

INT. FUNCTION ROOM. RESTAURANT. CONTINUOUS

One waiter carries a table over; another lays it.
    PARVEZ *and* BETTINA *are now sitting down – in the room previously
visited. It is a big room with only a few tables, and fewer people eating. It is
far less salubrious than downstairs, and* PARVEZ *is taken aback that his
friend has done this to him.*

Cut to: PARVEZ *chatting away, trying to make the best of it.*

PARVEZ

You can't force anyone to be sensible.

BETTINA

I made a resolution – to try something new every day. I've even
signed up for evening classes.

PARVEZ

In what?

BETTINA

Singing.

PARVEZ

Singing? Good idea. In school I loved the hymns. One thing I regret. Farid wanted to study music and arts and all . . . and I didn't listen, but forced him into science and maths. It caused a resentment.

(*Pause.*)

You were telling me, that thing about your mother and –

BETTINA

Well, she –

(*She looks up and* PARVEZ *is stuffing his face with food. She laughs. He looks quizzically at her.*)

BETTINA

You look like a hamster.

PARVEZ

I'm not used to being looked at with curiosity.

BETTINA

Nor me, really.

(*They look at one another, as if trying to work something out.*)

When you meet a new person you don't know where you are. There is . . . possibility.

(*They are both feeling awkward.*)

Why did you come here?

PARVEZ

To feed my family only. I never saw further. You have been a dreamer?

BETTINA

I wanted to be a teacher. But my children were too young. Then my man died and I had debts. I had a friend who was doing this. If you had the choice what would you do?

PARVEZ

It's been so long since I have thought about anything.

(FIZZY *comes over.*)

FIZZY

What is date for engagement booking?

PARVEZ

(*Looking at* BETTINA)
At this moment, Fizzy brother, I am completely engaged and
booked elsewhere.

FIZZY

(*Banging his fist on the table*)
Parvez, yaar –
(PARVEZ *quickly leads him away from the table.* FIZZY *is furious.*)

PARVEZ

Whole question of engagement is off, yaar, for time being, at
the moment, for now –

FIZZY

What?

PARVEZ

I am stuffed up, far into rear end. The boy doesn't like the girl.
The girl is fighting with –

FIZZY

You are giving Fingerhut the finger! But we were expecting
community policing at last.
(PARVEZ *notices that* FIZZY *is looking quizzically at him.*)
What's happened to your eyebrows?
(FIZZY *looks over at* BETTINA *and is about to say something, but*
PARVEZ *moves away from* FIZZY *and sits down again.*
    BETTINA *seems agitated. She gets up.*)

BETTINA

Sorry, I can't stay.
(*She walks out.* PARVEZ *gets up and watches her go, not knowing*
what to do. At that moment a waiter brings the food.)

INT./EXT. RESTAURANT. NIGHT

FIZZY *at the window. He watches an anxious* PARVEZ *run to* BETTINA
and take her arm. She puts her arm around him.

INT. BETTINA'S HOUSE. NIGHT

BETTINA *is getting changed in the bedroom.* PARVEZ *watches her through*

*the open door. He sees that new clothes are hanging from door handles
and the tops of doors.*

PARVEZ

All that is new?

BETTINA

The big Shit is paying.

PARVEZ

You're seeing him often.

BETTINA

Saves me seeing anyone else.

PARVEZ

You don't . . . talk to him.

BETTINA

That's not what he wants.
(*He glimpses a bruise on her forearm.*)

PARVEZ

That him, too?

BETTINA

I think I look excellent. If you don't like it, you can go. Go on.
(*Beat.*)
You like me today don't you? Sometimes you're not so sure.
Do you know why you like me?

PARVEZ

It's only that I can't help thinking that you are a magnificent,
special woman. It's a feeling I want to push away. It makes me
feel good, and as if I'm going mad.

BETTINA

You know what I've always wanted to do?
(*She puts her hand in his hair and tugs it, quite hard. He winces and
smiles.*)
Does your wife do that?

PARVEZ

Why are you asking?

BETTINA

It's something I can't help thinking about.

PARVEZ

She's too bloody ugly.
(BETTINA *laughs.* PARVEZ *is horrified by what he has said. She stands in the doorway of her bedroom.*)

Cut to: PARVEZ *and* BETTINA *standing by her bedroom door, not together.*

BETTINA

I lie in bed with the music on. When I think of you I get a warm feeling in my stomach and I have to close my eyes. No other man has come in here.

Cut to: Bettina's face. Parvez's hands on her face. He caresses her forehead, eyes, mouth, exploring.

Cut to: She examines the palms of his hands and his fingers; kisses them. She kisses her own hands and rubs them over his face. Hands; lips; kisses; bits of body.

INT. PARVEZ'S HOUSE. CELLAR. NIGHT

Parvez's trembling fingers unbuttoning his shirt.
    He has come home at last. He removes his shirt, burying his face in her scent. He changes into another shirt, crumpled up on the side, doing up the buttons wrong.

INT. PARVEZ'S HOUSE. BEDROOM

Upstairs. PARVEZ *is going to bed, exhausted.* MINOO *is standing in front of him.* PARVEZ *looks at her guiltily.*
    He moves past her and turns the corner on the upper landing. He sees FARID *sleeping outside his own bedroom. Taken aback, he steps over him, opens the bedroom door, and sees and hears the snoring* MAULVI *in his son's bed.*

PARVEZ

These people are even taking over our beds.
(MINOO *puts her finger to her lips.* PARVEZ *shakes his head in disbelief and goes past.*)

IN. PARVEZ'S HOUSE. KITCHEN. DAY

In the kitchen the MAULVI *is having breakfast watching cartoons on TV.* FARID *is in the room waiting on him.* PARVEZ *comes in, dressed and ready for work.*

PARVEZ

(*Sarcastically*)
What can I get you?
(*The* MAULVI *continues to watch TV. Finally he looks at* PARVEZ *and gives a little shiver.*)

MAULVI

To be honest . . . I am a little chilly.
(MINOO *rushes in from the kitchen.*)

MINOO

Chilly?
(*To* FARID)
He's chilly.

FARID

Chilly?
(MINOO *looks around, spots a blanket lying on the back of a chair and puts it over the Maulvi's legs. The* MAULVI *sighs contentedly. They look at him. He gives another little shiver.*)
I'll get the fan-heater!
(FARID *goes to leave, rushing out but returning immediately.* PARVEZ *looks on incredulously.*)

FARID

(*To* MINOO)
Where is it? The heater!
(*She rushes out of the room to help* FARID.
   Hearing the phone ring, PARVEZ *goes, shaking his head.*)

INT. PARVEZ'S HOUSE. HALL. DAY

PARVEZ *on the phone in the hall.*

> PARVEZ
> (*Whispers urgently into phone*)
> Herr Schitz, Herr Schitz, I am only driver but am arranging
> everything with red-hot tarts toot suite. I know where it is, yes.
> (*As he speaks* MINOO *rushes past with the heater.*)

INT. CAB OFFICE. DAY

PARVEZ *arrives at the cab office. As he hurries through the entrance he finds the addict* PROSTITUTE *coming at him.*

> PROSTITUTE
> Parvez, are you going my way? I know you are –
> (*He brushes past her. Looks over at another* DRIVER. *As the* PROSTITUTE *turns back to him, he shakes his head, also refusing to take her. She is too out of it.*)

> DRIVER
> You girls are going to be in bloody big trouble. 'Bout time too!

> PROSTITUTE
> You men are a load of hypocrites!

> CONTROLLER
> How's things at home? The boy.
> (PARVEZ *shakes his head.*)

> PARVEZ
> I need a couple of drivers to help me out later.

> CONTROLLER
> See who's around.

INT. TAXI OFFICE. DAY

PARVEZ *comes into the main taxi office.*
  Across the room, RASHID *has clearly been gossiping with the* CONTROLLER *and other* DRIVERS *about the just-arrived* MAULVI. *Some nod gravely, others smirk and laugh, others look on. But everybody knows and has an opinion.*

On the video in the corner a porn film is playing. One of the DRIVERS
stands in front of it mockingly to prevent PARVEZ *from seeing it.*

PARVEZ *looks at* RASHID *reproachfully, and at the others, and sighs.*
Then he notices that two of the DRIVERS *are playing cricket with a*
rolled-up ball of paper and bat. PARVEZ *does a double-take at the bat*
and grabs it.

DRIVER

Signed by Imran. Open the batting, yaar.
(*Thinking* PARVEZ *wants to play, the* DRIVER *hands him the bat.*
PARVEZ *examines it. It is the bat from Farid's room, signed by the*
Pakistan cricket team.)

PARVEZ

Where did you find this?

DRIVER

My boy.

PARVEZ

It's not his.

DRIVER

Your son sold it.

DRIVER 2

How's your new lodger, yaar?

DRIVER 3

Given up all your bad vices? No more bacon butties!

DRIVER 2

They say you can't even get a drink in your place now. Is it true
you're living under stairs like a troll?

DRIVER 3

The Ayatollah's moving in permanently, has he?

. DRIVER

These demonstrations he has in mind are starting, they say. It's
a bloody nuisance and all, affecting our work.

RASHID

They are vile girls! There is too much unbelieving going on.
Everywhere there is evil to be cured. Parvez has right idea!
(PARVEZ *opens his wallet and contemptuously throws money at the*
DRIVER *from whom he's snatched the bat.*

A DRIVER *stands in front of him, smirking.* PARVEZ *pushes past
him and raises his hand as if to hit him.*

Behind him the DRIVERS *laugh.*)

Cut to: PARVEZ *is leaving the outer office, carrying the cricket bat.*

PARVEZ

I am on urgent business. Tonight, later, I will work. But you
must get me two drivers.

CONTROLLER

Taking your girlfriend somewhere nice?

PARVEZ

Girlfriend?

CONTROLLER

What name she use?
(PARVEZ *looks blank.*)
Bettina? Everybody says –

PARVEZ

Everybody says nothing – bloody fool!
(*Parvez rushes out.*)

EXT. STREET. DAY

PARVEZ *drives up the street of prostitutes towards* MARGOT.

Along the street a brother is tying a poster to a tree.

Further along, the MAULVI, FARID *and a couple of other brothers
standing on a corner watching the proceedings, and talking
concentratedly with one another.*

*He backs the car off a little in order to watch them without being
observed himself.*

A punter in a car approaches one of the women. FARID *ostentatiously
brandishes a notebook and writes down his registration number.*

The car drives off.
The woman abuses FARID. *He abuses her back.*

FARID

Get out of here, you filthy women!
(PARVEZ *looks on. Finally he turns the car round. We see that* FARID
has looked up and noticed his father's car.)

CONTROLLER

Parvez, the boys are ready!

INT. CAR. EVENING

Cut to: a PROSTITUTE *making up her face.*
   A harassed PARVEZ *has, in his car, three of the more salubrious*
PROSTITUTES, *who have dressed up for the occasion, and* MARGOT.

Cut to: PARVEZ *is driving them towards the mill we have already seen.*
The car is full of loud music, perfume, and cigarette and dope smoke.
Coughing, PARVEZ *waves his hand to try and clear the air. The*
PROSTITUTES *exchange cosmetics and look in mirrors.*

PARVEZ

They're the top pillars of the whole community.

MARGOT

(*Laughing*)
Pillocks, more like.

PARVEZ

Don't drop the food.
(MARGOT *has her fingers in the dall.*)
Margot, I am observing naughty fingers! Keep them for nimble
uses later.

PROSTITUTE I

Nimble uses!

MARGOT

So what's going on with you and Bettina?

PROSTITUTE 2

Yeah.

PARVEZ

What has she told you?

PROSTITUTE I

She won't tell us nothing.

PROSTITUTE 3

That's how we know it's serious!

PARVEZ

You silly girls imagine romances everywhere.
(*Pause.*)
What makes you think she likes me?

PROSTITUTE I

She doesn't!

PARVEZ

What?

MARGOT

(*Leans forward and whispers*)
But when she mentions you – she smiles a little bit.
(*Tears spring into Parvez's eyes.*)

PROSTITUTE 3

You're not like your son, then.

PROSTITUTE 2

That lad and his people look at you like scum and frighten the
punters.

PARVEZ

What do they say?

PROSTITUTE I

Abuse.

PROSTITUTE 3

A little one was beaten up.

PROSTITUTE I

The dirty bastards carried her up to the moors and did her all
over. She was only fifteen. No one touches me!

PROSTITUTE 2

Everyone touches you!

PROSTITUTE 1

Shut it!

PARVEZ

(*Interrupting*)

How many times has my boy been there?

MARGOT

A few.

PARVEZ

I apologize for his behaviour. He's got many problems.

MARGOT

Why's he taking it out on us?

(PARVEZ *hangs his head.*)

EXT. OUTSIDE MILL. NIGHT

SCHITZ *stands waiting at the door, smoking a cigar. He walks down and kisses the girls as* PARVEZ *drops them off. Rashid's cab turns up with another two girls inside.*

SCHITZ

Welcome, delicious tarts. Everything is ready but you!

Cut to:

Come, little man, we are all thirsty and everyone is standing still! Bring the drink!

(*As* PARVEZ *goes to the boot of his cab,* SCHITZ *kicks him up the arse and laughs.* PARVEZ *slips and falls, before getting up and wiping his muddy ripped trousers.*)

PARVEZ

Please, don't ever do that to me, sir!

(*Angrily he goes towards* SCHITZ, *who grabs and restrains him.*)

INT. INSIDE MILL NIGHT

A group of businessmen, a couple of Sikhs among them, are standing around in a cluster. BETTINA *is chatting to some of them. They perk up when Schitz leads the girls into the room.*

SCHITZ

This way, gentlemen, for entertainment.
(*The girls and the businessmen eye each other up.* PARVEZ *and* RASHID *in the meantime bring in the crates of drink and the food.*)

INT. MILL. NIGHT

The party is in full swing. Two of the girls are stripping. Some of the men are yelling encouragement. Other men and girls lie on couches. BETTINA *stands with Schitz.*

The two strippers start trying to undress the men. One Sikh businessman has his shirt off and trousers down. Another man is resisting, as the stripper sits on his chest and tries pulling his shirt off.

The unselfconscious women seem to attack the men, pulling at them, humiliating them.

PARVEZ, *frantically pouring drinks and handing them to people, looks on. He and* BETTINA *talk during all this.* (*This conversation should be broken up.*)

BETTINA

The religious man still sleeps in your house?

PARVEZ

Until late in the morning when Farid brings his breakfast. He's so comfortable perhaps he will stay for ten years.

SCHITZ

(*Interrupts*)
Come along, big girl. You are wearing too many clothes, as usual.

PARVEZ

The boys gather up and never stop talking about good and bad, or God says do this or that, or burn in hell, or celebrate in Paradise.
(*Pause.*)
Sandra, I am tired of being instructed, as if I am a fool or a bad man without my own mind.

(*Pause.*)
You're right, they thirst for something. But why is there so
much violence and hatred there?
(*Pause.*)
It is true that Farid must go his own way. It must be inevitable,
with the children. If life for the parents isn't to end, there must
be . . . other interests.

Cut to: A drunk BETTINA *goes over to* PARVEZ, *and kisses his face.*
RASHID *gesticulates at the wild scenes which have become a fracas.*
PARVEZ *shrugs.*

Cut to: BETTINA *and* PARVEZ *standing with their arms around each
other: she whispers in his ear, he laughs. They start doing a little
improvised dance together.*

EXT. OUTSIDE THE MILL. NIGHT

PARVEZ *is paying the women from a fat wad. They wait in a line,
shivering in their skimpy clothes. Cold; raining; silent.* SCHITZ *sits in a
car watching.*

  RASHID *leans against his car, watching scornfully.* BETTINA *watches
from a distance.*

                              RASHID
  (*In Urdu, subtitled*)
  Money from immorality.

                              PARVEZ
  (*In Urdu, subtitled*)
  Is it wrong to help someone out?

                              RASHID
  (*In Urdu, subtitled*)
  Funny how it's whores and not your own kind. And you living
  with the Maulvi in your very own house.
  (PARVEZ *suddenly loses his temper.*)

                              PARVEZ
  (*In Urdu, subtitled*)
  What right do you have to judge me, or these women? Come
  near me and I'll swipe you with the bat!

(RASHID *slinks off, cursing.*)
Good show, girls.

MARGOT

Ta very much for the work.
(SCHITZ, *sitting in a car, indicates to* BETTINA.)

SCHITZ

Come along, my love, back to the hotel.
(BETTINA *looks at him. Looks at* PARVEZ.)

BETTINA

I am going with this one.

SCHITZ

He can't afford your prices.
(BETTINA *shakes her head at him.* SCHITZ *crooks his finger at
another girl.*)
I'll have to make do with you!
(*To* PARVEZ)
She is hard to satisfy, little man!

INT. BETTINA'S BEDROOM

BETTINA, *exhausted, lies naked in the bed. She and* PARVEZ *have made
love.* PARVEZ, *beside the bed, has almost finished putting his clothes on.
He strokes and kisses her face.* BETTINA *swoons.*

BETTINA

I love you looking after me.
(*She pulls him by the hand.*)
Lie on top of me for a little while.

PARVEZ

I must go.

BETTINA

I want to hold you. Please.
(*He does so. Their faces together.*)
Oh man, I'm so tired.

PARVEZ

Sandra.
(PARVEZ *starts to move.*
    BETTINA *grabs him and pins him to the bed.*)

BETTINA

Now you must stay.

PARVEZ

I wish I could.
(*Beat.*)
Let me go.

BETTINA

No! Why should I?
(PARVEZ *struggles with her. They fight and kiss. He pulls away and gets to the door. Out in the hall he hears her voice behind him.*)
Never leave me! Never, never, never!

INT. PARVEZ'S BEDROOM. NIGHT

MINOO *lies in bed.* PARVEZ *undresses.*

PARVEZ

I'm bloody pleased to be back.

MINOO

Again you're muddy.

PARVEZ

This Schitz is getting my full value.
(*He indicates some money that he put on his bedside table.*)
Here. Today I received a nice tip.
(*She takes the money. He watches her put it under her pillow.*)

PARVEZ

What will you do with it?

MINOO

Put it away for a better time.

PARVEZ

You know I want to take you to that place I saw. Can't we go on Sunday?

> MINOO

It is the first time you have asked me to go out, and I am going to be too busy.

> PARVEZ

Doing what?

> MINOO

Looking after some things.

Cut to: They lie at each side of the bed. She turns off the light.

INT. PARVEZ'S HOUSE. HALL. MORNING

PARVEZ *is picking the mail off the mat.*
   He seems very weary, emotionally and physically exhausted.
   Downstairs a young Asian kid is talking on a portable phone in the hall. Another kid is with him. PARVEZ *slides, with difficulty, around them.*
   The house seems full of people. As we follow him through the house we see someone yelling into a mobile phone; others are talking frantically; someone is making placards.

INT. PARVEZ'S HOUSE. LIVING ROOM. MORNING

He looks into the living room where the MAULVI *is giving instructions to his young deputies.*

INT. PARVEZ'S HOUSE. KITCHEN. MORNING

> PARVEZ

Minoo.
   (*He opens the kitchen door. Inside he finds young women in the hijab cooking for the troops outside, someone else washing up. Meanwhile* MINOO, *in a comfortable chair, with her feet up, chats to the women, enjoying their company, and the hustle and bustle.*
   Parvez stands outside the door, not knowing what to do with himself.)

> PARVEZ

You boys are busy, eh?

LAD

Community spirit.

PARVEZ

Haven't I seen you?

LAD

Rashid's young brother – he works with you.

INT. PARVEZ'S HOUSE. LIVING ROOM. MORNING

In the living room Farid's young friends are making placards and preparing for today's demonstration. Opening the mail which consists mainly of bills, PARVEZ surveys the scene.
   The MAULVI goes to PARVEZ.

MAULVI

One word please.

INT. PARVEZ'S HOUSE. CUBBY HOLE. MORNING

The MAULVI and PARVEZ are alone in Parvez's cubby hole.

MAULVI

I am in need of some legal advices.
(*Pause. He looks up to see that three of Farid's companions are standing outside the door. The MAULVI indicates for one of them to close the door.*)
My work is here. I will stay.

PARVEZ

And bring your family?

MAULVI

You knew that?

PARVEZ

You are so patriotic about Pakistan. It is always a sign of imminent departure.

MAULVI

Can you help me? In our own country we are treated badly, and everywhere else we are what? Pakis.
(*Pause.*)

The point is . . .

(*The* MAULVI *drones on interminably while* PARVEZ *studies the phone bill which is for more than £500. Stunned, he immediately examines the rest of the mail. All of the bills are inordinately high; there is a threatening letter from the bank.*)

There are many who reject the teaching, they close their minds and choose atheism, thinking that bread is all that men need to live by, and that the sky is empty, but right conduct is possible provided the preacher warns and advises that in the military-industrial state the greatness of God's guidance is essential in guaranteeing repentance . . . Loss of faith in all areas is common here, but poor preachers can move mountains, that is all I am here to inform the masses of . . .

(PARVEZ *stares at the burbling* MAULVI.)

INT. PARVEZ'S HOUSE. HALL. MORNING

In the hall PARVEZ *leans against the wall in a state of virtual collapse.*

PARVEZ

(*Calls*)
Farid!
(MINOO *hurries towards him.* FARID *comes out of the front room.*)

MINOO

What's the matter?

PARVEZ

Now I will never pay off mortgage!

MINOO

I will get a glass of water!
(FARID *holds on to Parvez's arm, looking at the bills.*)

PARVEZ

I can't breathe!

FARID

Papa! A few pounds is worth it for what we are trying to achieve. The house price will increase once the tarts have gone.

PARVEZ

One of the little ones was beaten up on the moors.

FARID

Propaganda. Why are you taking their side?

PARVEZ

Your great long-beard friend wants to stay in this immoral
country. Knowing of my Fingerhut connections he asked me
to help him with the immigration.
(FARID *looks at his father and turns away.*
   MINOO *has opened the front door and let several young men into
the house, who look at* PARVEZ, *yelling.*
   FARID *turns away to greet the visitors.*
   PARVEZ *puts his head in his hands.*
   MINOO *holds the telephone receiver.*)

MINOO

The German is calling you.

EXT. OUTSIDE PARVEZ'S HOUSE. DAY

As PARVEZ *gets into his car and drives away, the* MAULVI, FARID *and
their companions are leaving the house with banners and placards.*

INT. FIZZY'S RESTAURANT. DAY

FIZZY *is sitting in the restaurant doing his paperwork. (Perhaps there is a
screen around his table.) He looks up as* PARVEZ *goes slowly towards him.
Seeing Parvez's expression he becomes concerned.*

Cut to: They sit across the table, FIZZY *examining the bills as* PARVEZ
points out their worst features.

PARVEZ

Can you believe it?

FIZZY

They say you have lost control of him.

PARVEZ

(*Impatiently*)
The boy will grow less zealous when he improves overall.

FIZZY

Everyone says it was him, personally, who invited this man into your house. They're agitated, yaar, and complaining to me like mad.

PARVEZ

If he doesn't bugger off I'll report him to immigration authorities.
(*Trying to change the subject*)
Fizzy, friend . . . I've never come to you before.
(FIZZY *extracts his chequebook with a flourish and begins to write a cheque.*)

FIZZY

Yes, yes, shut up. But I haven't signed.
(*Beat.*)
You came with that tart here. The community is small but the big mouths say you two are doing something together.

PARVEZ

All the drivers are up to it – everyone in England full-time in fact.

FIZZY

You have never been a cheap man. But she –

PARVEZ

Even you, friend, are divorced, let me –

FIZZY

She is an old whore that even a taxi-driver could afford! Everybody fucks her – thousands of dicks.

PARVEZ

Shut up!
(*And adds much extra abuse, in Urdu.*)

FIZZY

Perhaps it is lucky that your new lodger is sending them away. You've always been naïve, Parvez.

PARVEZ

Naïve?

FIZZY

Minoo's parents paid my fare to England! I came to your wedding!

PARVEZ

I know, I know –

FIZZY

You will stop seeing the woman. Otherwise –
(*He stops writing the cheque and looks at* PARVEZ. PARVEZ *looks back at him. He begins to boil; he loses his temper.*)

PARVEZ

Stick it in your backside! I won't beg, Fizzy!

FIZZY

You don't like this woman, do you? So you do. I can tell.

PARVEZ

What else is there for me, yaar, but sitting behind the wheel without tenderness? That's it for me, is it, until I drop dead, and not another human touch.
(PARVEZ *starts to sob.*)
You are too certain of what everyone else should do! Minoo has never given me satisfaction. Who am I satisfying? You? Go to hell!
(*He gets up and walks out.*)

EXT. STREET. DAY

PARVEZ *is striding down the street towards his car. We see* FIZZY *hurrying behind him.*

FIZZY

Here, here!
(FIZZY *hands* PARVEZ *the cheque.*

  PARVEZ *turns and, in front of* FIZZY, *rips up the cheque. The bits of paper scatter in the wind.*)

INT./EXT. PARVEZ'S TAXI. DAY

PARVEZ *is taking* SCHITZ *to the airport.*

> SCHITZ
>
> At last I'm going home, little man. The women are the one good thing about this town.
> (PARVEZ *is taking another route and loses his way. He notices the traffic is bad, and there are a lot of people heading in one direction.*)

> PARVEZ
>
> (*Mutters*)
> What the hell is all this? What are these bloody people doing now?

> SCHITZ
>
> Look out! Where are you going man! I'll miss my flight!

> PARVEZ
>
> (*Driving in another direction*)
> Sir, special short cut.

> SCHITZ
>
> What are they doing here! We don't have time . . . Turn around now . . . don't get out!

INT./EXT. SEEDY STREET. DAY

PARVEZ *takes a turn and there, on the street, is the anti-prostitutes demonstration. People are waving banners, and shouting. The women stand in their places swearing, cursing, brandishing fists. The atmosphere is tense.*

SCHITZ *is first exasperated, then incredulous.*

PARVEZ *tries to drive through the crowd beeping his horn, but can't make any progress.*

Some of the crowd start hammering on the roof and the few police that are there shout at PARVEZ *to get his taxi away. But the cab is stuck, unable to move forward or back and all* PARVEZ *can do is sit there in a daze.*

Then PARVEZ *catches sight through the* mêlée *of the* MAULVI *with* FARID *next to him.*

Next to them is one of the drivers – RASHID *– and all of them are*

*exchanging insults with a group of prostitutes among whom, at the back,
is* BETTINA.

At the head of the prostitutes is the addict prostitute who points at
RASHID *and shouts out that he was fucking her only last week and makes
derogatory remarks about the size of his dick, etc.*

Furious, RASHID, *breaking rank, races forward and strikes the addict,
knocking her to the floor. Immediately the other prostitutes set upon him
and all hell breaks loose as the demonstrators also join in.*

To the German's horror, PARVEZ *gets out of the cab. He is trying
desperately to locate* BETTINA.

Suddenly she finds herself facing FARID *and stops short. The boy looks
at her for a moment, then, with the Maulvi's eye on him, spits in her face.*

Incensed, PARVEZ *barges his way through the crowd until he gets to her.
He wipes her face with his handkerchief.*

He looks around for FARID. *When he sees him, he grabs him by the
scruff of his neck and drags him back towards the cab. Reaching it, he sees
that some of the crowd are venting their anger on it, rocking it violently
from side to side with the terrified* SCHITZ *still inside.*

PARVEZ *shoves the demonstrators away before throwing his son into the
front passenger seat. When* SCHITZ *screams and swears at* PARVEZ *for
leaving him* PARVEZ *reaches for his cricket bat and brandishes it.*

PARVEZ
Get out of my car! Out!
(*As the hapless* SCHITZ *tries to take himself and his luggage out of
harm's way* PARVEZ *drives off, the crowd parting in front of his
accelerating cab.*)

INT. PARVEZ'S HOUSE

A distraught MINOO *watches* PARVEZ *drag* FARID *upstairs to his
bedroom. Hurling the boy into the room* PARVEZ *regards the Maulvi's
possessions with disgust.*

Behind them MINOO *pushes at the door.* PARVEZ *bangs it shut and
sticks a chair under the handle.*

PARVEZ
Get this crap out!
(FARID *hesitates.* PARVEZ *starts to throw the Maulvi's clothes, toilet
articles and learned books into his suitcase.*)

FARID

No!

PARVEZ

He could be Jesus Christ himself, but he is leaving!
(FARID *tries to stop him by pulling the things from Parvez's hands.*
PARVEZ *pulls them back and pushes his son away.*)

FARID

If you shame me, I am going away too! Put in my things!

PARVEZ

(*Staring at* FARID)
All right! I won't stand for the extremity of anti-democratic
and anti-Jewish rubbish! And he eats too much!

FARID

Only the corrupt would say it is extreme to want goodness!

PARVEZ

But there is nothing of God in spitting on a woman's face! This
cannot be the way for us to take!

FARID

(*Slyly*)
Why are you so interested in dirty whores? Is it because –
(*Behind them* MINOO *is pushing at the door. She can see and hear
through the gap.*)

PARVEZ

What nonsense is this?

FARID

You do it to one of them, don't you? It's been going on for –

PARVEZ

Farid!

FARID

Answer!

PARVEZ

You listen to the gossip of fools?

FARID

They know you better than we do!

PARVEZ

Would they be drivers if they weren't ignorant fools? We drive the women and they pay us.

FARID

It is all around, everyone says so . . . it makes me feel sick to have such a father! I never thought you were such a man! . . . You are a pimp who organizes sexual parties!
(PARVEZ *grabs him and starts to hit him around the head.* FARID *falls backwards.* PARVEZ *is so angry he grabs him again and continues to whack him.*)
You call me fanatic, dirty man, but who is the fanatic now?
(*Father and son struggle desperately.*
     MINOO *has broken into the room.*)

MINOO

You have killed him!

PARVEZ

He will recover, I am afraid.

MINOO

These minutes have made me into an old woman.
(MINOO *goes to* FARID *and helps him up, kissing and holding him.*
     PARVEZ *looks at them.*)

INT. HOUSE. DAY

An agitated, disturbed and regretful PARVEZ *is walking around the house with a glass in his hand.*
     He smashes an unused placard over his knee and throws it in the bin.
MINOO *comes in.*

MINOO

Papu, please, don't let him go.

PARVEZ

Yes, it will be only us.

MINOO

I will be here alone, like the English women, waiting to die.

PARVEZ

He will do what he wants.
(*Beat.*)
Minoo, just tell me, what can I do to make you happy? If you
just tell me once, then I will know for good!

MINOO

Is it true – you have a friendship with one of those
women?

PARVEZ

Yes, a friendship.

MINOO

Filthy selfish man!

PARVEZ

Friendship is . . . good, Minoo. I think it can be found . . .
in the funniest places. Other people can be useful, and
nice.

MINOO

All this time I stayed here to serve you, and you were out,
laughing with low-class people! What a fool I've been made
into! What a waste.
(*He watches her howling. He considers going to comfort her, but is
unable to do so. He turns away.*)
Papu.
(*He turns. She throws a glass at his head.*
    PARVEZ *looks up and sees* FARID *standing at the door with his
bag.* MINOO *turns and sees too.*
    The front door bangs.)
Go to him! Go!

EXT. STREET. DAY

PARVEZ, *in his taxi, drives along the street beside* FARID, *who is carrying
his suitcases.*

PARVEZ

Remember two things. There are many ways of being a good man. And I will be at home. Will you come to see me?

(PARVEZ *stops and watches him go. Out of the shadows several of Farid's companions emerge, waiting for him.*

PARVEZ *watches the boy go.*)

INT. THE BEDROOM. DAY

MINOO *is going through her cupboards, sorting her clothes out. Suitcases on the bed.*

PARVEZ

What is this?

MINOO

I will see everyone who loves me, my brothers and sisters and all! Come, Papu, I am begging you, husband.

PARVEZ

There is nothing there for me.

MINOO

You are not Prime Minister. They require drivers –

PARVEZ

You can't go home, Minoo. It isn't like that now. This is our home.

MINOO

I hate this dirty place! The men brought us here and then left us alone!

PARVEZ

Oh you make me ashamed, so ashamed! But I have done nothing wrong, I know I haven't.

MINOO

Oh yes, one unforgivable thing.

(*He looks at her.*)

Put self before family.

PARVEZ

Oh God, yes. The first time! But not the last!

MINOO

Is it because of her that you won't come? Yes, yes.

PARVEZ

(*Shaking his head*)
Perhaps one day the boy will tire of his moral exertions and will
need me. I will wait. You will come home?

MINOO

Do you want me to?

PARVEZ

If you want to.

MINOO

I will then.
(PARVEZ *with his head in his hands.*)

PARVEZ

Otherwise I will come to get you. It is too late now for us to be
parted for good.

MINOO

No it is not. I can tell you have lost your feeling for me.

EXT. COUNTRYSIDE. DAY

BETTINA *and* PARVEZ *are walking through a wood with some distance
between them. She picks up leaves and pieces of tree bark.*

PARVEZ

I have managed to destroy everything. I have never felt
worse . . . or better.

Cut to: Another part of the wood.

BETTINA

Can't we leave?

PARVEZ

Where?

BETTINA

I thought . . . India. Parvez, a few weeks. You can show me the good places. We can live cheaply, everybody says.

PARVEZ

That's a young people's thing, yaar.

BETTINA

Why have you never been back?

PARVEZ

No time, no money –

BETTINA

Come away. It's a chance! Otherwise . . . what will we do but the same thing every day!

PARVEZ

You put such ideas in my head!

BETTINA

Good. Good.
(*She holds him. They kiss.*)

PARVEZ

What do you want?

BETTINA

More than I've ever had before.
(*Pause. He looks at her questioningly.*)
Your face, your hands, you, all of you, you.

INT. PARVEZ'S HOUSE. NIGHT

PARVEZ *comes into the darkened house. Everyone has gone. It is eerily silent. He puts the lights on.*
    Still wearing his coat, he pushes the doors of the various rooms – kitchen, bedroom, Farid's room – putting on the lights as he walks through the empty place.

Finally he sits down, alone, and pours himself a drink. He holds the glass up, swirls the liquid around and drinks.

He puts on his favourite Louis Armstrong (or similar) record. Music fills the house. He dances.

EXT. PARVEZ'S HOUSE. NIGHT

Parvez's house, its windows blazing with light in the middle of a dark terrace.